W9-BMN-070

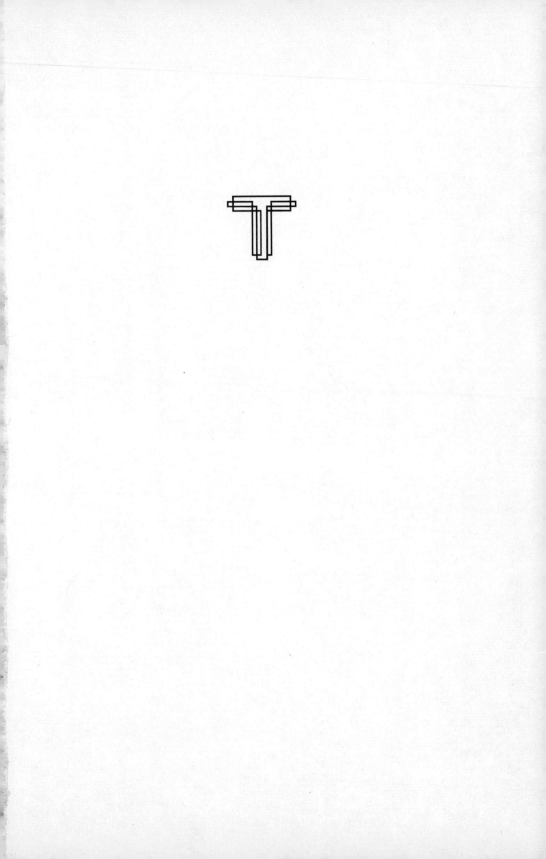

THE KINGDOM
OF HAPPINESS

INSIDE TONY HSIEH'S
ZAPPONIAN UTOPIA

AIMEE GROTH

Annalisa, and Trey!
Thank you for all
your ♡ support &
encouragement!
Aimee

TOUCHSTONE
NEW YORK LONDON TORONTO SYDNEY NEW DELHI

Touchstone
An Imprint of Simon & Schuster, Inc.
1230 Avenue of the Americas
New York, NY 10020

First Touchstone hardcover edition February 2017

For information about special discounts for bulk purchases,
please contact Simon & Schuster Special Sales at 1-866-506-1949
or business@simonandschuster.com

The Simon & Schuster Speakers Bureau can bring authors to your
live event. For more information or to book an event contact the
Simon & Schuster Speakers Bureau at 866-248-3049 or visit our
website at www.simonspeakers.com.

Interior design by Kyle Kabel

Manufactured in the United States of America

10 9 8 7 6 5 4 3 2 1

Library of Congress Cataloging-in-Publication Data is available.

ISBN 978-1-5011-2990-2
ISBN 978-1-5011-2992-6 (ebook)

For Lauren

You're right, happiness is just persistence and sheer will.

CONTENTS

INTRODUCTION

Black Rock City, Nevada

August 2013

We pedaled slowly through the alkaline playa dust, surrounded by a sea of neon lights, navigating our way through the magnificent art cars. Electronica music echoed eerily from the mountains that surrounded this pop-up desert city. Some revelers were on stilts, others breathing out fire. It felt as if we were at a circus on the moon.

Tony turned around and yelled back at us, "This way! I see the fire installations!" Taiwanese and soft-spoken, he rarely raised his voice. "Let's follow the octopus!" he said, referring to one of the most popular art cars. It was easy to follow him because of the bright yellow flag with a smiley face hooked to the back of his bike.

Burning Man, the massive rave and futuristic arts festival that draws around sixty thousand revelers every year, has become popular among tech CEOs in the last decade, drawing the likes of the Google guys, Amazon CEO Jeff Bezos, and Facebook founder Mark Zuckerberg. Tony Hsieh, who is CEO of online shoe store

Zappos, is a religious attendee. It wouldn't be the last time I would follow him under the desert's crystalline night sky.

Black Rock City is arranged in a half moon, from two o'clock to ten o'clock. The streets run in circles around the center, beginning with the Esplanade and then fanning out from A through L. This evening, we were pedaling into the center of the clock, where all of the fire installations are.

Burning Man was a huge inspiration for Tony's own plans: after Amazon bought Zappos for $1.2 billion in 2009, he decided to invest his windfall into creating his own desert utopia in downtown Las Vegas, just six hundred miles from Black Rock City. Just as the PLUR (peace, love, unity, and respect) code of conduct governed the raves of his youth, Burning Man's Ten Principles –including radical self-reliance, self-expression, and immediacy–have a way of pushing humanity to operate at a higher potential in this alternate reality. Many "Burners" call Black Rock City "home" and regular life "the default world." For about 7 days each year (the event runs up to 10 days, though most stay for no longer than a week), Burners get to experience a slice of heaven on earth. The other 358 days are subpar, all preparation for the 7 days. Tony was on a mission to re-create the Burning Man ethos in the area surrounding Zappos' new headquarters in downtown Las Vegas.

Arriving at our destination, we threw down our bikes and walked over to the fire Skee Ball, where white-hot flames whistled into the air as players tried to hit the center target. The desert air had dropped to a cool breeze, but I could feel the warmth of the fire on my skin.

"Imagine if we had this downtown," Tony said in a low voice, turning to his longtime right-hand man, Fred Mossler. Both were wearing cargo shorts, white T-shirts, and bandanas, making them stand out plainly amidst all the outlandish costumes.

"It would be quite something," nodded Fred, whose skin was tanned from the desert sun. He readily compares Tony to Steve Jobs and counts himself one of the luckiest guys in the world. Though that sort of partnership doesn't come without a price: Fred has sacrificed a lot for his millions.

"How would you get around city code?" I asked.

"Um, we'd figure out some way around it," Tony replied, his voice trailing. He had already found a way to park a forty-foot fire-spitting praying mantis from Burning Man in front of Container Park, one of his cornerstone properties. Container Park is a shipping container mall licensed as a tavern so that adults can walk around with alcohol while children play on The Treehouse jungle gym. His Downtown Project continues to find creative ways to circumvent red tape and retrofit urban spaces.

Tony's tag line for Downtown Project is a "City as a Start-up." He set out an ambitious and audacious goal of transforming downtown Las Vegas in five years in what would normally take fifteen to twenty years. His $350 million investment vehicle is focused most heavily on real estate, allocating at least $200 million, and then on small business and technology investments ($50 million each). Additionally, he personally earmarked $50 million to support education, arts, and culture within the investment property footprint and beyond. Several million went toward a private school that would raise children as entrepreneurs beginning at infancy, and also into an annual festival called Life Is Beautiful, inspired by the grandeur of events such as Burning Man and the annual South by Southwest (SXSW) conference and festivals in Austin, Texas.

We followed Tony to the roped-off area, where two players were dressed like astronauts in their silver fireproof gear. Whenever the players missed a beat, fire would flame up into their faces.

An announcer stood before the cordoned-off section on a large platform like the Wizard of Oz.

Burning Man attracts all walks of life, but it's become a destination for the Silicon Valley elite in recent years. Tesla and SpaceX CEO Elon Musk, who came up with the idea for SolarCity with his cousin while en route to the desert playa, insists that Burning Man *is* Silicon Valley. "If you haven't been, you just don't get it," he said of Mike Judge, the co-creator of HBO television series *Silicon Valley*.

Except in Black Rock City, there is no commerce. Before my pilgrimage there, Burners told me that I could manifest anything. All I had to do was desire it, and it would appear. That happened once that week, when I had a vision of fruit in my mind's eye and looked up to see a man carrying a crate of oranges on the desert path before me.

"Here, let's go over to the Dance, Dance Revolution!" Tony yelled with enthusiasm to the group, approaching the roped-off area.

The difference between Tony and most other Burners is that he wants to make every day a bit more like Burning Man—and he can afford to create his own universe. He launched a media campaign in earnest around his intention to create a city of the future back in 2012, and that's how our worlds collided. I met him at a Venture for America gala in New York City, where he was on the speaking circuit evangelizing the gospel of Downtown Project. (Venture for America is the equivalent of Teach for America for start-ups: the organization targets students from the nation's top schools to convince them to move to depressed cities instead of launching careers on Wall Street.) He told audiences, as he did that night in Manhattan, "If you fix cities, you kind of fix the world." Tony embodies the libertarian Silicon Valley ethos: a belief that the private sector is more capable of fixing the world's problems than government will ever be. Despite his introversion, he attracts people like a magnet. I was inspired by his vision and was willing to follow him anywhere.

As we stood in awe of the scene, Jenn Lim, the CEO of Delivering Happiness, the title of Tony's 2010 book and an offshoot consultancy created as a result of its success, walked over to us, her combat boots kicking up the playa dust. "There's a party at Ashram Galactica," she told the group, referring to one of the nicest camps at Burning Man; it even had a hotel. We hopped on our bikes to head over to 6:45 & D, its location on the playa.

Las Vegas bar owner Michael Cornthwaite stood waiting for us outside the entrance. Michael is a big reason that Tony decided to invest in downtown Las Vegas, but we'll get to that. Inside was a long bar that served specialty cocktails; it even had a menu. I handed over my thermos, and the bartender filled it with a vodka and cranberry juice on ice. Inside the cavernous tent reminded me of Michael's dimly lit Downtown Cocktail Room on Las Vegas Boulevard.

Someone gave us a tour of the camp and led us through several different luxury tents. Our guide shared that visitors could win a night in one of the tents through a raffle. Michael encouraged me to drop in my name. It looked a whole lot more comfortable than my arrangement across the playa: a small tent with no air conditioning, where it was nearly impossible to sleep during the day when temperatures rose above 100 degrees.

I secured a ticket to Burning Man at the eleventh hour and had little time to prepare. Downtown Project's cultural attaché–a Burner retained by Tony and tasked with bringing the Burning Man ethos to downtown Las Vegas–connected me to the young Venture for America fellow who gave me the golden ticket etched with the words "Cargo Cult," the theme for that year's festival. The term "cargo cult" is in reference to cult worship in Oceania a half century ago, when islanders built airports in anticipation of the miraculous arrival of a messiah-like figure bearing goods and other riches. Some Burners deemed cargo cult a "daring and dangerous theme" because it mirrored the very essence of the festival. The VFA fellow presented the golden ticket to me wearing bunny ears as his friend played guitar. In hindsight, that moment was really the beginning of my adventure falling down the rabbit hole into Tony's world.

I found a camp led by a group of Vegas entertainers (DJs, burlesque dancers, performers) and a ride from a stranger on Facebook–modern-day hitchhiking–days before the festival. There's no reliable cell phone service on the desert playa, so it was serendipity that I ended up spending that evening with Tony and his crew at all.

Earlier that afternoon, I had attempted to use the makeshift pulley shower system at my camp, to no avail. After trying and failing to get the bucket of water to fall over my head, I put my towel back on and ventured through my camp looking for help, and that's when I saw Tony, Fred Mossler, and the others. The group had arrived on their bikes, and Tony unfolded a piece of white paper, where he had written down names and camps. He invited me to join them for dinner at the 3 Seasons, one of the luxury "turnkey" camps on the playa where Tony was staying, and wrote the camp address (8:45 & H) on my forearm with a black marker.

Over dinner that evening, one of the guests stood up and spoke with reverence about the meaning behind the Temple at Burning Man. The Temple is one of the most sacred places on the playa: it is the space to honor the dead. Inside the tall wooden structure, there are notes, photos, and mementos for those who have passed away. On the last day of Burning Man, a Sunday, the Temple goes up in flames. It's an act of catharsis. "We've lost many to suicide, and let us not allow these people to burn in our memories in shame," the guest shared with the group, silent around the table inside the tent.

I didn't realize it at the time, but attending Burning Man that year foreshadowed many of the events that would unfold in downtown Las Vegas.

"If most people had the kind of money that Tony has, they'd ride off into the sunset," early Zappos investor Erik Moore remarked once. That comment never sat quite right with me because in many respects, Tony already has, in his own way.

For one, his yearly festival circuit is densely packed. Beyond Burning Man, there's Tomorrowland, Lightning in a Bottle, Coachella, Further Future, Electric Daisy Carnival, and many others. But more than anything, it seemed that what he was doing with his Downtown Project was nothing more than an experiment. Life on an island would be much worse: he would have no real influence.

Over the next three years, I came to know intimately many of the people who make up Tony's utopia, through being invited into their inner lives and understanding what motivates them, what they fear most, and why they too were drawn into its vortex.

You could say that it was a dare that brought me into Tony's world. After I met him at the VFA gala in New York City, I convinced my editors at the website *Business Insider* to send me out to Vegas to report on his Downtown Project. I returned with the same puff piece that nearly all of his media visitors came back with: an excitable profile of a tech visionary revitalizing a city.

Only when I decided to return to Vegas two months later on my own account did I begin to see the real story emerge. Through a series of fortuitous events (opportunistic decisions), I decided to leave *Business Insider* and my life in Brooklyn and move to Vegas to write a book about Tony's quest to create his own version of Burning Man. I saw it mostly as an adventure; a once-in-a-lifetime opportunity. I knew these things didn't happen very often.

Along with many others who gave up everything to follow Tony to Vegas, I rode the roller coaster of extremes in a city where people travel from far and wide to risk it all. Only when I too decided to risk it all did things get really interesting.

But before we dive back into the story, I'll brief you on Zappos' history and how Downtown Project got started–then I'll bring you back inside Tony's social engineering experiment.

DAWN OF THE PROJECT

In Silicon Valley, start-ups live and die by their stories. Tony understands the enduring power of the origin story and wrote one that would stick with people in *Delivering Happiness: A Path to Profits, Passion, and Purpose.* His version of events leaves out some people and the decisions they made that influenced Zappos's success, but it's a high-level view of the company's trajectory.

He opens his book with the Amazon sale, describing how employees stood before him with tears in their eyes when he delivered the news in July 2009. He recounts how PLUR principles helped him create a billion-dollar brand.

Like many storied start-ups, Zappos's origins trace back to the halls of Harvard University, where Tony met Alfred Lin, the person who would become integral to all of his future success. Both sons of Taiwanese immigrants, they bonded over the high expectations that their parents had for them. Their mothers wanted them to become doctors and lawyers, but both leaned toward business because it wasn't such a rigid and predictable path.

The bond that they formed would transcend years, even as their paths diverged and converged again. After graduation, Tony went to work for the enterprise software company Oracle, while Alfred went to work on his PhD in statistics at Stanford University. They found each other again when Tony asked Alfred to join his online advertising company, LinkExchange, which he cofounded with another Harvard grad, Sanjay Madan, in 1996. Alfred joined LinkExchange as VP of finance after the Internet start-up got funding from Sequoia Capital. Two years later, they sold the company to Microsoft near the peak of the dot-com bubble in November 1998 for $265 million.

Alfred and Tony then created a venture capital fund, Venture Frogs, to support new start-ups. Most of the firm's capital came from Tony and outside investors. They made twenty-seven investments and had about seven successes, including Zappos—a well-performing fund by industry standards.

The young investors made some real gambles. In 1999, Tony purchased the domain Drugs.com for $823,456 in a public auction. Its previous owner discovered that the sale of pharmaceuticals is regulated pretty heavily. Venture Frogs apparently came to a similar conclusion and sold the domain in 2001. "They'd rather be shoe salesmen than drug dealers," a tech news site proclaimed.

"Our decision to focus on [Zappos.com] is that it seemed like a much bigger opportunity than developing Drugs.com on our own," Tony told *Wired* magazine. "Initially, we just felt it was a good value. The equivalent of real estate on the Internet."

The idea for Shoesite.com (now Zappos) came from Nick Swinmurn, who had graduated from the University of California at Santa Barbara a few years earlier. He was looking for someone to invest in his idea, and a lawyer told him about Venture Frogs. He pitched Tony and Alfred at their loft office space at 1000 Van Ness Avenue in San Francisco. Tony describes the idea in his book:

Nick summarized his entire pitch in three sentences: Footwear is a $40 billion industry in the United States, of which catalog sales make up $2 billion. It is likely that e-commerce will continue to grow. And it is likely that people will continue to wear shoes in the foreseeable future.

Tony and Alfred agreed to invest only if Nick could find someone with merchandising experience to join the team. So Nick called up Fred Mossler, then a rising shoe buyer with Nordstrom department stores in San Francisco. Lacking the confidence to jump fully into a risky endeavor solo, Fred accepted the offer on the condition that his boss, John Alteio, also came on board.

For a while, Tony and Alfred stayed on the sidelines, but then when they decided to double down on Zappos, Tony joined the company and made it his full-time job. (Alfred opted to join another one of their investments, Tellme Networks, which also experienced success.) He was extremely confident in his abilities from early on. "Tony's always the smartest guy in the room," Nick said, speaking to Tony's demeanor.

The Zappos origin story is filled with near-death experiences. Tony's risk tolerance is very high. After the LinkExchange sale, he got into day trading and Alfred remembers how his friend received a letter from the Charles Schwab brokerage firm warning Tony that he was losing too much money too fast. Alfred says he's never seen anyone operate so close to zero in his life.

"It felt like every day we were betting the farm," Nick recalls.

By the early 2000s, several employees were living in Tony's lofts at 1000 Van Ness, including Nick, in order to keep salaries and expenses low. Operating close to zero was the only way that the company could possibly survive. Tony took over as CEO, and the online shoe retailer grew to just under a hundred employees in San Francisco.

In 2004, Tony decided to move the company to Las Vegas–where he had been spending many weekends playing poker–to grow its call center in a city that runs on a 24/7 hospitality industry. About seventy employees chose to relocate to its new headquarters on Warm Springs Road, a nondescript office in an Allstate building near McCarran International Airport. The company's work-hard, play-hard culture was really established in Sin City. "We only knew each other," reflected a longtime call center worker who made the move and is still with the company today. "So we really bonded." Vegas was a great option for Zappos not only for its hospitality focus but also because Nevada is a corporate tax haven like Delaware.

Upon arriving in Las Vegas, Tony also made a double-down bet to grow the company by focusing on its culture. At the time, companies like Google were investing in company culture (it was trending in Silicon Valley), but creating an enjoyable place to work was a foreign concept for call center workers in Las Vegas. That focus gave Zappos its edge. Alfred joined Zappos full-time in 2005, and together they were unstoppable: Tony as the visionary, and Alfred as the finance and operations man.

Recruiters in the area began to take notice of the start-up's unique culture, sending their favorite candidates to Zappos. Two of those recruiters, Jamie Naughton and Christa Foley, eventually joined the company and helped establish the distinct culture that exists today.

The Warm Springs Road office was designed with two separate areas: one room filled with mostly call center workers, and the other, on the opposite side of the lobby, where the executive team and others worked.

Still, there was a natural cohesion. "It was very start-up; it was very everyone-does-everything, everyone-jumps-in-and-helps," Christa remembered. "It's a call center and collection agency town." She named a few: Citibank, HSBC, Ford Motor Credit, Expedia, Williams-Sonoma. "Some people are used to being told what they can do, and that open door of 'What do *you* think the right thing to do is?' takes people aback."

Different factions in the organization started to gel when it decided to invest in hiring call center workers full-time and established more of a universal hiring guidebook. On Valentine's Day 2006 the company rolled out its Ten Core Values (including directives such as "Create fun and a little weirdness"), against which Tony and the recruiting team would measure new hires. Many were corporate misfits, sporting colorful streaks in their hair and tattoos down their arms. The office environment evolved into a zany place, complete with office parades and numerous happy hours. In the early years, Tony would take shots of vodka with new hires as part of the initiation process.

A decade later, Zappos still evaluates job candidates on culture fit based on the company's Ten Core Values. "I'm not trying to get someone who is one hundred percent on all Ten Core Values–that's impossible," said Christa, who herself experimented with red hair and sports tattoos. "But I do want to make sure that I filter out anyone who would be in direct opposition to one of the core values. Maybe they don't do parades, but they aren't rolling their eyes when a parade is going by, either."

In order to ensure that new employees fit the culture, Zappos holds a month-long initiation process and even pays candidates to quit, a strategy that Amazon has adopted. Zappos describes its new hire training as a "probationary period in that employees are held to high standards and are evaluated based on their performance, providing the Zappos experience to customers, and their embodiment of the Zappos culture and core values." In other words, the process consists as much of Zappos evaluating its candidates before extending the offer (which is presented after the second week) as it does of prospective employees assessing the company. Those who successfully complete training and decide to stay celebrate by dressing up and parading through the office at the end of their initiation. "It's made very clear that you are choosing Zappos over money," says a former employee.

Some employees have called Zappos the "land of misfit toys." It's a brilliant tactic to give people who normally feel cast aside by society the opportunity to feel special; like they can express themselves while doing the routine work of answering phones.

For all the fanfare around its culture, it's important to remember that Zappos is a retailer that sells shoes online. It's successful because its customers like free shipping and its 365-day return policy. The call center workers are given loose scripts and are encouraged to be highly personable, to the point of staying on the phone for hours if that's what it takes to establish rapport with customers.

The company moved to a sprawling office park in the Las Vegas suburb of Henderson and grew rapidly to around a thousand employees. As the organization's culture strengthened and became something that Tony was really proud of, he began going out on the speaking circuit to talk about Zappos and closed his talks by telling audience members that they should stop by the office for a tour. Over time, that grew into a tours team and a revenue stream for Zappos. (Today tours cost anywhere from ten dollars to $15,000, according to its website, depending upon the type of tour and group size. On any given day it's common to see Zapponians guiding tour groups throughout the campus.)

Nick left the company in 2006: after seven years, he was ready to move on to something else. There was no good-bye party but no real animosity either, though there was frustration a few years later when Nick contacted Zappos to cash out a few hundred thousand shares. It was days before the Amazon sale was announced. He lost out on about $2 million. We'll get to more on his story later.

Zappos's strong brand, customer loyalty, sales, and market share are what attracted Jeff Bezos, who first approached Tony in 2005 and then again in 2009. The second time, the country was in a recession and Zappos was still operating on a revolving $100 million line of credit to purchase inventory. When Amazon came calling again, Sequoia Capital (which had already invested $48 million) was pressing Zappos to either go public or sell. The latter was something that Tony never wanted to do, because it meant losing the freedom to run the company as he pleased. Zappos would likely have gotten crushed in public markets, observes one former employee, in part because the sales figures it projected to the world painted a slightly rosier view than what was actually happening. The online retailer was in a tough spot.

As part of the deal, they negotiated that Zappos continue to operate independently. In the tech world, it's not uncommon for companies to become acquired and then get absorbed into the parent company. But Tony was determined to maintain Zappos's independence.

As long as Zappos hits its numbers, Jeff Bezos generally allows Tony to do what he wants. But of course, that could change any day. "Let's be clear: Amazon owns one hundred percent of Zappos," said Alfred. "They could have ripped up the tenets the day we were acquired. There's nothing formally binding about it."

DOWNTOWN COCKTAIL ROOM

In December 2009, about a month after the Amazon deal was finalized, Tony shared with his friend Sarah Nisperos a dream he had about investing his financial windfall into creating a city district with happiness as the number one goal. Sarah immediately thought of entrepreneur Michael Cornthwaite, who was working to develop a more attractive downtown through his Future Restaurant Group–that area could certainly use an infusion of happiness. Michael had a good relationship with Mayor Oscar Goodman, who was also working to build a better downtown.

Within twenty minutes after Sarah connected the two, Tony appeared at Michael's Downtown Cocktail Room (DCR) alone, which is rare–he always travels with others. Tony was wearing his signature Zappos T-shirt and Michael wore a plaid button-down shirt with the sleeves rolled up to his elbows. They ordered drinks, and then he started peppering Michael with questions: *Why did you move downtown? Why do you believe in it? What do you think the potential is? What is your end goal?* Many of the most pivotal decisions in Tony's life happen over drinks in the back of a bar.

And then it turned into a series of meetings several times a week that went on for months. At the time, Tony had been looking into other suburban locations for Zappos, with a vision of creating his own Disneyland and a sprawling corporate campus like Apple or Facebook.

Michael was particularly excited about one meeting where Tony asked a series of questions that made it sound like he wanted to expand Zappos into the walls of a city: *How could the whole area be so controlled so that it didn't matter so much about money or status, and it was just filled with nice people?* They'd walk into the neighboring bars, such as the Beauty Bar and the Griffin, and talk to the bar owners.

Both Tony and Michael were thirty-six at the time, but their lives were worlds apart: after Tony sold LinkExchange to Microsoft at age twenty-four, he technically never had to work another day in his life. Michael built his bar from the ground up and still sweated when his rent checks came due each month. He was engaged to his now-wife Jennifer, and his shoulder-length hair, salt-and-pepper beard, and already-weathered skin revealed his years working late into the night in Vegas's underbelly. Tony, a bachelor, sports a buzz cut and looks much younger than his years.

Directly across the street from DCR is the Fremont Street Experience, a poor man's Vegas Strip where older half-naked men and women walk around in string bikinis and other costumes and try to make a buck from unassuming tourists. Mayor Oscar Goodman, a former mob lawyer (who had a cameo in Martin Scorsese's 1995 film *Casino*) with a gregarious personality and an insistence on being flanked by show girls during his press conferences, wanted to leave his mark on Las Vegas's downtown and had been trying to revitalize the area for years.

Aside from a few notable establishments, in 2009 the area was filled with shuttered shops, a dollar store, and a hole-in-the-wall kabob restaurant. It wasn't always this way. In fact, downtown Las Vegas is the original Vegas. The city emerged in the early 1900s, a half-century after the Church of Jesus Christ of Latter-Day Saints set up a Mormon fort between Salt Lake City and Los Angeles on the land that would become Sin City proper. Nevada legalized casino gambling in the 1930s (before then, it took place in speakeasies and illicit casinos), and the downtown area became a destination in the 1950s with the opening of the Moulin Rouge casino-hotel. Real estate magnate Steve Wynn renovated the downtown Golden Nugget casino in the 1970s, making it a destination for high-end clientele. Wynn turned his attention and changed the center of gravity to what is now the Las Vegas Strip in the 1980s and 1990s, when he built the Mirage, the city's first megaresort, and then the Bellagio. Over the next few decades, the downtown area became increasingly neglected and known for its pay-by-the-hour hotel rooms and seedy, smoke-filled casinos. There are still remnants from the downtown's past, including the El Cortez casino hotel–built in 1941, making it one of the oldest–on Fremont and Sixth Street, but the area devolved into a skeleton of what it once was.

When the real estate bubble burst, Nevada and the city of Las Vegas were hit harder than nearly any place in America, and 70 percent of all homes went underwater. Over the next few years, a chilling number of properties went vacant, and construction froze across the city. "It was a leveraged, false environment, and we all bought into the Kool-Aid," a Las Vegas resident told a local reporter during that time. "The mentality was to go borrow credit and put money into the house and get it back before it was finished."

The high foreclosure and climbing unemployment rates would also drive many people to despair: the suicide rate in Las Vegas was already among the nation's highest, but during those years, it spiked. In many ways, Las Vegas is a microcosm of America, amplifying its shadow nature in plain sight.

Over his far-reaching conversations with Michael, Tony wanted to gather as much data as possible to determine whether the area was worth investing in. It is proven historically that when a large company relocates, investment in the area typically follows. Tony considered his employees: many were young and unmarried, and reflected the demographic Richard Florida predicted would migrate into cities in his 2002 book, *The Rise of the Creative Class: And How It's Transforming Work, Leisure, Community, and Everyday Life.*

Tony and his number two, Fred Mossler, continued to look at properties around Las Vegas, even considering renovating a casino on the edge of the Strip for Zappos's new home. But nothing felt right. When Michael shared with them that city hall was becoming available, a light bulb went off. Tony and Fred looked immediately for someone who could secure the building for them. They were introduced to Andrew Donner, a real estate mogul who looks and acts like Bruce Willis. Vegas is a town where you need to know someone to get anything done, and Andrew, who lives in California, is related through marriage to ex–City Council member Michael Mack. Mayor Oscar Goodman described Andrew as a "pleasant-enough fellow, a cheerleader."

Walking around downtown with Andrew one afternoon, Tony pointed to the city hall building, a large, white structure shaped like a half moon. "What about that?" he asked. Andrew explained that the building was already claimed, but Tony pushed him to look into it further.

Mayor Goodman took a meeting with Andrew, who told him that he had an interested buyer for city hall. "I see anybody as long as they have money in the bank," Mayor Goodman explained. Andrew said at first that he couldn't offer details on the prospective buyer. But eventually he arranged for a black town car and took the mayor out to Henderson. There Goodman encountered Zappos for the first time. "People were running around with flags, dolls at their desks, marionettes, lying down eating candy. I had never seen anything like it," he recalled with bemusement, which says a lot coming from the mayor of Las Vegas. "This is extraordinary.

What kind of business can be run this way?" Oscar Goodman's wife, Carolyn, who went on to become mayor, described her experience at Zappos as watching employees "do their circus thing."

Around that same time, Tony departed for a twenty-three-city bus tour across America pitching his *Delivering Happiness* message to the world. He purchased a tour bus from the Dave Matthews Band and replaced the signage with the *Delivering Happiness* logo: a now-iconic winky face. He solicited the services of a company that specializes in turning books into bestsellers and bought a substantial number of copies himself.

A notable Barbara Walters interview and a *CBS Sunday Morning* segment gave him even more name recognition. The media push from his book likely elevated Zappos even higher on *Fortune* magazine's annual list of the best companies to work for. *Delivering Happiness* earned Zappos respect as a leader in company culture and positioned Tony as an inspirational happiness guru.

His message was also the right one at the right time: the United States was still reeling after the Great Recession, the unemployment rate was hovering at 9 percent, and Americans were looking for signs of hope. They had put President Barack Obama in office and were searching for leaders who could reinstate their belief in capitalism and the government, after Wall Street had failed the country.

Against this economic backdrop, tech CEOs were gaining momentum again as the country's leading thinkers and attracting young talent to join their start-ups instead of heading to Wall Street or taking high-paying consulting gigs. Entrepreneurship was an extremely appealing narrative to Americans, especially to Millennials who were entering the workforce at a time when faith in traditional employers had dropped significantly. This segment of the population was searching for purpose in its daily work. Shared values mattered more than a paycheck. *Delivering Happiness* was the sort of message they were seeking.

Tony's net worth had skyrocketed with the Amazon sale, his employees were happy, and he had a *New York Times* bestseller. The bus tour propelled Tony into semicelebrity status, and it launched a revolution of sorts around happiness at work. To the American public, Tony Hsieh *was* the American Dream.

Meanwhile, Andrew was working hard behind the scenes to bring Tony's vision to fruition. He made an unsolicited bid to purchase the old city hall and convinced Mayor Goodman and the City Council to backpedal on its deal with real estate developer Cordish Companies–a respected century-old firm based in Baltimore, Maryland–which had secured the rights to the property to build an arena. Asking City Council to get out of its deal with Cordish was not a minor request: taxpayer dollars were on the line, as the mayor was already investing in an expensive new city hall blocks away. If the deal fell through and the old building remained empty, there would surely be a public outcry. "We made a sweetheart deal with Cordish," Mayor Oscar Goodman explained to me. "Moved them to Symphony Park."

Tony teared up at the City Council meeting when its members approved the sale of the city hall building to Zappos. "And mayor," he looked at Oscar. "I think you're sitting in my future seat." The universe was bending for him.

In the final months before it was set to close, the *Las Vegas Sun* reported that Andrew gave $10,000 to Carolyn Goodman, who was soon to take over her husband's job in summer 2011. In the final days of Oscar Goodman's administration, the sale price dropped from $25 million to $18 million. City officials cited

Zappos's promise to bring even more employees downtown as among the reasons they lowered the price. At the City Council meeting where lowering the price of the deal was on the agenda, two hundred Zapponians wearing bright blue T-shirts with the faces of the mayor on them descended into the council chambers, flash-mob style, dancing with pom-poms. The mayor and others stood up and danced. "That's why we're doing what we're doing," Oscar Goodman concluded.

The occasional light moment aside, it was a grueling, months-long marathon deal process that led to Andrew's boutique real estate agency, Resort Gaming Group (RGG), becoming the landlord to the Amazon-owned retailer. Once the deal terms were nearly finalized, Andrew was hospitalized for exhaustion. "I cannot impress enough on you, that transaction took everything out of me," Andrew told me later. "Everything I had. The pressure and the stakes were very high. Can you imagine if it didn't happen, after the city voted for Cordish to leave?"

The Goodmans were thrilled to have someone with as much international cache as Tony enter their sphere. "Whatever Tony did is electrifying," Carolyn Goodman told me resolutely. "There was nothing better coming out of this recession than the name Tony Hsieh. He's the king of the Millennials."

The stars were aligning, except for one thing. Alfred Lin left Zappos in late 2010, as Tony was completing his book tour and as the city hall deal was becoming a reality. Alfred's wife was pregnant with their first child, and they wanted to be closer to family in the Bay Area. He was also not interested in working on the Downtown Project.

• • •

RGG played a major role in the formation of Downtown Project (DTP). "We had an option on expansion land," Andrew Donner explained. "We were looking to expand and redevelop in different areas. I suppose we were probably the driver to say, 'We should start acquiring this real estate before we secure city hall.'"

With the Zappos/city hall deal in motion, Tony signed a lease on a luxury high-rise around the corner from his future campus. The Ogden was a tall, white structure that had struggled to attract occupants during the recession. It filed for Chapter 11 bankruptcy in 2009 and was acquired by new owners.

Down the street, DCR became the de facto headquarters for Downtown Project–DTP even put a sign on the dark door that stated as much. Walking into Michael's bar feels like walking into a sacred space. DCR is on Las Vegas Boulevard, tucked inside an exposed brick wall with a door that is just inside an awning. The bar is filled with black leather chairs. The menu consists of specialty cocktails and a slim assortment of bar food such as pretzels and nuts. If you're going to spend a lot of time at DCR, you need to emerge back into the Fremont East District every few hours to find real sustenance.

Tony connected with Zach Ware, a young Zappos product manager who expressed a shared interest in urban revitalization and hacking ways to make downtown better for company employees. Together they read Harvard economist Edward Glaeser's *Triumph of the City: How Our Greatest Invention Makes Us Richer, Smarter, Greener, Healthier, and Happier* and spent hours brainstorming over drinks. They bonded over Glaeser's manifesto about how the world is concentrating in cities, which is spurring higher innovation because of the high population density. Tony became obsessed with the idea of sparking more innovation at

Zappos by investing in the area and turning a cultural wasteland into a creative capital.

Zappos's planned move downtown reflected a trend in Silicon Valley: tech companies were moving outside of the office parks and into the city. For instance, Twitter, swayed by generous and controversial tax breaks, moved its headquarters to San Francisco's gritty Mid-Market District.

"What if we could create the coworking capital of the world? The shipping container capital of the world? The fire capital of the world? What if we could do that in five years?" Tony proposed. "There's a story about how once someone broke the four-minute mile, then everyone followed." Tony formed the DTP investment vehicle with a proclaimed mission of making downtown Vegas "the most community-focused large city in the world."

Initially, Zach declined the opportunity to work on the campus redevelopment and what would become Downtown Project. "I was shortsighted," he reflected. "I didn't realize that this was the future." He continued to work his day job at Zappos, but his nights became more exciting: he'd break away from drinks with out-of-town visitors to jump on an eleven o'clock Skype call with a Danish architect in China, for example. Momentum was building. With access to Tony and his money, those sorts of late-night Skype calls weren't theoretical: Zach actually got to start working on the idea of creating a "City as a Start-Up."

By June 2011, Tony had moved into his apartment on the twenty-third floor of the Ogden, and Zach had moved in down the hall. Fred Mossler and his now-wife Meghan Boyd, a former Zappos buyer, soon followed suit, as did Tony's chief of staff, Jamie Naughton; his longtime life manager Mimi Pham; Zappos's life coach, Augusta "Coach" Scott; and others. The building began to sharply increase the rent, capitalizing on the influx of new residents because of Tony's decision to move there.

Tony wanted to replicate the feeling of being in a college dorm, which he first experimented with at 1000 Van Ness in San Francisco–where he lived next to all his friends, including Alfred, and other Zappos investors and employees–now it was just a different luxury apartment building, different city. Living in close proximity to coworkers was something that felt natural to an otherwise introverted person.

The idea of having everyone in closer proximity in the Ogden was also strategic, as it would increase the number of interactions people would have with one another, and, ideally, fuel ideas and collaborations (which he coined "collisions"). Tony and Zach began giving tours that started in Tony's apartment, where there was a wall filled with Post-its with ideas for businesses downtown. Visitors were encouraged to add an idea to the wall. It was a brilliant marketing strategy.

Overnight, Tony's platform had elevated to happiness guru and seller of dreams. In a city like Vegas, his message had unique resonance. There was no city in America where it would ring so well, though Detroit was a close second, where another billionaire* started a similar reinvestment project around the same time: Quicken Loans founder Dan Gilbert moved his company HQ to the city's core and invested more than $1 billion to invigorate the area.

In addition to giving tours and entertaining out-of-town visitors, Zach was working hard on transforming city hall into a corporate campus. Despite having no experience in construc-

---

* Although Tony has not publicly disclosed his net worth, many sources point to his net worth to be around a billion dollars.

tion, city planning, or investing, he was tasked with overseeing the $40 million renovation. Soon he also was given the responsibility of managing the $50 million Vegas Tech Fund, which was the venture capital arm of Downtown Project that would invest in early-stage companies. It was created a few months after Tony invited Zappos's tech team to a brainstorming session at his Southern Highlands mansion about the formation of DTP and offered would-be entrepreneurs incentives to start their own companies. He encouraged engineers–already a scarce resource for the e-commerce company in Vegas–to come up with start-up ideas to get the culture off the ground.

A handful of the Zappos engineers took Tony up on his offer, and conceptualized a garage sale app (Rumgr) and an online polling platform (Wedgies). The Zappos network had ties to tech talent in Salt Lake City (Ticket Cake, an online ticketing company, and the other half of the Wedgies cofounding team), and encouraged them to move to Las Vegas. All three companies received early seed funding. It was more important to attract tech talent in the first place; the quality of the idea was less important.

Downtown Project's focus on becoming the most community-minded city in the world meant that it wanted start-ups to invest in ROC, or "return on community." It was stated explicitly in its mission statement: The measure of any start-up was whether it could add value to the community, spark news, and eventually, deliver financial returns. Being "story worthy" was very important. That would attract the press, and in turn, more potential recruits. Tony's focus on the media is why he offered to invest $100,000 in journalist Paul Carr's NSFWCORP media site ("NSWF" is short for "not safe for work") with zero equity, as long as Paul stayed in Vegas. (Tony ended up investing $600,000 into Paul's NSFWCORP through his Vegas Tech Fund.)

Tony identified very quickly the start-up that he hoped would deliver a healthy return on his money. Through a fortuitous chain of events, he met a young Harvard grad named Keller Rinaudo, who was traveling the world as a professional rock climber while also developing a company called Romotive that sold personal iPhone robots ("Romo"). Keller happened to be in Vegas for a climbing event and was crashing on the couch of a Zappos employee. It didn't take long for Vegas Tech Fund (VTF) to invest $500,000, the maximum allocated amount at the time. VTF was then exclusively focused on early-stage companies. Keller moved his team to Vegas, and they leased an apartment in the Ogden, with the entire team living and working there.

Romotive was the early Vegas Tech darling, and one that Tony favored through gestures such as bringing down leftover pizza after Downtown Project events. Soon after the company moved there in 2011, Keller sent out this email to Ogden residents:

From: Keller Rinaudo <keller@romotive.com>
Date: Thu, Dec 1, 2011 at 1:52 AM
Subject: Community dinners at the Ogden
To: ogdenpeeps <ogdenpeeps@googlegroups.com>
Cc: peter@romotive.com, phu@romotive.com,
jen@habitlabs.com, info@rumgr.com, tony@zappos.com

Hi Ogden family,

As many of you know, we've decided to move Romotive to Las Vegas. We couldn't be more excited about joining the downtown community. We love everything about the Ogden, and we want to play a major role in turning it into a unique and awesome place to live. Along those lines, we'd like to propose a new tradition.

Since we started Romotive four months ago, we've eaten out for 75% of all our meals (usually take out, food trucks, etc). We're tired of eating greasy food off disposable plates with disposable utensils. So we're going to start cooking a healthy, fresh, local dinner every Wednesday and Sunday, and we want you all to join us. We know everyone is super busy, so come for 20 minutes anytime between 7:30 and 9:30, say hi to your friends, eat good food off a real plate, and then take off.

We'd like these dinners to help us create a sense of family and trust. We think that it would be awesome to live in a building where our living space is not limited to the apartments that we live in. On that note, we live in unit 1714, and we never lock our door. If you ever want to hang out, work, or sumo wrestle, please come by. Eat food out of our fridge. Play with our robots.

We are moving here because of the crazy potential we saw in this place. Thanks for welcoming us so graciously, and we hope to see you all on Sunday.

Much love,

Keller and the robot guys

Aside from the dinners and other events, Romotive went dark: everyone was in creation mode. One of its team members emerged occasionally, when he carried a Santa Claus–style bag filled with

Romo orders to the post office on Las Vegas Boulevard and Carson Avenue, two blocks from the Ogden.

"I loved the idea of building a city from scratch, and worked every day I was there to try to build a community around things like technology, art, friendship, and hard work," said Keller.

Tony explained to me once what he was going for with Downtown Project by using the Massachusetts Institute of Technology's online Media Lab as a tool. (MIT's Media Lab in Cambridge, Massachusetts, is a hub for innovation; its online extension reveals some of its discoveries and prototypes.) He asked me to put in my email address, and the Media Lab's algorithm generated a visual web showing how all of my contacts were interconnected. "Imagine that's the fashion incubator, and that's tech start-ups," he said, pointing to two disparate groups of dots that appeared on his laptop screen. "Now imagine if they collided."

The idea is to create exponential idea generation, in the way that popular science author Steven Johnson describes in his book *Where Good Ideas Come From: The Natural History of Innovation*. Tony explained that he wanted to see this happen daily, in real life, with the people that he brought to the community. He said he wanted to see how quickly he could inspire innovative ideas.

THE COLLECTION PROCESS

By late 2011, Downtown Project consisted of a few employees, including Tony's cousin Connie Yeh, who would manage the education fund, and her then-fiancé, Don Welch, who would run the $50 million small business fund. On a whim, after reading a glowing profile of Tony in a local magazine, Zach asked its author, Kim Schaefer, a woman in her early forties who was known to enjoy a good martini, if she would join Downtown Project as its communications officer. Kim would become one of the most loyal Tony evangelists, calling herself the "Mama Bear" of the entire project.

The core team was built of a group of generalists: people with little to zero experience in their area. But that was the idea: Tony saw DTP as an opportunity to give people the chance to try things entirely outside of their fields. He used ride-hailing app service Uber, now valued at several billion dollars, as an example: "Uber wasn't founded by people who came from the taxi industry," he said. (As Uber grew, the company brought in more experts, as would DTP.) Andrew Donner had the core competency in real estate, but aside from that, many of the key people were new to their fields or had only peripheral experience. They relied on expertise from others, and it was mostly trial by fire.

Hiring generalists is also a closely held personal philosophy. In the early days of Zappos, Nick remembers how Tony once fired a very senior person in favor of a junior graphic designer. It's cheaper, usually, and also the person doesn't come in with preconceived notions of how things should be done. About 25 percent of Zappos employees come in through the call center, many of them while in their twenties, and they become versed in Zappos's core competency before moving elsewhere in the organization. That way, it's easier to adopt the cognitive and cultural norms of the company.

The small DTP team began working out of Tony's apartment on the twenty-third floor of the Ogden, with near-360-degree views overlooking Las Vegas. Most of the original team leased apartments in the Ogden, and Downtown Project was in the process of taking over leases all throughout the building and turning them into crash pads for guests. By 2013, DTP owned close to a hundred leases.

Downtown Project arranged for VIP guests and advisors such as Sal Kahn, the education guru known for Kahn Academy, to visit via private jet chartering company JetSuite and stay in Tony's apartment or one of the nicest crash pads. (Tony is an investor in JetSuite and on its board of directors.) Most of the hundreds of visitors over the recruiting season were personal guests of Tony. That said, it was relatively easy to get an invitation. At the end of his stump speeches, Tony would display a slide with an image of the Ogden and the words "Our Secret Weapon," and then display his email, encouraging attendees to reach out to him directly. He was addressing curated audiences at venues such as the Aspen Ideas Festival and SXSW to encourage them to transplant to Las Vegas. One of his biggest early mistakes was not seeking out more local talent–something that would become a tension point for Las Vegans, sparking some negative press.

Most of Tony's early recruiting occurred on his yearly festival and events circuit. Through tech circles Tony met a serial entrepreneur named Jody Sherman, an eccentric man with a shock of curly hair and tattoos lining his body. Jody and Tony were both members of Summit Series, an invite-only group of entrepreneurs. Tony convinced him to move to Las Vegas and help recruit other entrepreneurs there in exchange for an investment in his start-up, Ecomom. Jody became one of the first entrepreneurs to receive funding from Downtown Project, and soon helped recruit another Summit attendee with rough edges: Matt Berman, who owned the eclectic Bolt Barbers shop.

Don Welch–who went from a job in sales and technology at Citigroup to managing a $50 million fund–could be easily spotted downtown wearing a button-up shirt and a backpack, and always holding a cigarette. He began to meet with local business owners. One of the first was Natalie Young, a former chef on the

Las Vegas Strip. Michael, who spent years on the Strip, including a stint as a parking attendant at the Stratosphere in 1996, introduced Natalie to Tony. DTP invested $225,000 in her restaurant Eat, it taking 50 percent equity and 50 percent in lifetime profits. All small business deals were structured fifty-fifty, an arrangement that led some more seasoned restaurateurs to walk away (although DTP would still attract chefs with proven star power, like the late Kerry Simon). The early investments were designed to attract those who would likely otherwise not receive funding elsewhere, giving them little leverage in negotiations. A big draw was the interest-free loan and the owner's ability to walk away at any time without paying back the loan.

But DTP also developed relationships and went above and beyond for its investments in ways that other investment vehicles wouldn't. For example, when Matt Berman decided to open up a Bolt Barbers location in Container Park, he decided that he wanted to purchase a train caboose for the shop, instead of a shipping container. When he found a caboose for sale in Henderson, Matt told me that Don Welch stepped in and personally insured the caboose. Not only was Matt a seasoned entrepreneur, his business was newsworthy: it was a first, unique, best.

Everyone was moving so fast that a lot of what was set in motion during those early years was simply shooting from the hip. That went for the official public launch of DTP, which happened when an *Inc.* magazine reporter spent some time in town and published a story in January 2012 titled "Tony Hsieh's Excellent Las Vegas Adventure." The story launched a tidal wave of press that would keep on flowing over the next few years. "Our hero," Max Chafkin wrote, "attempts to reinvent his city, Zappos-style."

SHOOTING BULLETS

On Sunday, January 15, 2012, Zappos experienced its worst security breach in its history. Someone hacked into the company's servers in Kentucky, putting its twenty-four million customers at risk. That night, Tony sent out an email to his employees telling them he needed all hands on deck.

The next day an entertainment executive from the Cosmopolitan hotel and casino by the name of Rehan Choudhry arrived at the Henderson campus for a tour. It also happened to be Pajama Day at Zappos.

"I couldn't believe it," Rehan recalled later. "It was the worst day in the company's history, and everyone is as happy as they could be, walking around in pajamas." Blown away by the corporate culture, the visit convinced Rehan to quit his job, build out a concept that he had been playing around with for years, and pitch Downtown Project on funding him. He spent his days at Michael Cornthwaite's The Beat Coffeehouse and Records on the corner of Sixth and Fremont Streets. After suffering a heart attack at age twenty-three, he changed his priorities and began only chasing after the things that truly mattered to him. "I have never felt that time was on my side," Rehan explained to a reporter.

He conceptualized Life Is Beautiful as a massive festival of music, food, art, and learning. "Imagine if you're a hospitality worker–how far do your dreams go?" he offered, referring to the city's backbone of hospitality and service workers. Life Is Beautiful was exactly the kind of branding that Downtown Project was looking for, and Tony bankrolled Rehan almost immediately somewhere between $22 and $24 million dollars. For Rehan, then thirty-two, it was the manifestation of his wildest dreams.

With a promise to transform downtown Vegas in five years or less, Tony planned on high-risk ventures and failing fast when necessary, applying the same principles of running a start-up to a city. Life Is Beautiful was one investment that DTP decided it would risk taking a significant loss on. The idea was that the festival would serve as a marketing tool for Downtown Project.

The data breach at Zappos happened just as the company was beginning its massive move to adopt Amazon's technical infrastructure, which would require the focus of its engineering talent for years. It was also a moment where the company's culture was stronger than ever before. "If you study tribes, when there's an external threat, they band together," Tony's chief of staff, Jamie Naughton, explained. "That's what happened to us. It was like 9/11."

Ever since the hacking incident, the company hasn't quite found its way back to that same collective energy. The planned move downtown led to resistance from some employees, but many stayed with the company nonetheless–Zappos was still a better place to work than most call centers in Vegas were. It was hard to come by a place where you could sport tattoos and commission office parades.

During Downtown Project's first year, Tony encouraged everyone to move quickly, take chances, and fail fast. It's what led to the rapid hiring of Andy White, who was part of the start-up community in Salt Lake City.

At a tech conference in San Francisco, Andy ran into a Zappos employee who was also a partner in the Vegas Tech Fund; this led to an interview with Zach at SXSW in March 2012. Andy was then invited onto the *Delivering Happiness* party bus, where he met the core DTP team. Everyone was dressed in raver gear; he was wearing a rainbow wig. He was told that as part of the vetting process, he would be given a list of ten companies to evaluate. But after meeting Tony on the party bus, he was in. That list of ten companies never materialized; he had already passed Tony's culture test.

It's the kind of recruiting that is typical in Silicon Valley to assess for culture fit, where candidates are observed in a casual social environment, usually at a bar. At the end of the weekend, Zach extended Andy an offer to lead the $50 million Vegas Tech Fund under his management–just like that.

It's some combination of idealism and the promise of a blank canvas that attracted people into Tony's world. University of Iowa professor David Gould decided to become part of what he describes as a "fascinating social experiment" after being struck by the way his students followed Tony around the college town during his *Delivering Happiness* book tour. Former TEDMED speaker curator Lisa Shufro wrote in a *Medium* blog post that it was a "*Good Will Hunting* moment" that led her to quit her job in DC and "go see about a city." Then there are followers like the Dancetronauts, an electronic music performance group that Tony met at Burning Man and convinced to relocate from California. "Tony collects people," a downtown Vegas resident once told a reporter.

And that's exactly what he does: collect people everywhere he goes. I could trace being collected back to the evening I met Tony in June 2012. The event was hosted by strategic partner Andrew Yang, founder of Venture for America. Tony donated $1 million to VFA in exchange for a stream of VFA fellows to support DTP, the sort of youthful energy that projects like this are built upon.

After delivering his keynote Tony was flanked by the Agrawal twins, Miki and Radha, whom he met at Summit Series. Miki Agrawal invited Tony to her gluten-free pizza restaurant in Williamsburg, Brooklyn, and he agreed to invest in a second location in Vegas. Andrew Yang grabbed Tony before the twins could steer him too far and introduced us. He invited both my colleague Lauren Brown and me to visit Vegas, and then walked back into the crowd.

I'm sure I didn't make an impression that night, but I could understand why enthusiastic entrepreneurs like the Agrawal twins hung on to him like a magnet. Tony seemed genuinely interested in other people. I didn't know much about Zappos, so I didn't have many questions for him that night, but he had questions about *Business Insider*. In hindsight, I realized that one of his superpowers is just listening well to other people.

As it turned out, *Business Insider* could send only one of us. Over sushi later that week, Lauren told me that I should be the one to go. "It'll be a great opportunity," she said. And just like that, it was decided.

THE BLUEPRINT

Downtown Vegas felt like a blank canvas in September 2012. Fremont Street was filled with taped-up storefronts and empty parking lots.

Coterie, a clothing boutique owned by Sarah Nisperos, the woman who'd connected Tony and Michael, was the first brick-and-mortar DTP small business to open its doors. It received funding in the low millions of dollars. Sarah pulled out racks of high-priced hipster clothing onto the floor on opening day. Outside, show girls with large feather headdresses stood in the middle of the street. The upside-down Checks Cashed signage–left from the store's previous owner–was a visual cue to the community of Tony's influence in downtown Las Vegas.

Sarah earned her nickname, the Sorceress, in part for her role in the origin of Downtown Project. When Sarah stayed at Tony's place (he maintains several rooms for guests), he would ask her every morning to brainstorm ideas with him for how to change the world.

Coterie means "gathering place" in French, Sarah explained (the term actually means "intimate and exclusive group," something that she later told me got lost in translation when she was searching for synonyms for "community"). "We're a place to hang out first, and a business second." She was referring to DTP's unique philosophy and approach to investing by focusing on ROC–return on community–above all else. The idea was that by focusing on people and community, "the rest would just work itself out," Tony told audiences during his keynote. Later, when many companies struggled to turn a profit, DTP would abandon that strategy. But today anything was possible.

Sarah's story of how she met Tony is, like many others, a spiritual awakening of sorts. At the time, she was working in the fashion epicenter of the world. "I remember dancing at a party next to Jay Z and Kanye West, and I was a hundred pounds and *so unhappy*," she explained. Tony convinced her to quit her job and launch a yoga clothing line, Naked Yoga, which Zappos sold on its site. The business didn't work out, and she says that she decided to live on $400 a month while doing a 365-day Bikram yoga challenge "to shed all of my layers." She recalls meeting Tony at a bar that year while wearing cheap drugstore makeup. "I have never been so happy in my life," she told him, and now me, as her face lit up. "We're all just broken dolls. And Tony has brought us together in this beautiful way."

In the early days of Downtown Project, Sarah would bring people into Tony's apartment and do yoga with weed to calm them down. After she opened up her store, Tony would still send people to her to figure out how to better acclimatize to the downtown ecosystem.

Coterie was where start-up employees went to complain about being overworked and underpaid, and where Downtown Project's chief evangelists troubleshot how to do their jobs when they no longer believed in Tony's mission. Before the social sharing app Secret, a multimillion-dollar backed start-up that created a platform where users aired their "secrets" anonymously, became popular, frustrated Downtown Project employees aired their concerns behind the boutique's counter. (Secret's popularity ultimately led to its demise.) Incidentally, on the other side of the mirrored wall was Downtown Project's office: a single room with a big whiteboard for members of the construction and finance teams who sometimes needed more privacy than sitting in bars with their laptops.

The strategy the first year or two (2012–2013) was to recruit as many people as possible to Las Vegas and to shoot bullets–that is, make a lot of bets. DTP attracted tech talent who found it difficult to attract investors in the Bay Area and other major tech centers such as New York, Seattle, and Boulder, Colorado. Like its small business investments, many of its early tech investments were first-time entrepreneurs who were not in a place to negotiate the terms of their contracts. One of the key expectations was that the company had to move to Las Vegas and contribute to ROC.

The start-up scene was scrappy, just like the downtown area. A Vegas Tech pitch night was hosted in a no-frills room above the Emergency Arts center, an artists' collective in an old medical building on Fremont and Sixth Streets, owned by the Cornthwaites and where the Beat is also located across from the El Cortez casino. Guests pitched apps and other unimpressive consumer-focused technology; most were variations on existing products. The collective Tech Jelly involved the cofounders of the garage sale app Rumgr at the Insert Coins bar on Fremont Street, a bar featuring classic arcade games located a few doors down from Emergency Arts. Near the end of the week, a larger crowd gathered for the Vegas Tech weekly community dinner at Romotive's Ogden apartment.

Zach Ware led me on my first tour of downtown Vegas. It began with the Post-it wall in Tony's apartment, continued through the Jungle Room–designed to look like a jungle with plants on the walls and hanging from the ceiling, with dark purple lighting–and then took us into the far room overlooking the new Zappos headquarters. (Tony's twenty-third floor Ogden apartment is actually three apartments combined.) If you wanted to meet with Tony, it was a requirement that you went on the tour first.

"This is the blueprint for Container Park," Zach told us, sporting jeans, flip-flops, and a button-up shirt. The architecture rendering depicted a park filled with stacked shipping containers, a playground in the center, and families walking around the park at the corner of Fremont and Seventh Streets, which, at present, was a desolate street corner. It was inspired in part by another shipping container park in San Francisco. "We'll break ground on that soon, and it will open next year," he continued.

Downtown Project had brought in consultants in the urban-planning space such as Richard Florida, whom Zach characterized as not all that helpful. They were going to do their own thing, a new kind of flexible urbanism (as some involved in the project would describe: a "shoot-from-the-hip" version). Zach told our small tour group, which included a couple from the Netherlands, that he initially declined Tony's offer to join Downtown Project but was later convinced over a bottle of wine.

A few doors down from Tony's apartment lived Augusta "Coach" Scott, whose job it was to motivate Zappos employees to pursue their dreams; and an elevator ride away, to the fifteenth floor, was the new headquarters for Tech Cocktail, which had just received $2.5 million in funding. I joined Tony the day that the media and event company's founders arrived in Las Vegas. Cofounder Frank Gruber invited us into the new condo-office, complete with cherrywood floors and granite countertops. Frank and his cofounder and fiancé, Jen Consalvo, whom he met at AOL, bootstrapped their company for six years before securing outside funding. Frank and Jen's mission with Tech Cocktail was to showcase start-up communities in cities across the United States (by the time they moved to Vegas they'd hosted events in forty cities). A 2009 *Washington Post* story called them "digital nomads" for being on the precipice of a much larger trend, part of a growing segment of the workforce that works remotely while traveling the world. They met Tony at the Las Vegas Consumer Electronics Show (CES) that same year and sparked a friendship. ("No one knew Tony in 2008, 2009," Frank told me. "It was before his book. At least, they didn't know him like they know him today.") At SXSW in 2012 Tony invited them to visit downtown, and they took him up on his offer. "Then we just packed up our bags and moved across the country," said Jen. Although there was never any formal agreement to host events for Downtown Project, Frank and Jen signed on to invite a fleet of entrepreneurs, investors, and media to downtown Las Vegas every month and put them up in the Ogden. They would absorb the costs of the events if Downtown Project provided the housing. "It was a train that just kept on coming," said Jen. "It was hard because it wasn't central to our business. It was a bit of an offshoot we'd capitalize on."

This particular afternoon was a calm before the storm. Tony walked over to the balcony, where Frank was standing, and looked out onto the horizon. His eyes were set just beyond the Lady Luck Casino. I captured a photo of Frank and Tony standing there in that moment, and later noticed that Tony's head covered the word "Lady" so it seemed he was looking squarely at the word "Luck." That was the perfect photo to headline my *Business Insider* story.

An elevator ride away on the tenth floor, digital marketing firm Digital Royalty was also opening up an office. The company played a key role in publicizing *Delivering Happiness* through social media, and its founder Amy Jo Martin spent a lot of time on the bus tour. Tony wrote the forward for her book, *Renegades Write The Rules: How The Digital Royalty Use Social Media To Innovate*, and she used the same marketing company as he did (Result Source) to ensure that her book was a bestseller. Tony also bought up a number of copies of her book, as he did with other authors in his ecosystem.

Digital Royalty fell into a broad, growing category of companies that helped support Tony's broader publicity and business goals around Downtown Project and Zappos. They weren't in the same category as start-ups like Romotive, which could potentially deliver real exponential returns; instead, they were part of the PR arm. Providing seed-fund money for start-ups that were, in fact, marketing expenses, was part of the entire veneer of Downtown Project that would hopefully attract companies that could add more value to the tech fund. When I asked Tony about this, he provided a term that he used for these companies: "community investments."

Although Amy, Frank, and Jen had worked for years to bootstrap their companies (Amy founded Digital Royalty in 2009), a number of community investments were new companies and appeared to provide its founders with a brand of lifestyle entrepreneurship.

One outsider, a young woman who noticed some of Tony's community investments at events that she attended, the ones that typically cost several thousand dollars and a special invitation to attend–such as TEDActive (the experiential side of TED) and Summit Series–asked innocently enough, "What is going on? Are there *scholarships*?" She'd gone through traditional means to secure venture capital funding for her fashion tech start-up. "But then someone pulled me aside and explained, 'Oh, honey, they're not real companies. They just have founder titles to support the cult of personality.' Meanwhile, I'm living off of five dollars a day because I want to create a company that matters."

Another way to look at community investments is to view them as a loose experiment with universal basic income–a much-talked-about system that would alleviate the jobs lost to robots and provide everyone with a paycheck. The idea is that universal basic income will allow more people to follow their passions and ultimately elevate universal consciousness. That's the theory, at least.

When I was weighing my decision to move to Las Vegas, I had lunch with one of my colleagues, Jim Edwards, a deputy editor at *Business Insider*. I told him that I had a start-up idea, but it wasn't fully formed. "Listen, Tony isn't going to pay you to figure out what you want to do with your life," he told me as we sat on the patio at Almond, a restaurant in the Gramercy neighborhood of Manhattan. He was half right. Tony did, in fact, pay people to figure out what to do with their lives. He saw value in community investments.

The entire DTP/Zappos/Delivering Happiness ecosystem is designed in such a way that all of these interests are interconnected and feed one another–sort of in the way that Alphabet is the holding company of an ecosystem of Google divisions, and Google Ventures (now simply called GV) invests in outside start-ups (some founded by ex-Googlers) that could potentially support the larger brand. All of the investments are intended to support the larger ecosystem. The broader alignment in Tony's world is that most everyone needs to be a culture fit.

CULTURE FIT

Sitting in the very back of DCR, behind the heavy black curtain and in black leather seats, Vegas Tech Fund lead Andy White explained to me how he vetted entrepreneurs. He was dressed plainly in cargo pants and a T-shirt, in line with the unofficial uniform for Downtown Project. His close-cropped hair and measured way of speaking, along with his perceived self-discipline, could make Andy pass as being in the military. His low-key demeanor was a good fit for DTP: he appeared quick to take marching orders and support the culture of personality.

"It's all about ROC and culture fit," he explained with gusto. "They need to deliver a return on the community and fit in with the community." Downtown Project took a page out of the Zappos playbook by investing in strict culture fits. But unlike Zappos, DTP doesn't have a set of core values that determines the sort of person it hopes to find. If you asked him or any of the other investors–Fred Mossler, Tony, Zach Ware–what culture fit *was*, exactly, or how they measured ROC, the answer was ambiguous. It was mostly about finding nice people, they said.

Most investments were the laid-back engineering types who are more comfortable behind the scenes; not the sort that would raise hell. (After all, those types were pounding the pavement in San Francisco and Silicon Valley.) They often reflected the young, male Silicon Valley founder archetype that has since been parodied on the popular HBO show *Silicon Valley*.

Research shows that venture capitalists tend to invest in those who remind them of themselves, and the Vegas Tech Fund was no exception.

"If I had come out of a traditional VC firm, this would drive me nuts," Andy told me. "No traditional due diligence materials to work with," referring to the typical review process that entrepreneurs go through that helps investors weigh whether they are a reliable and trustworthy investment. "It's all about how much you believe in the team."

When Brooklyn writer Jay Dixit pitched Tony on funding a writer's colony, Tony mostly looked at him with his poker face and then asked what kind of writers he was planning to invite: "Just as long as they're not *mean* writers."

At Zappos, job candidates are screened in multiple ways. The company sends a driver to pick up candidates from the airport. Later, the driver, along with the folks at the front desk, are asked what they thought of the candidate. "Was the person kind? How did they treat you?" Downtown Project also took a page from this: when entrepreneurs visited, Andy, Zach, or whoever the host was would send out an email to the Downtown Project staff with questions like: "What do you think of this person? Did you run into them at the Beat or DCR? Were they the same person at night as they are during the day?"

The Downtown Project mission is lofty and intentionally vague: to be the most community-focused large city in the world. Yet, for all of its perceived transparency around its goals and accessibility with the tours and the Post-it notes, the unspoken message is that "community" applied only to a certain subset of people. After Tony, those on the front lines vetting for culture fit were primarily Andy White, Zach Ware, Don Welch, and Maggie Hsu, a young McKinsey & Company–trained analyst who was a contractor for Downtown Project. Fred Mossler has always deferred to Tony. Even then, their tests weren't foolproof. Casting such a broad net inevitably attracted a range of people, including a club owner with a history of bank fraud and massive financial liabilities. Las Vegas resident Joshua Ellis, who even worked for one of its startups, raised some red flags early on about the insularity of Tony's initiative. He wrote a pointed blog post titled, "Vegas Tech, We Need To Talk," echoing the sentiment of other longtime residents. He criticized Downtown Project for aggrandizing its noble intentions, arguing that it masked more capitalistic and libertarian goals. Time proved both to be true:

Like a growing number of locals, I am deeply, deeply conflicted about the vision for Downtown that's being laid out by
Tony Hsieh and his circle of friends, employees, and business
partners. The problem, I think, is how one defines the words
"community" and "happiness," which are words you hear a hell
of a lot in Vegas Tech. Hsieh wrote a best-selling autobiography/
manual for success, in fact, entitled *Delivering Happiness*, and
"community-building" is the number one activity that Vegas
Tech people engage in, with an enthusiasm that often borders
on the unnerving. A phrase you often hear muttered around
Vegas these days is "drinking the Kool-Aid," and you often
hear Zappos and the Downtown Project–and Vegas Tech at
large–compared to a cult. . . . When I began to venture downtown every week to go to the new Tech Jelly meetups/geek
hangouts at the Beat, there was very much the same feeling
that Tom Wolfe described about Ken Kesey's Merry Pranksters
in *The Electric Kool-Aid Acid Test*: you were either On The Bus,
or Off The Bus.

Like the many yes-men and yes-women around Tony, Andy White
filled his role well: he always stayed on message. At a Zappos "En-
lightenment" party, in the vein of the movie *The Matrix* (which
evokes Zen Buddhism philosophy), he wore a red sweater with
a piece of paper attached and the question "How far down the
rabbit hole will you go?" Tony guarded the entrance dressed as
Morpheus from *The Matrix*, a character he quotes in *Delivering
Happiness*. ("There's a difference between knowing the path and
walking the path.")

Andy subscribed to the system: he went to all the community
dinners, Downtown Lowdowns (monthly community events at
which Downtown Project employees showcased their progress),

and devoted his evenings to entertaining visiting entrepreneurs. He leased a place at the Ogden with his Russian-born wife, Oksana, and together they lived and breathed the culture (though she didn't work for the Project). Andy told me that he doesn't drink (and clarified that, though he previously lived in Salt Lake City, is not Mormon). It's difficult not to drink–especially when Tony is bonding the group over shots–but it's not a requirement for entering his ecosystem.

Andy previously worked with entrepreneurs at an accelerator start-up in Salt Lake City called BoomStartup. Accelerators are short-term, cohort-based programs that provide mentorship and resources to help founders develop ideas and get companies off the ground. His right hand was a young VFA fellow who had just graduated from college, Laura Berk. Together they were tasked with figuring out how to manage the $50 million fund. In the early days, you could find the two sitting at small tables at the Beat, a vintage coffeehouse that was filled with old records and an adjoining Burlesque Hall of Fame shop that played fuzzy black-and-white videos. If not at the Beat, they were sitting at the high tables under the dim lights in DCR. With infinite capital at their disposal and no failures just yet, it was an exciting if not overly romanticized time in Downtown Project's history.

MODERN-DAY CLUB BIO

One of the most integral guardians of Tony's reputation is Jenn Lim, CEO of Delivering Happiness. They met at the height of the nineties rave scene in San Francisco, in his penthouse suite at 1000 Van Ness. Tony had recently sold LinkExchange and was enjoying a season of immediacy, extraordinary wealth, and no obligations. He had conquered the world by age twenty-four. For a young millionaire in Silicon Valley, that meant sharing the wealth with his friends in order to attract more friends. It was a season of excess, reminiscent of the Roaring Twenties in New York City, as depicted by F. Scott Fitzgerald in *The Great Gatsby*. It was an era marked by Prohibition that spawned an underground market for bootlegged alcohol. But instead of Prohibition, during the dot-com boom, there were laws around recreational drugs; and instead of speakeasies with jazz, there were gritty warehouses playing house, trance, and other electronic dance music. There was a shared belief that there would never be a time in history quite like this again.

At a rave in Oakland in 1999, Tony ran up to a booth on the edge of the crowd, shirtless and sweating from dancing. The booth was managed by DanceSafe, a nonprofit that advocates for awareness around safe use of MDMA, the base form of the popular party drug Molly. DanceSafe founder Emanuel Sferios recalls how Tony asked if he could donate, and then escaped back into the crowd.

During the dot-com boom, a number of DanceSafe's donors were millionaire tech CEOs. MDMA, a recreational drug, is not legal, although it's being used in clinical trials to study its effectiveness for therapeutic use (to treat post-traumatic stress disorder, for example). The value that researchers place on MDMA is its ability to rewire the brain and allow for feelings of empathy to arise for most users. In the way that Prohibition led to the black market and bootlegged alcohol that had fatal repercussions, MDMA is sold on its own online black market and can be fatal when users ingest unknown chemicals. Tony didn't discuss MDMA in his book, but he wrote about the profound impact that raving had on his worldview and how it increased feelings of connectedness with his tribe. When I asked him about MDMA, he told me that "I stay away from talking about religion, politics, or drugs in general because those topics are very polarizing and people have already made up their minds on what side of the issues they want to be on."

One evening at Club Bio, which is what they nicknamed his penthouse, Jenn watched as the DJ announced Tony on the stage. "Now let's bring all the ladies up to the house!" the DJ called out. "At that moment, I thought, 'Aw, that's too bad; he's just like all the others," she recalled. "But then the next night, I saw him for who he really was." She joined Tony's tribe, and they developed a friendship. Over time, Tony entrusted Jenn with culture work for Zappos and with Delivering Happiness, the offshoot consultancy connected to the Zappos brand. When I later asked Jenn who Tony was, she didn't provide an answer. I had a difficult time figuring out exactly who he was too.

During my last night on that first trip to Vegas, I watched as revelers moved in syncopation with the Dancetronauts, who were directing the crowd in the courtyard behind the Ogden as fog machines filled the area with mist. Tony and his posse swept into the scene in a Flying V formation. I stood on the edge of the crowd with Andy White; Michael Cornthwaite and his wife, Jennifer, were standing farther outside the dancing, near a food truck.

Jenn Lim noticed I was standing on the periphery. "Here," she said, taking my hand and inviting me into the circle to dance. We had met earlier that day during a tour of the Shadow Lane house, a mansion in the nearby Scotch 80s neighborhood that Tony recently purchased to host parties. He brought a group of friends to tour the place, which was reminiscent of a funhouse, with rooms filled with dolls, mirrors, and whimsical artwork–a perfect sort of setting for a masquerade ball.

Jenn's invitation into the circle was the split second that put me on a crash course with Tony and his great experiment. That encounter in the fog machine mist led to the elevator ride up to the twenty-third floor of the Ogden, where I encountered Tony's modern-day Club Bio. A collection of mostly young people were mingling around the living room and sitting in colorful roller chairs. In the corner of the couch sat Tony's cousin Connie Yeh, who was joking about how her husband, Don Welch, was passed out in the hallway somewhere. They are an unlikely couple: Connie is Asian, petite, and unassuming, while Don embodies the "bro" fraternity brother archetype. They met at Citigroup, where Connie was a derivatives trader and Don worked in sales and technology, and neither had prior experience in education or small business, something they wear on their sleeves with a dose of insecurity and humility.

For Connie and Don, joining Tony's mission was the opportunity of a lifetime. They were living and working on Wall Street as the country reeled from the Great Recession when Tony started courting them over multiple dinners in New York. "I sat at my desk on Wall Street one day, looking at all of my screens, and thought, 'There is *so much more* in Vegas,'" Connie recalled. "But I had no experience in education. I asked Tony, 'What if I fail? What if I don't know what I'm doing?' And he said, 'Then you'll learn.'"

As Alfred Lin explained to me once from Sequoia Capital's then-sparse Silicon Valley offices, "When you're doing something as crazy as Tony's doing, you've got to surround yourself with yes-men and -women. At least at the start."

Across the way in the kitchen, members of the hipster rock band Rabbit were raiding the cupboards for chips and EZ Cheese. Tony collected the musicians at the Fairmont Orchid hotel in Kona, Hawaii, where they were performing at a venture capital conference in 2010. At the time, the Florida-based musicians were living in a van while touring the East Coast. Tony was attracted to Rabbit because its music is "happy," he told me, featuring only upbeat tonality and lyrics. In fact, he ensured that Rabbit's music is what Zappos customers heard when they were placed on hold after calling the customer service line. It didn't take much convincing for the two male members of Rabbit to leave their nomadic life and build out the music scene in downtown Las Vegas.

Tony walked out of the kitchen carrying a tray with shot glasses and a bottle of Italian fernet liqueur, wearing his usual Zappos T-shirt and jeans, a uniform that he rarely deviates from. He passed them around to everyone, including a Zappos employee and his fiancé sitting in the roller chairs. The Zappos employee announced that Tony was going to officiate at their wedding.

"How many weddings have you officiated by now?" someone asked.

"Um . . ." Tony's voice trailed off in the way he does when he is uncomfortable. He's received a number of requests ever since marrying a couple onstage at a Zappos All-Hands a few years ago. Zappos All-Hands are the company's much-anticipated quarterly meetings that involve a general business update and also spectacle, complete with entertainment and talks by famous guests, and an afterparty.

Jenn was falling asleep on the oversize beanbag, still listening to the hum of conversation into the early hours of the morning. She became especially accustomed to Tony's pace of life during the *Delivering Happiness* bus tour and when she supported his book writing process, a marathon two weeks fueled by vodka and coffee beans just before the Amazon sale closed.

After downing the shots of fernet, a young female Zappos buyer sat next to me on the couch. As everyone began trickling out of Tony's apartment, we walked over to the balcony overlooking Fremont Street.

"It's not New York, I know," the young blonde buyer hedged. "But it's exciting. I left FIT [Fashion Institute of Technology] to come out for this."

The music from the bars below bounced off the walls of the Ogden. We could see patrons standing outside the Beauty Bar, the Griffin, DCR, and the crowds across the street just inside the Fremont Street Experience.

Meanwhile, Tony was lying on another beanbag in the next room, which was filled with architectural renderings and all of the colorful Post-its with ideas for businesses downtown. The young Zappos buyer explained Tony's plans for downtown Las Vegas, pointing to different properties, all within the shape of a llama. Somewhere along the way, Tony decided that he had a thing for llamas and that fetish has been integrated into various aspects of Downtown Project–even determining the shape of his $200 million property investment. The goal was to increase the number of downtown residents significantly over the next five years. Tony explained it to us this way: "If you do the math of one hundred thousand collisionable hours per acre per year, that translates to something like 2.3 collisionable hours per square foot per year."

Tony's investment in downtown coincided with investment from Wendoh Media, an influential entity in Las Vegas. Wendoh and Downtown Project both shared a vision for turning downtown into a Brooklyn, an Austin, a Seattle–with its own spin of course–transforming it into a creative capital brimming with young hipsters, entrepreneurs, and artists. Wendoh's young male founders also share a similar belief system around the fusion of work and play. To attract the demographic that would make the vision a reality over time, first they needed to get people there– *anyone* who vaguely fit that description.

I must have fit the description, because early in the morning, before we all trickled out of Tony's apartment, he told me that he was going to be in New York the following week. Did I want to join him at a charity gala? Of course I did.

"IT'S LIKE MAGIC"

"If you could do anything in the world, what would you do?" Tony asked me while we sat on the couches atop the Hudson Terrace, a high-end nightclub on the Hudson River overlooking Manhattan. I was intrigued.

It was a simple question that led many people to relocate to Vegas and support his Downtown Project, which was largely about selling dreams–the same sort of escapism that Vegas has always sold, just repackaged for the aspiring entrepreneurial set. I responded with something about owning a media site–and then poured my second straight glass of vodka out of nervousness.

"The decisions you make this year will dramatically change the course of your life," he responded, sounding more like a prophet than a CEO.

On paper, I had a great job and an exciting life in New York. I had just been promoted to a senior editor position at *Business Insider*. But I realized that I wanted to be outside the office, on the ground, meeting interesting people. I wanted to set the rules.

That night, I continued to treat the Grey Goose like water. In fact, I partied so hard that my cab driver decided to drop me off at a Brooklyn hospital instead of at my apartment because he thought I had alcohol poisoning. I was surprised when Tony and his date appeared to pick me up. Apparently the cab driver had called one of them before he dropped me off.

I would later discover that partying hard was the norm when

people entered Tony's world–and surely stranger things had happened. Zappos is different from most companies in that employees are rewarded for partying with their CEO. I never heard of anyone in his sphere suffering repercussions from doing something outrageous or unsavory. Those sorts of events only seem to bond the tribe.

The very next day, I joined Tony, his date for the weekend, and a few others on a tour of a micro-apartment in Soho designed by architect Graham Hill who pitched Tony on investing in his company, LifeEdited. The progression of the week's events led to a night at the Ainsworth on East Eighteenth Street in Manhattan and the Ace Hotel, when I met a charismatic young woman named Amanda Slavin.

"It's like magic," Amanda told me in a hushed voice, sitting on the rooftop of Soho House in New York City later that week. "Tony plants seeds." Amanda met Tony while at Summit Series, one of the original inspirations for his utopian vision, where she was working one of its events. When she traveled to Vegas to check out Downtown Project, she was surprised to see Graham Hill sitting next to her in the Zappos airport shuttle. "I couldn't believe it: one of my favorite TED speakers was sitting right next to me," she continued. "It was a sign that I just had to be there."

Over a two-hour brunch in downtown Vegas, she and Tony worked out the details of a potential partnership. "What do you want to do with your life?" he asked. Amanda, a petite and fashionable brunette in her midtwenties, was working for Paige Hospitality Group, a NYC-based events company. She was overworked and downing several drinks a night at the events she hosted regularly in Manhattan, the Hamptons, and LA. "It wasn't healthy," Amanda lamented. She told Tony that she wanted to combine her backgrounds in education and events management. He asked her how many of her friends she could get to Vegas every month to re-create an event like Summit Series. She had an extensive network through Paige Hospitality and guaranteed that she could attract a good turnout. Amanda is originally from New Jersey and a natural hustler, something that Tony picked up on immediately.

He agreed to fund her to form an events company, Catalyst-Creativ. Their main focus was "human capital ROI," similar to ROC. And they did a good job of creating experiences to attract talent: around 30 percent to 40 percent of the people came back to visit, she told me. While the public will likely judge Tony's efforts by measurable impact in downtown Las Vegas, that does not account for a very important demographic: the many people who passed through, or heard his keynote, and took the idea to create something in their own city–perhaps completely unrelated and unreported. Tony's message was powerful like that. For every person who acted upon a solution in Vegas, there are likely several more who made even microimprovements in their lives and/or work elsewhere.

Tony had this idea that the Summit community would become a key part of his plan for Vegas; many of its entrepreneurs have developed an ability to stretch limited amounts of capital to solve big problems. CatalystCreativ would brand its vision as a community design firm; the intention was to get as many young entrepreneurs to Las Vegas as possible, and, hopefully, some would relocate. Amanda immersed herself into the craft of hosting a speakers' series, often falling asleep while listening to TED Talks. Alongside Tech Cocktail, CatalystCreativ would become one of the primary recruiting tools for Downtown Project. When she invited me to attend the first Catalyst Week, I said yes.

The inaugural Catalyst Week occurred the weekend before Thanksgiving 2012. Several people from the Summit Series community flew in, including a few Googlers, social entrepreneurs, and an independent filmmaker. Some had been on the ground in the New York area supporting relief efforts after Hurricane Sandy devastated parts of the Northeast. For this crew, Vegas literally was the calm after the storm. Two tech entrepreneurs-turned-nomads even showed up after driving across the country in their Airstream.

"That's the lifestyle. One woman I know traveled around the world and didn't have an apartment for a year. It's just the Summit way–they all live like that," one Catalyst employee observed. "They figure it out."

The inaugural group included Google engineer Dan Fredinburg, who was hacking his way into Google X, a division of the company devoted to "moonshot projects" such as self-driving cars (now just called "X" through the reorganization under Alphabet); Adventure Project cofounder Becky Straw, whose nonprofit funds entrepreneurs in developing countries; and a host of other social entrepreneurs and rising stars with equal ambitions. Meredith Perry, who was on the verge of raising several million from investors (including Tony) for her start-up uBeam, with a mission of providing wireless charging technology to the world, was my roommate in the Ogden.

Like Summit Series, the week's events were designed to spark breakthroughs and social bonding. Everyone gave talks in the trailers in the Learning Village with his or her grand visions for changing the world, and the week culminated in a vulnerability session. During a morning yoga session with the group on the twenty-fifth floor, I was able to finally get into a pose that had been impossible for years. Dan Fredinburg, who was training to climb Mount Everest to take photos for Google Streetview, was sitting on the yoga mat next to mine.

During a community dinner, I asked one of the two men who

arrived in an Airstream what they did for a living. "I'm here for one reason: love," he responded. I later learned that he sold an advertising company for millions and was now living a nomadic life, traveling the world and engaging with indigenous tribal communities. I wanted to know exactly how one gets to a place where he can live so freely.

The week was highly curated and wasn't an entirely accurate picture of the place: it incorporated all the best elements from downtown and resembled the festivals that Tony experiences around the world. This group primarily saw his investment in the same way he did: as an experiment that they could enjoy from above and afar, without getting too involved.

During the week, I felt so out of my element that I opted out of spending too much time socializing with the group after hours. The last day, instead of traveling with them in the Airstream and partying just outside the city center, I chose to stay downtown and find some of the DTP employees I had met that week. They felt more accessible.

While meandering around Fremont Street late Saturday night, I walked by Le Thai, which was packed with patrons celebrating the Thai eatery's one-year anniversary. Next door, Wendoh Media–owned Commonwealth, which describes itself as a "pre-Prohibition style cocktail bar" complete with a semi-secret speakeasy, was celebrating its grand opening. I saw Tony inside the entrance to Le Thai, and he pulled me inside and handed me a shot of fernet. I was relieved to have found him, since I'd been walking around alone with no real destination. I joined his growing posse on the way to DCR, where we picked up Michael Cornthwaite, and ended up at Drink N' Drag inside the Fremont Street Experience.

Under the strobe lights at Drink N' Drag, a gay nightclub on the other side of Las Vegas Boulevard in the Neonopolis, Tony turned to me and asked, "Why don't you write the real story of what it's really like to live here?" For someone who plants ideas all the time, I don't know if he even remembers saying it, especially a few drinks in on a Saturday night. But that was the dare, and I wanted to take him up on it. The bar was loud, and moments later, Michael walked up to us and handed us more drinks. I don't know if Michael also had a tab open that night, but usually anytime you're out with Tony, he covers the bill for anyone in his periphery. Coach and the Tech Cocktail founders made their way over and pulled us onto the dance floor, where we stayed for a while.

After that, I lost the group somewhere along the way and ended up in the Ogden, where a DTP employee was DJ-ing for a small group until dawn.

Coach, who was celebrating her sixty-second birthday that night, told me that the energy rises when Tony is there and falls when he's away. It was true: the lifeblood of downtown, at least in that moment in time, was connected largely to one person.

UTOPIA OR DYSTOPIA?

On January 28, 2013, news spread quickly downtown. Jody Sherman, the eccentric entrepreneur and one of the Vegas Tech Fund's first investments, had taken his own life. His body was found in his car near Mount Charleston, about twenty-five miles outside Las Vegas. He died of a gunshot wound to the head.

A few days earlier, he had sent out a mass email to all of the CEOs from the Vegas Tech Fund. On Jan 23, 2013, at 6:04 p.m., Jody Sherman <jody@ecomom.com> wrote:

> I'd like to propose that we find a time, once a month, to meet as a group outside of the VTF meeting.
>
> Each of us is so busy and has so much on our plates. Oftentimes I find myself with no one to talk to about the challenges I might be facing, the frustrations, the excitement, and the stress that comes from being a CEO/founder.
>
> I thought, "Hey, I know a bunch of other founders who probably find themselves in similar situations, I should hang with them!"

So why not pick a night once a month, and let's get together?
We can move the venue around to keep it interesting.

This doesn't just have to be for VTF companies. If any of you
know other founders from the area who we should invite,
let's get them too.

I propose the first one either for next Monday or Wednesday
after work.

Who's comin' with me?!

js

Elizabeth Yin, who was part of the Vegas Tech ecosystem, recalled
how many founders responded immediately. Everyone wanted
to discuss what is all-too-often a taboo topic. "Then that night
came, and Jody never made it," she said, sighing.

He ended his life days before a scheduled board meeting would
have likely ousted him from the company. It was soon revealed
that his start-up Ecomom, which had raised $5 million six months
earlier and $12 million in total (including from the Vegas Tech
Fund), had run out of cash. This blindsided his investors, including Tony, who had hoped that Jody would be a key recruiter for
Downtown Project. He had convinced Jody to move from LA,
where his network of friends and family were, to Vegas. My colleague Alyson Shontell at *Business Insider* reported that "although
Sherman was vocally supportive of the tech scene in Vegas, close
friends say he was never happy there."

Aside from disclosing his company's financial troubles, Jody
didn't have a problem speaking his mind. He was among the OGs

a middle- to high-income bracket, but not so high where life was already frictionless, so to speak.

Money was still moving like water. That spring, Downtown Project put down a reported $22 million to purchase the Gold Spike Hotel & Casino on Ogden Avenue between Fourth Street and Las Vegas Boulevard, just behind the new Zappos campus. DTP transformed the property into a 24/7 bar and restaurant, retaining the gaming license by bringing out one or two slot machines for twenty-four hours once a quarter. By stripping out the slot machines, Tony sought to draw a new, younger crowd. The hotel was also renovated into boutique hotel rooms, some of which were used as crash pads for his many guests from around the world.

There were warning signs of volatility, but the excitement around the new, bright, shiny objects were a distraction enough for those in the ecosystem.

AMANDA'S PITCH

"You've got to try this," Amanda Slavin said to me, holding out a piece of avocado toast. She was wearing a bright red shirt, black leather pants, and high heels. Amanda arranged for us to meet at Cafe Gitane in the Soho neighborhood of New York City one frigid February morning, and she was dressed to the nines.

She ordered several drinks, just like she did at Soho House: watermelon juice, cucumber juice, espresso. I followed suit with the drinks, but not with the toast.

After a few moments of small talk, she dove right into why we were there: Vegas. It was her job to bring back as many people from Catalyst Weeks as possible and to generate news coverage.

"You know if you come up with an idea, Tony will totally fund it, right?" she said, as I looked down at my meal of cold quinoa. It didn't look half as good as the avocado toast.

"Tony asked me, if I could do anything, what would it be," I began. She looked at me and nodded her head knowingly. "And I told him I'd start a news site. But I don't know what that would look like in Vegas. PR?"

"You can make it whatever you want it to be," she said.

"Doesn't it cost a lot of money to be an entrepreneur? How do you do it?" I asked, at that point naively not understanding the nature of community investments.

"You can take, like, a fifty-thousand-dollar salary, and, honestly, you don't need much in Vegas," she responded. "I'm totally happy just working from the Beat and eating an apple." However, taking that statement at face value was slightly misleading. Amanda didn't mention that through CatalystCreativ, Tony was paying for her apartments at the Ogden and in Santa Monica (she explained to me later it was because she had clients in both cities). Like some of the women who received investment money from Tony, she split her time between Vegas and California. Amanda lived in Santa Monica; Mimi Pham, who was given $1 million to open Fremont East Studios (a digital media production company, to document Downtown Project's trajectory, led by Freeman White III), lived on the water in Marina del Ray. Both Mimi and Sarah Nisperos had rooms in Tony's apartment. Evangelists like Amanda pitched newcomers on a world that even they didn't want to live in full-time. They also experienced this world in a way that not everyone could, with unique protections and all. That was the genius of the crash pads at the Ogden: guests were given the option to stay for extended periods of time, under the illusion that they would be taken care of when they chose to uproot their lives and move to America's underbelly. "It basically tricks them into coming," Tony said of the crash pads to reporter Timothy Pratt, who wrote the *New York Times* feature story, "What Happens in Brooklyn Moves to Vegas."

I nodded, thinking back to hanging out with the Catalyst crew at the Beat a few months earlier. That was my first exposure to this group of people who all seemed to be pursuing their dreams and living like vagabonds, traveling like a tribe from festival to festival. I could not understand how to get there, but I wanted to find a way.

As we walked back along Bowery, she told me about another idea she was pitching to early Zappos investor Erik Moore, whom she had gotten to know through Tony. Her investor had opened up his network to her, and her world was expanding exponentially.

When I got to the *Business Insider* office, I messaged a colleague on the tech beat to see how much founders typically take as a salary. He pinged me an article that listed figures in a range of $0 to $150,000. "Actually, this is interesting," he said. "I think I'm going to write a post about this."

In a vulnerable yet hopeful state on Sunday afternoon, I texted Tony: "I finally get what you're trying to do with the community thing in Vegas." He invited me to come out and meet him in another city, sending me his travel schedule. I chose to meet him in Hawaii.

BLANK CANVAS

Tony made it clear that this was a platonic trip. I didn't really understand his lifestyle but went along with the strangeness of it anyway.

Kona, Hawaii, is where Tony introduced me to Silicon Valley.

The March 2013 wedding of investor Kevin Rose, who is best known for founding news aggregator Digg, and foodie entrepreneur Darya Pino included an array of high-profile guests such as venture capitalist Chris Sacca and Instagram founder Kevin Systrom. The total net worth among the attendees was several billion dollars.

When we arrived, Tony shared with me a messaging group chat with all the guests. Entrepreneur/investors Loic Le Meur, Evan Williams, Tim Ferriss–all the bros of Silicon Valley who invest in one another's companies. Philip Rosedale, founder of the virtual world Second Life, an early inspiration for Downtown Project, was there too. At the time, I didn't recognize any of them, so Tony emailed me a *Fast Company* article on Kevin Rose, covered by Max Chafkin, the same reporter who had announced Tony's Downtown Project. Chafkin wrote about getting caught up in Kevin's world to the point where he even considered changing careers and becoming an entrepreneur after the Digg founder alluded to investing in him.

In that moment in Kona, I could understand the temptation that Max felt. On the plane ride from San Francisco to Hawaii, Tony shared with me an email from my colleague Alyson Shontell at *Business Insider*. She was fact-checking an article about Jody Sherman's suicide. I felt like a traitor to my profession.

On the beach before the ceremony, I met Elle Luna, who had just left her job as design lead for the app Mailbox, which sold for $100 million to Dropbox earlier that month. "I kept having this *dream*," she said, looking out onto the ocean, her eyes glowing. "I had this dream of a white room. And I decided that I simply *had* to find this white room." Elle is one of Silicon Valley's most sought-after designers who had the sort of cachet to approach

Uber's CEO, Travis Kalanick, at a party about redesigning his app, and he asked her to execute on it. After that project she joined Mailbox, where she slowly became discontent with start-up life. Now she was pursuing art: the real dream. "I found the white room on Craigslist, and now it's my studio," she said, still processing her lifestyle change. (She wrote about the white room in her 2015 book, *The Crossroads of Should and Must: Find and Follow Your Passion*.) If stepping into the rave behind the Ogden with Jenn Lim had been the moment I joined the story, this was the moment that pushed me to return to Vegas.

At the luau-themed reception, Elle walked over to Tony and told him that advice he'd once given her for how to restructure Mailbox had worked brilliantly.

Elle's comment about the white room resonated because she embraced this sense of possibility that Tony was trying to convey through his messaging: *anything is possible*. It was easier to believe when surrounded by people who had really *made* it. In downtown Las Vegas, Tony stands in stark contrast to most in terms of personal wealth and success.

There he's the seller of dreams *and* promising a sense of community: two powerful things that strike at the deepest desires of human nature. In some way, everyone who traveled into Tony's universe was a "broken doll," as Sarah Nisperos put it. I could identify with that description. At the time, I felt that I no longer fit the work culture at *Business Insider* and was eager to do something entrepreneurial. My sense of community came from helping plant a nondenominational church in Brooklyn. But as much as I admired my pastor and his wife–an unlikely pair; my pastor has tattoos running down his arms, and his Indian-American wife teaches boot camp workout classes–they could not give me a paycheck to start a company.

On Easter Sunday in Kona, Tony asked me what I would want to do in Vegas. Despite Amanda's advice, I hadn't prepared a pitch, so I suggested that someone should plant a church downtown; it seemed like people could use a gathering place like that. He asked me if I wanted to host a week like Amanda had, perhaps focused on creative professionals. I told him that I didn't think I had a large enough network to convince many people to fly out to Vegas. It was approaching eleven o'clock in the morning, and I said that I had to leave if I was going to get to church on time. I charged $80 to his account to take a taxi across the island. That was the only time I have ever seen him get frustrated with where his money was going. "Why don't you just send them your money instead?" he asked me as we walked to the gym later that afternoon. "I think they'd rather have people there," I responded. "They don't need your money."

That weekend, he asked me to brainstorm ideas for the name of the new DTP-funded health clinic in Vegas. Zubin Damania, an eccentric physician whose YouTube videos mocking the medical profession earned him a following as ZDoggMD, was one of Tony's most pivotal investments. They knew each other through his physician wife, who was friends with Tony at Harvard. Over dinner one evening, Zubin shared that he was unhappy working as an internal medicine doctor at Stanford University Medical Center. Tony asked him outright if he wanted to transform the future of medicine in Las Vegas. "My jaw dropped," Zubin recounted later. That's the sort of blank canvas that few people encounter in their lifetimes.

In the first couple months after Zubin moved to Vegas with his wife and daughters, Tony introduced him to people as "the guy who is going to revolutionize health care." Zubin considered various concepts, and helped the community by arranging for flu shots in the Gold Spike bar. As with many that Tony courted to work on a major aspect of Downtown Project, he provided Zubin with financial capital and the time to explore different ideas.

One afternoon as we walked on the beach, Tony explained why Romotive left. He said that Sequoia probably put some pressure on the company to go and that Romotive didn't add that much to ROC because its employees were in their apartment working all the time. Keller Rinaudo and Alfred Lin later told me that the first statement wasn't true (although Paul Carr reported that Sequoia did put pressure on Romotive to move as a condition of its Series A round of funding); and Keller mostly just felt bad about the second. ROC seemed to mean spending time at the bar, which the Romotive team didn't do all that often because it was busy working on its start-up.

One of its employees, Jen McCabe, stayed behind to support Tony's Vegas Tech ecosystem. He told her to take three months to figure out exactly what she wanted to do. Her task was to come up with lots of ideas. This sort of broad latitude was common in the first two years of Downtown Project, before there was any way to measure success or failure.

Whatever Elle–and Zubin, and Jen, and Amanda–had was exactly what I wanted: a blank canvas.

THE UNICORN ROOM

"If there's *anything* you need, don't hesitate to text me," Paul Iserino III, the boyish-looking hospitality manager for Downtown Project, said to me with overcompensating enthusiasm, the sort in which Zappos call center employees and other Las Vegas hospitality workers are trained. Previously Paul was a concierge at the Ogden front desk; Tony took notice of him and asked Paul to join Downtown Project. He upgraded to the twenty-fifth floor with the small hospitality team managing crash pads and tours. Their office is painted deep purple with a mythical theme; there's a life-sized black unicorn statue, a golden Buddha, and a slightly hidden, moveable wall into the next room that reminded me of C. S. Lewis's *The Lion, the Witch and the Wardrobe*. Lining the bookshelf along the wall is an array of classics including *Alice in Wonderland* and *Peter Pan*, juxtaposed against a collection of erotic anime comic books. *Alice in Wonderland* is a theme that's evoked throughout Tony's properties: for example, inside what would become the Airstream Park is a graffiti-painted school bus with images of Alice, the Mad Hatters, and the white rabbit next to the words "It's always tea time in Wonderland."

Paul, whose official title was "gatekeeper" of Downtown Project, handed me the door passcode for the nineteenth-floor apartment I'd be staying in for the next month. "Again, anything, don't hesitate to holler," he said. During that season in Downtown Project's history, guests would text Paul in the middle of the night with random requests, as if it were a hotel. With Downtown Project attached to the Zappos brand, some had very high expectations for how they would be treated.

It only took two months after Kona to leave my job. My heart was already in Vegas–or at least the idea of Vegas as Tony had presented it–and I joined the ranks of the many who took him up on the opportunity to stay in a crash pad for a few weeks and figure out something to contribute. I arrived with a loose idea, based on my conversation with Amanda at Cafe Gitane, but it wasn't fully formed. "Know what problem you are trying to solve," an entrepreneur friend cautioned me before I traveled to Vegas. I had told him that I was going to help with Downtown Project's

PR efforts and purchased the domain names CityAsAStartup.com and .co in advance. My friend, whom I had met at Catalyst Week and was familiar with DTP, pushed back presciently: "But do they think they need help with that?"

Summer 2013 was a season of high momentum and on the cusp of several initiatives coming to fruition: the new Zappos campus opening, inaugural Life Is Beautiful festival, and Container Park grand opening were all just around the corner, in short succession. It was the height of the Las Vegas summer heat and the apex in many ways of Downtown Project. The energy was electric, chaotic, and frenzied.

At the time, there were nearly a hundred furnished crash pads in the Ogden and just under half as many in the Eighth Street Apartments, another Downtown Project–owned property.

Real estate mogul Andrew Donner and his partner Todd Kessler were tasked with the dirty work of gentrification, which included evictions and displacing longtime residents in order to secure a hundred properties within fifty-eight acres of land downtown. When DTP left eviction notices on the doors of all residents who lived in the downtown apartment complex Towne Terrace, the media quickly picked up on it, and the residents were given the option to stay. "We made some bad assumptions," Tony told reporter Timothy Pratt. "Next time, we'll dig deeper." From a real estate perspective, Tony's decision to publicly announce his plans to spend $350 million ended up working against him. As soon as the word got out, downtown property owners started marking up their properties two, three, and even four or more times their estimated value. Sometimes DTP would take a pass. For example, Todd reportedly initially passed on purchasing a parcel of land behind an old motel called Fergusons at the edge of the Fremont East District near Eleventh Street. Its owner ended up selling the

0.17 acre of land for $125,000 to Iranian real estate mogul Kamran Fouladbakhsh, who flipped it to Downtown Project for $700,000 five months later. Through Andrew and Todd's Resort Gaming Group, DTP paid top dollar for downtown property, including $5 million for an old Motel 6 and the same amount for the crumbling Fergusons. Early on, Downtown Project had simply given a directive to spend money on initiatives and worry less about P&L (profit & loss) statements. "When you're at that size, you don't need to have really tight expense policies," said Rob Solomon, a Venture for America fellow who eventually became DTP's director of finance. "There's good communication." RGG stepped in and handled the books, at least for a while.

A local real estate broker who worked on some of the deals likens Tony's presence to that of Walt Disney. "The mistake I think he made was he announced what he was doing," he explained. "I liken it back to the sixties when Walt Disney was buying up Disney World. He told the attorneys to not identify him as the buyer when he was buying up thousands of acres of swampland, because people will double their price. Tony should have done what Disney did: acquire the land without people knowing."

But publicity was a primary part of Tony's project, which he was intent on completing in five years. It appeared that he was willing to pay any price. And he hired people who were eager to accomplish that mission for him.

"Tony hires people who are hungry, not polished," an early DTP employee observed.

That meant that some things fell through the cracks. For example, DTP partnered with Phantom Entertainment owner Kelly Murphy to create Krave Massive, which was intended to be the biggest gay nightclub in the world. It was soon unearthed that

Krave did not have the necessary permits to open up its club, and its owner had a history of bank fraud, among other financial liabilities. The local press closely documented the story. The turn of events was an embarrassment to DTP, which was already being scrutinized for its lack of due diligence among untrained professionals at the top.

Meanwhile, Zach Ware and Andy White were busy spending the $50 million tech budget to find someone to deliver exponential returns, should everything else fail. No matter: the real estate would always deliver a return, and it was the cornerstone of Tony's project.

As the downtown area attracted more visitors through the popularity of DTP, and with its new bar and restaurant openings, DTP took it upon itself to provide its own protective force in the area, the Downtown Rangers (who happen to dress similarly as the Rangers at Burning Man, with their brown Boy Scout–style shirts).

Locals were on the fence about whether they wanted in or out with DTP. Ron Corso, a longtime Las Vegas resident, received a call from DTPer Ashton Allen who was in charge of building up a music scene. Ashton, who was part of the band Rabbit, had done some research on the local music scene and came across his name. Ron was taken aback that his caller didn't realize there already was a music scene in downtown Vegas.

"Where are you from?" he asked the DTPer, who told him Florida.

"Well, then stop bringing in your people from Florida to build a music scene."

DTP ended up asking Ron if he wanted to start a business, and they became partners in creating 11th Street Records, an old-school record store and recording studio at the very far edge of downtown, across the street from the Fergusons Motel. He was pitched a vision for a vibrant Eleventh Street, with other stores opening nearby. The potential of the area was factored into the price of rent, but currently his location wasn't on the way to anywhere. When he presented Don Welch with a detailed business plan, Don told him that it was the most meticulous business plan he had received to date, remarking about plans written on napkins. Ron couldn't tell if he was half joking or entirely serious.

Entrepreneurs like Ron didn't really understand how DTP was acting as both his investor and landlord. "We always had this weird dynamic as both a landlord and the investor for a lot of these businesses," explained VFA fellow Rob Solomon. "You don't usually have to negotiate with your investors with rent price. It's an interesting position to put the business in."

There was a small subset of people who were exposed to the project and got in early to the opportunity, and knew to seize it. It was one of those sorts of chances that venture capitalist Marc Andreessen describes as once in a lifetime.* They will likely never present themselves again. Tony wanted to fund anyone and anything, and the quality of the idea was less important than the fact that people wanted to move to Las Vegas. There was a sense of urgency, too. The project had to be completed in five years: January 2017 would be the assessment date for measuring success or failure.

Jake Bronstein, founder of fashion tech start-up Flint and Tinder, understood this window. He'd pitched Tony and Fred over cocktails at DCR a few months earlier and arranged to continue working from New York and visit Vegas monthly as a Downtown

---

* Marc Andreessen describes these once-in-a-lifetime opportunities in his popular career-planning guide (pmarchive.com/guide_to_career_planning_part1.html).

Project "subscriber." Bronstein had leverage because he had already created one of the most successful Kickstarter campaigns to date and would become part of Tony's keynote presentation along with Coterie's Sarah Nisperos and Natalie Young, the owner and chef of Eat. Yet Tony still remarked to a *New York Times* reporter, "He needed us more than we needed him." I met Jake in the Ogden (where I collided with many visitors in the hallways and elevators, just as Tony had envisioned), and he drew up his analysis for what was going on:

> This is how many people who get a chance to pitch someone like Tony:
>
> xxxxxxxxxxxxxxxxxxxxxxxxxxxxxx
>
> This is how many people *know* how to pitch someone like Tony:
>
> xxxxxxxxxxxxxxxxxxx
>
> This is how many people end up with funding:
>
> xxxxxxxxx
>
> This is how many people know how to execute after getting funding:
>
> xxx

Tony funded many nascent entrepreneurs who lacked the proven ability to execute. Everything was new for Zach and Andy too, who were learning as they went. In that way, many entrepreneurs were set up to fail. "Andy was too," a Vegas Tech founder told me once. "They didn't give him the resources *he* needed."

Tony's desire to support people without experience "is a beautiful thing," Alfred Lin observed. "But it doesn't always work."

A close Zappos advisor explained: "Just because you're passionate about something, and Tony says you should do it because you're passionate, doesn't mean that you'll *succeed*." An Indian-born Zappos engineer once explained it this way to me from the company headquarters: "Tony tells us to do what we want, as long as it's not illegal."

This entrepreneurial philosophy would attract many into his universe, like the young McKinsey-trained consultant Maggie Hsu and the University of Iowa professor David Gould who took on key strategy roles. Both had encountered Tony on a whim.

Maggie, then in her midtwenties, learned about what Tony was doing after seeing him speak at Harvard Business School. She emailed him, and he asked her to come out to Vegas, stay in a crash pad for a few months, and help "facilitate serendipity." In other words, make connections between the many people who were visiting downtown. She once connected me to a guy who was there to pitch Downtown Project on acquiring his artwork: a collection of street signs with messages around happiness. For a young Asian-American consultant who spoke of how she identified with Amy Chua's controversial 2011 book *The Battle Hymn of the Tiger Mother*, running around to local Vegas bars and trying to facilitate serendipity must have been humbling. Maggie later told me that even so, her parents were excited for her to work for Tony, as he was pushing the boundaries with what was typical in Asian culture. There was a lot to learn from him.

Professor David Gould, whose title at DTP was "director of imagination," shared with me that one time he'd prepared nervously for a pitch meeting with Tony. Afterward, Tony said to him, "Why are you asking my permission to do any of this? You should just do it."

"One day we'll all talk about how we stayed in the Ogden when Tony hosted people in Vegas," remarked someone who worked closely with country singer Garth Brooks, who toured downtown in 2014 with Tony when he was in Vegas for a performance. "This won't go on forever."

HOLACRACY PILOT GROUP

Zappos, meanwhile, was about to undergo an experiment. It hadn't been revealed to the company yet, but a pilot group with recruiters and human resources employees was testing out a radical new system called Holacracy. The method, designed by a software engineer named Brian Robertson, eliminates job titles and abandons traditional hierarchy. The ultimate goal is self-organization.

The pilot group didn't realize the full scope of what was happening. "We thought it was an experiment," one member disclosed. "But we didn't realize this was actually happening, no matter what." The top-down initiative would prove to push several employees the wrong way, leading to a slew of departures over the next few years.

Tony's fascination with self-organization traces back to the 1990s, when he and his friends were looking for a more efficient way to run LinkExchange. Tony was then in his early twenties and soon immersed in rave culture, which piqued his interest in complex systems design. "It was as if the existence of individual consciousness had disappeared and been replaced by a single unifying group consciousness," he wrote in *Delivering Happiness*, "the same way a flock of birds might seem like a single entity instead of a collection of individual birds."

Tony met Brian Robertson at a Conscious Capitalism conference in 2012 and decided that his model was the solution to help Zappos run more like a start-up again.

The Holacracy pilot group was led by recruiter Alexis Gonzales-Black and software developer John Bunch. Neither had any experience in change management or organizational design. John and Tony, who earned a computer science degree at Harvard, shared similar backgrounds and a love for poker. Alexis, a former teacher who served on Nevada's State Board of Education, proved her grit when she asked Tony more than once to donate to her campaign for election to the Board of Education; he eventually came through with $10,000 (so did Facebook COO Sheryl Sandberg). Resilience is a crucial quality that both Alexis and John shared, which was essential for guiding 1,500 employees through a complete upheaval of their day-to-day.

Tony's meta vision was to get Zappos *and* all of the Downtown Project start-ups and small businesses to "speak the same language," so that they could better communicate with one another, share ideas and talent, and spark more innovation. That was a major piece behind the "four-minute mile for cities" concept; together, it appeared that he and Brian Robertson, who created the consultancy HolacracyOne to commercialize Holacracy as a "social technology," wanted to create an off-the-shelf city-building formula that anyone could replicate.

Brian had come up with the system while leading Ternary Software. It draws from Sociocracy, an organizational structure meaningfully developed by Dutch entrepreneur Gerard Endenburg in the 1970s. Endenburg sought to eliminate bureaucracy and created a system of interconnected circles where power is decentralized and distributed fully. Sociologist John Buck furthered the framework and attempted to sell it to the masses with his 2007 coauthored book *We the People*: *Consenting to a Deeper Democracy*. While a technical writer at Boeing, he felt a sense of helplessness in the sea of cubicles. "I didn't want to be a slave at work," Buck told me over a Skype call, summarizing the introduction to his treatise. "It struck me that we are given all these freedoms as Americans, but then are suddenly slaves again in our jobs."

His lament is one that the management set, organizational thinkers, and futurists have been trying to tackle for decades. Sociocracy gained traction in the Netherlands and throughout Europe, but its academic language prevented it from ever really taking off. Buck was once told by an academic testing service that the system was a level 12 in complexity on a fourteen-point scale–a compliment to the system's sophistication but too complex for the masses.

Robertson found a way to develop the system for the general public. After a few years of operating in relative obscurity, he landed as a client Twitter cofounder Evan "Ev" Williams, who had been pushed out of his company and sought a new way to run his publishing platform *Medium*, which sparked Silicon Valley's interest in Holacracy.

Tony pitched his employees on Holacracy as a way for everyone to operate with more freedom and autonomy, which was correct; but it was also an ostensible way to eliminate expensive project managers and otherwise poor culture fits. "Tony basically said that he was tired of people not implementing his ideas fast enough," said Bud Caddell, a consultant who worked with Zappos on its move to Holacracy. Amazon had increasingly put more pressure on Zappos, as its previous competitive advantages such as overnight shipping and great customer service were now commonplace.

Jeff Bezos made it clear that he wanted to see better results.

Another Amazon executive relayed the message during a video conference call in early 2014: "This message is coming directly from Jeff Bezos," the executive said to Tony and Fred. Someone on the call remembers the two just looking at each other. Over the next few months, Arun Rajan, the chief technology officer who had just left the company, returned to Zappos, though this time as chief operating officer. "I'd say we weren't meeting our own expectations," Arun told me later (Zappos sets it own sales targets, which Amazon then approves). Tony announced a new pricing strategy in August 2014 called "Best Customer Strategy" where Zappos stopped discounting its inventory. To one observer it looked like a knee-jerk response to Bezos's directive: buying time with a new strategy.

BAPTISM IN THE GOLD SPIKE POOL

Approaching twenty-five-thousand feet, Tony's Phenom 100 hit moderate turbulence over the mountains that border Las Vegas. Tony was sitting comfortably across from his date for the weekend, working intently but still half listening; Maggie Hsu sat across from me in the four-seated plane, looking at her phone. We were en route to Santa Monica, where Tony was giving his "City as a Start-up" keynote at the advertising agency Ogilvy & Mather. After *Delivering Happiness* hit number one on the bestseller list, his speaking fees spiked, and he now spends a good portion of the year on the speaking circuit.

Tony suggested that Maggie and I find a way to meet up with Dave Logan, the coauthor of *Tribal Leadership: Leveraging Natural Groups to Build a Thriving Organization*, after the event. "Dave just needs to find a babysitter; maybe you guys can meet him closer to his home?" he offered. *Tribal Leadership* is strongly suggested reading for Zapponians and, by default, anyone with a strategic role in Tony's inner circle. In his book, the PhD researcher makes a case for five stages of organizational cultures, from stage 1 ("dog-eat-dog") cultures to stage 5 ("transcendent") cultures. The book reinforces Tony's beliefs around company culture, and he mentions it often in his keynote talks, as he would today.

We landed on the tarmac at the private Santa Monica airport and walked over to a black SUV, where his life manager, Mimi Pham, met us. She handed Tony a button-up shirt and made small talk about sharing-economy start-ups like TaskRabbit and the merits of creating a membership-only Downtown Project hotel chain. Tony mostly stayed focused on his laptop until we arrived.

"Look at all of Tony's women," Mimi remarked as we all stepped out of the car. "At the very least, he'll get a standing ovation from us."

There was one more: Amanda Slavin, who greeted us enthusiastically at the door of the Ogilvy & Mather office wearing a black cocktail dress and leopard-print ballet flats. She had arranged for the event, which also featured venture capitalist and Lady Gaga's then-manager Troy Carter. Part of Amanda's role was also to connect Tony to audiences like the one today. The office was a modern space designed for and filled with Millennials wearing Warby Parker glasses and J. Crew. Tony, his date, Maggie, Mimi and I wandered into the VIP lounge, where there were several bottles of VeeV vodka-like liqueur steeped in ice. I handed one to Tony to open it and then poured a few stiff drinks.

We all made our way out into the crowd again, and amidst the sea of young professionals, I found Dave Logan. I shared with him my diagnosis of my previous company's culture: "Stage 3, most definitely." *Business Insider*'s founder, Henry Blodget, is a Wall

Street veteran and ran the newsroom like a trading room floor. Stage 3 is defined by high competitiveness (*Business Insider* may have evolved to Stage 4 over the years).

"I've heard that diagnosis before," Dave said knowingly. "That's not a secret to anyone." He told me that he had a book about the dark side of leadership coming out soon, in which he would discuss how leaders need to address the darker, uncomfortable sides of themselves in order to hit real breakthroughs with their teams. From the way he spoke about it, it sounded like a counternarrative to the hero complex around founders and CEOs–a treatise on authentic leadership.

During the talk, Tony's date, Mimi, Amanda, and I sat on a row of pillows in the very front, just below the stage. I think Maggie was probably standing near the back of the room or sitting on a couch. We had all heard his talk several times before: the Zappos origin story, how visiting Michael Cornthwaite's bar inspired him to move the company downtown, and how he wanted downtown Vegas to become the four-minute mile of city building. "After the first man broke the four-minute mile, there was a domino effect around the world," he said. "And if you fix cities, you kind of fix the world." Amanda rested her head on Mimi's shoulder.

The talk concluded with an emotional appeal–a video promoting the upcoming Life Is Beautiful festival set to the music of the band Imagine Dragons and portraying scenes of wonder and discovery in the Fremont East District–and a challenge to the audience to pursue its dreams. "We live in an age where the greatest threats are not saber-toothed tigers running after us," Tony said. "The worst that can happen is that we have to stay on a friend's couch." The crowd erupted in applause and a standing ovation.

After the event, Dave Logan ran outside to the black SUV where

Tony and Mimi were standing. "I get it," he said breathlessly. "I finally get what you are doing, and I want to help."

When we returned to Vegas a few days later (we all went our separate ways after the event and met up again at the private airport hanger on Sunday morning), I joined Maggie and others at the Gold Spike. They were playing with the toys (flip cups, Jenga-like games, brain teasers) that Tony had purchased in Santa Monica near the bar. Outside in the backyard, Zappos employees were gathering for their annual pool party. It was a Sunday afternoon in August, and everyone in the ecosystem was hanging out together.

"So you drank the Kool-Aid, huh?" asked a familiar face sitting on the edge of the pool. I recognized the man from my first tour on the *Delivering Happiness* bus. Henry Kang, a former Wall Street banker who rented an apartment at the Ogden to support Tony's Downtown Project and Delivering Happiness mission, had seen this play out many times before. I nodded and then jumped into the water.

It was a quintessential Zappos party, marked by the sort of culture that has continually landed the company on *Fortune*'s "Best Companies to Work For" list. A DJ spun rap and Top Forty songs as employees played beer pong in the wading area, while others danced poolside. That afternoon, the heat index was 120 degrees Fahrenheit, nearly the same as Saudi Arabia.

When I emerged, I walked over to one of the high tables by the bar, where Tony was taking in the scene. "Here." He slid a shot of fernet to me across the table. Fernet is casually referred to as the "Kool-Aid" in downtown Vegas. As we downed the shots, a young woman wearing a black-and-white-striped swimsuit walked over to us holding a red plastic cup in the air and dancing to the music.

"Alexis [Gonzales-Black] is a key player to everything," Tony said of her, referring ambiguously to his larger plan for downtown

Las Vegas. "She's part of the Holacracy implementation team at Zappos."

Alexis set down her glass and described her mission as "busting bureaucracy" and replacing the traditional management structure at Zappos with a more agile system where power is distributed more evenly. "You know"–she turned to Tony abruptly–"we're trying, but people don't really listen or believe what we're saying until you walk into the room."

He cracked his Mona Lisa smile and offered a few suggestions. Alexis just stared at him in mock frustration. "Do you know that it's my birthday?" she said, changing the subject. "Where's my gift?"

"I'm going to give it to you later," he replied. "There's a lot of research that points to delayed gratification as creating increased happiness in the long run."

When Alexis walked back to the beer pong in the pool, I turned to Tony and asked him how to move forward with documenting the Downtown Project story. Specifically, would he fund the venture? "Why don't you couch surf? Make your way through the community," he said, begging off the question. "You could even coin a term, 'community surfing,' and call your book *365 Beds*." He throws these sorts of ideas out every day, like how he told Andrew Donner he wants to build a ski hill in the middle of downtown. People also spoke about his "MacGyver tests," where he wants to see how badly a person wants something first. I thought that might be the case with my book, so I decided to continue. Besides, I had already given up my apartment in New York City and saw entering Tony's world as an adventure. It felt like anything was possible.

"He's always had people following him around," Alfred Lin explained. "But that group just keeps getting larger and larger." That afternoon, I became part of that group.

As more Zapponians made their way over to the high table, I

watched as Tony joined hands with two employees and jumped cannonball-style into the water, sending huge waves throughout the tiny pool.

After partying with the Zapponians, I followed Tony back up to his apartment. Mimi Pham, who has a room there, was arranging his mail and handed him a new management book. The main living space is lined mostly with management books, many of which Tony recommends to his employees. The Zappos lobby holds all of them, and the company holds classes that teach the principles from *Tribal Leadership*, Jim Collins's *Good to Great: Why Some Companies Make the Leap . . . and Others Don't*, and Simon Sinek's *Start with Why: How Great Leaders Inspire Everyone to Take Action*. And over the coming months, just as employees would have the opportunity to get accredited as Holacracy trainers, they, too, could take classes about finding their personal "Why?" and become accredited in Sinek's leadership principles. One morning at the Beat, I overheard Fred Mossler strongly encourage a prospective Zappos employee to read *Start with Why*.

Tony is always looking for people who could be good brand evangelists. For example, Maggie Hsu's early initiative was largely to get to know the multitude of visitors who wanted to find a way to become involved. She had the support and ear of a well-respected CEO but also had to manage what it meant to facilitate serendipity, such as putting together a "Passport to Downtown"–a laminated mock passport with the faces and job titles ("Wizards," "Sorceresses")–for guests to take on scavenger hunts. The goal was to spark collisions by getting guests to track down all the different members of Downtown Project. For guests who weren't VIP, this was a clever way for the core team to avoid meetings. It also added a burden to the Downtown Project employees who didn't have a traditional office and were generally working in plain sight.

Zach Ware also worked on the scavenger hunts. Sitting at the Gold Spike bar one afternoon in August 2013, he opened his laptop and shared with me the guidelines. He said that so far, they'd had only one abuser of the scavenger hunt: a longtime friend of Tony's. "He chased down several employees around downtown," Zach said, cracking a smile and holding back laughter. "Unfortunately, he can never come back."

Part of what intrigues Tony is bringing into his circle people from all walks of life. One evening in Tony's apartment, the Dancetronauts and Downtown Project's Burning Man cultural attaché were sharing nachos at the center island in his kitchen. Michael Cornthwaite was in the hallway trying to break away; he wanted to get home to his wife and daughter. But Tony insisted that he join him in meeting a young musician who was performing at the Gold Spike later: "But she's really *interesting*."

"Tony is the master inviter to the table; the consummate gambler," a longtime Zappos manager shared with me. "It's usually some sort of dare. It's then up to you to decide what to do with it."

ENCOUNTERING THE SORCERESS

Zappos's Vendor Appreciation Party that August 2013 would foreshadow the series of events to unfold over the next couple months. It was a misty evening, and the streets were filled with hundreds of people dressed in Mardi Gras attire, wearing colorful beads and masks, and carrying around red plastic cups.

There I encountered Sarah Nisperos again inside Coterie. She was standing behind the maze of clothing racks next to the register. She wore a colorful top, and her hair was in braids, Burning Man style. "I need to be the most eccentric person in the room so

I can give others permission to do the same," she shared. Other Downtown Project employees were sitting near the cash register taking shots of whiskey and snacking on red licorice. In the year since it opened, Coterie had become a place that lived out its ROC ethos. (Meanwhile, its balance sheet was falling into the red, but more on that later.) People say that Sarah has a way of looking into people's souls, which is how she gained the nickname Sorceress.

"Everyone has their five days with Tony," she said. In an interview with *Playboy*, Tony alluded to his recruiting strategy for Downtown Project, explaining that he applies tactics from journalist Neil Strauss's seduction bible *The Game: Penetrating the Secret Society of Pickup Artists* to get people to move to Vegas. *Business Insider* ran a similar story titled "Zappos CEO Tony Hsieh Explains How Reading Guides on How to Pick Up Women Led to One of His Most Ambitious Projects." Strauss, who distanced himself from the pickup artist community with his 2015 book *The Truth: An Uncomfortable Book About Relationships*, describes the tactics as essentially manipulation.

As Sarah and I were talking, revelers with skeleton faces and other costumes made their way into the store for shots and face painting. Sarah's associate painted a galaxy on my cheek, we each took a shot, and I was on my way. Just like most everyone else who passes through Coterie's doors, I left happier.

A few doors down at DCR, Tony was dressed in a black-and-white court jester's costume and surprised guests by acting as a bouncer, checking IDs and determining whether people could enter. Michael stood to the side in bemusement. Later that night, Flint and Tinder founder Jake Bronstein and I saw him walking along Fremont Street with a fire thrower. As the construction lead for Downtown Project remarked to me later in the week, "Festivals like Mardi Gras allow you to suspend the rules for a few days and operate with a different set of norms. But there's a reason why festivals are contained to a few days. We can't handle it. We need order."

He was right: the "golden age" of Downtown Project would last only about a year. After that, people couldn't handle the chaos. Most did not hold the same appetite for risk—or at least have the same financial wherewithal—as Tony did.

Two weeks later, I attended Burning Man for the first time, where I spent twenty-four hours with Tony and his crew. Zappos Holacracy implementation lead Alexis Gonzales-Black even lent me her brand-new camping tent so that I could attend. Living on a very limited budget—I had saved virtually no money in advance of moving to Vegas—was a real constraint, though people like Alexis helped make my adventure possible. I don't think Tony realizes what it really means to go to zero.

A few days after Burning Man, Tony was having drinks at the Gold Spike with a young female bartender from the Arts District and showing her his photos. He called me over and asked what my favorite part of the festival was; I responded that it was a solo afternoon walk to the very edge of the deep playa, a vast open area that stretches beyond the clock-like city and toward the surrounding mountains. He shared that his favorite moment was dancing until dawn with the Dancetronauts on their art car. He has told reporters that his lifestyle hasn't changed much over the years, and, on one hand, that's true. This escapist view of the world is seductive, but it doesn't ring true for all of the Zapponians who are making around $11 per hour in its call center, supporting families and worried about paying rent. Some employees complain of an empathy gap.

"I'M DIFFERENT"

For all of the mixed feelings around the company's move, September 9, 2013–the day Zappos moved into its new headquarters–was one for the organization's history books. The Las Vegas skies were a brilliant blue, and there was a buzz of excitement in the air. The Ogden lobby, less than two blocks away from the campus, was filled with Zappos and Downtown Project employees and others within the ecosystem.

Everyone walked to the new campus in the way that die-hard baseball fans walk toward a stadium during the World Series. Gatekeepers with clipboards checked off the names of attendees and handed them blue plastic scissors for the ribbon cutting. Everyone filled the white circular structure and its three levels surrounding the exposed open space, wrapping around the courtyard. Following Zach Ware's introduction, Tony stepped up to the podium and shared that he felt like "Mad Max in the Thunderdome." Mayor Carolyn Goodman, Andrew Donner, Michael Cornthwaite, and an Asian woman with bleached blond hair holding a llama on a leash stood off to the side.

The Record Setter, a DTP-funded start-up that documents events to incorporate them into its own version of the *Guinness Book of World Records*, announced the countdown, and as soon as the blue ribbon fell to the ground, the Jabbawockeez, a performance group defined by their white masks, stormed the stage to the song "I'm Different" by the rapper 2 Chainz. That afternoon, they were trying to set the record for the longest ribbon cutting in the world (in terms of ribbon length and number of participants). In that moment, a rare convergence of grey clouds took over the skies, and rain started pouring down into the atrium. Zapponians ran across the street and into the Gold Spike, where waitresses carried around trays of fernet shots and Blue Edition Red Bull and vodka. Employees entertained themselves by playing cornhole and giant-sized Operation and Connect Four games. I pushed through the crowds and emerged outside, where the rain was clearing up and a rainbow had started to appear. I saw Tony surrounded by a few women and walked over.

"How do you feel now, after all of this?" I asked him.

"Um, I heard there are mermaids by the pool," he demurred and then disappeared back into the crowd.

Meanwhile, hours later Zach Ware was being pulled onto a stretcher to the hospital for what he thought was a heart attack; it turns out he was suffering from exhaustion over the schedule leading up to the Zappos campus opening. I admired him for having the vulnerability to share the incident on his personal blog:

> September 9th marked the culmination of nearly three years of work with the opening of Zappos's new HQ at the former Las Vegas City Hall. I had labored, stressed and taken bullets over that development and felt a pride I can't describe when I stood in front of our entire company gathered in the Plaza and said "Welcome Home." Twenty-four hours later I was en route to the hospital, this time to spend 24 hours enduring a battery of tests to see if my heart was compromised. As it turns out, it's not . . . it fact it's very healthy. So what was causing this?
>
> The weeks that followed included a few small incidents, including one that erupted in the middle of what I considered the most important meeting we've had at Project 100 since launching it. I left the table, ran in circles behind the restaurant, calmed down, then continued the meeting. I had a few glasses of wine the night before, so a pattern could be established.

The worst came on a Friday night. With a pulse of 150 and blood pressure off the charts, I felt like I was surely dying.

To uphold the promise of delivering happiness, there is a price to be paid.

COUCH SURFING

Between my stays in the Downtown Project crash pads, Tony encouraged me to stay with members of the community, and I took him up on the challenge. Holacracy implementation lead John Bunch was one of the few to open his door. Many Zapponians had moved to Vegas just to play poker and turned to Zappos when they realized they wanted a corporate day job. That was the case for John. He has made a few hundred thousand dollars from tournaments alone. If you want to find him, just search for the tall guy wearing a baseball cap at the Wynn casino on the Las Vegas Strip. Once I understood this about John, I made sense of his resting poker face and his fascination with rolling out Holacracy. Like Tony and Brian Robertson, John is a computer programmer at heart. *Holacracy is just a game for John, too*, I thought to myself. "Tony knew what he was doing in getting John," a Harvard professor of organizational design shared with me, referring to the similar coder mentality.

Before taking on his role as Holacracy implementation lead, John handled special projects for Tony as a technical advisor. He spent the year living "in Tony's shadow," he explained at an All-Hands meeting, with a photo on the screen of him standing quite literally in Tony's shadow in front of Zappos. (Jeff Bezos is known for his "league of shadows," a longstanding tradition at Amazon where deputies are tasked with finding ways to execute on his craziest ideas.) And as with all who play a key role in Tony's life, John adopted work-life integration. He once attended a pick-up artist convention with Tony to better understand "real social dynamics," he told me, "to learn more about the psychology behind why this works and how it might apply to other situations." Although he continues to reinforce the fact that in a Holacracy there are no titles and no managers, John's LinkedIn profile indicates that he has an expertise in management as an advisor to the CEO of Zappos.

As we sat on the balcony of his apartment in the Ogden overlooking Fremont Street one evening, he strategized with me. "So, three hundred sixty-five days, on average two nights per place?" he estimated. "You'll be staying with about a hundred eighty people over this next year. I tried couch surfing once. It's hard because you never know if you're a liability or not. Tony's a big optimist, perhaps to a fault. He doesn't think, 'What if this doesn't work out?'"

Many challenges like this start with a drunken bet. One Downtown Project visitor confided in me that Tony had roped her into running at six in the morning with the Downtown Project running team after a night of drinking. "I don't want to go–I'm a mother, I'm exhausted," she confessed to me about what was going on in her head at the time. The drunken bet was essentially how Tony himself made a deal with Michael Cornthwaite to move Zappos downtown and invest his windfall from the Amazon sale into a city.

"Does this whole thing trace back to Tony at a bar? Do I really think that?" Zappos founder Nick Swinmurn posed to me. "Yes, I do."

From his new company's headquarters in Silicon Valley, Nick shared with me how everything was an experiment. "We'd go to a bar, and Tony and the woman he was dating at the time would pretend to be single and see how many people the other attracted. One day I decided that I didn't want to be part of a damn experiment anymore."

DOWNTOWN LOWDOWN

After the September 2013 Downtown Lowdown, a monthly event open to the public where Downtown Project gives the community an update on the state of its investments and progress, Henry Kang (the Wall Street banker whom I met on the *Delivering Happiness* bus) invited an early Downtown Project employee and me up to his apartment in the Ogden and poured us a round of drinks. A copy of *Delivering Happiness* displayed in his office decorated with Zen garden stones, and he kept a bottle of fernet in his refrigerator in case Tony ever came around.

The Downtown Project employee told us the story of how he got drawn into the community. He was working in the hospitality industry in LA when Mimi Pham and Tony invited him to join the *Delivering Happiness* bus tour around the country. By the end of the tour, he had secured a job handling hospitality for Downtown Project, and Mimi handed him the comic book version of *Delivering Happiness* so that he could better acclimatize himself to the culture.

One of the first things he did after arriving in Vegas in fall 2011 was attend a Zappos All-Hands. "It was at the Palms, in this magnificent room that felt like a church," he told us, taking a sip of his drink. He said it reminded him of the Church of Scientology.

A few months earlier, he was the first to be fired from Downtown Project and was still recovering from its aftermath. "If Tony doesn't want me, then who does?" he said, taking another drink of his vodka Red Bull. When he couldn't find another job in the ecosystem, he went back to his acting roots and joined the cast of a theater show in Las Vegas, which was raising money to support a cause. In the weeks leading up to the performance he had come alive again.

That afternoon in Henry's apartment, the former employee told us about how he used to spend evenings drinking and smoking with Downtown Project employees on their balconies at the Ogden. In the weeks after being let go, he walked around the apartment complex with his sunglasses on to hide tears. "When you're in, you're in," he said, exasperated. "When you're out, you're out."

At one point during his tenure, he discovered what other employees were making and asked for a raise. Mimi Pham responded by ordering him a book from Amazon about how you don't need money to be happy.

No one understands exactly who Mimi is or why she has so much influence over Tony. Some identify her as the woman with the dragon tattoo on her back. One evening I walked into Downtown Project's hospitality headquarters and saw a whiteboard that showed the occupancy of all the crash pads in the Ogden. Everything was mapped out in red and blue marker, except for several rooms that were blocked out in black: MIMI VIP.

BOLT BARBERS

One morning in the Beat, I was having coffee with Downtown Project's Burning Man cultural attaché when she turned to the man sitting next to us. "Are those scissors on your bracelet?" she asked Matt Berman, founder of Bolt Barbers.

"Yeah, they are, in fact!" He looked up, pleasantly surprised. Berman explained that he was opening up Bolt Barbers in a black train caboose at the far end of Container Park. He had just relocated to Las Vegas and moved in with a couple other guys he met on Craigslist. "I've been going through a divorce for years, and so I kind of just want to live like a college guy," he told us. "I was lonely in LA. From the moment people get to LA, they're posing. They have two groups of friends, two lives they lead: one they have to get by, and the other that they want." He created Bolt Barbers to bridge the gap between the two, "so guys have a place to kick back and relax," he explained. "A barbershop is the essence of community."

"Why not get hot girls with big tits who can cut hair and lean over the guys while they do that? Wouldn't that be a great thing for Vegas?" the cultural attaché asked.

"It's been done before," he said nonchalantly. His earrings, bald head, and tattoos made him look like a member of the Hells Angels. "There are a few start-ups. But it sounds better than it is in reality. Guys just want to shoot the shit in the barber chair."

He finally walked over to us and sat down. He shared that Bolt Barbers has been on the Bravo network's *Million Dollar Listing* and other television shows, and showed us a picture of one of his clients with a clown tattoo on his face. The cultural attaché mentioned that her husband dresses up as a clown sometimes. (I didn't ask her to clarify, but I think she meant at Burning Man.)

Then Matt shared with us the story of finding the black caboose. He had told Jody Sherman his idea during their meeting at the Palms and called him the moment that he found one listed on

Craigslist. "You'll never believe it," he told Jody. "It's in Henderson!" Together they drove out to the location, not far from the Zappos headquarters, checked it out, and immediately put down $10,000 after Don Welch agreed to insure it.

"Most people don't understand just how tough it is to be an entrepreneur," Matt said, looking each of us in the eye. "And that's part of why I want to be here. You're surrounded by people who are doing the same thing." For Matt, the early excitement and energy would eventually wear off, as it would for many.

"WE'RE LIVING ON MARS"

Between the Ogden, the Gold Spike, which is a bar, hotel, and room-rental property, and other Downtown Project–owned properties, for a season, Tony's entire ecosystem lived within a few thousand square feet of one another. There were unique benefits, such as engaging with African penguins at Tony's apartment on a random weeknight, and real drawbacks. Outsiders were calling out the absurdities over the years. Tech reporter Paul Carr, whose VTF-funded company NSFWCORP folded into the website *PandoDaily*, which chronicles tech culture and describes itself as "speaking truth to the new power," was one of the most vocal critics. He captured the project's sometimes vapid nature in his March 2015 story "Tony Hsieh's Vegas Downtown Project Finally Accepts It Can't Operate a Lemonade Stand in the Desert." In an article for *Slate*, "The Dark Side of Techtopia," reporter Alison Griswold (now with *Quartz*) asked whether "Downtown Project was a legitimate venture or the egomaniacal whim of a wealthy technocrat."

"We're living on Mars!" one outsider lamented during a Catalyst dinner in Tony's apartment, as he evaluated the food:

a gluten-free pudding from a new Downtown Project–funded restaurant. "For some reason, we're all accepting this as normal life, but it isn't." He glanced over at other attendees crying after an emotional night of talks in the double-wide trailers.

At one of the Catalyst dinners, I sat next to an educator from the Bronx and an employee of SoulPancake, a digital platform known for its uplifting content, such as the viral video-turned-television show *Kid President*. After a night of talks, the educator broke down in tears. Outbursts like this were a common occurrence and I wasn't immune. It was an emotionally exhausting environment. There were benefits to that too. At the end of the inaugural Catalyst Week, Amanda and an ex-Googler hosted a vulnerability session, which bound my Catalyst group indefinitely. Tony had tapped into Amanda's superpower, which was to bring together entrepreneurs and change-makers and create a safe place for them to process their emotions. But Catalyst was an anomaly within the Downtown Project ecosystem, and most of the guests still chose not to move to Vegas: it was a tough sell for that community. Still, she hosted around twenty-two weeks and two thousand guests over two years.

"Get me out of here!" another Catalyst attendee yelled in mock frustration. She had arranged for an extended two-week stay to see if she could find a way to collaborate with Downtown Project but was already worn out from the food and the politics. After trying to arrange meetings with multiple players in the ecosystem, she was given the runaround and told to rely on serendipitous collisions instead. "They won't even tell me who's in charge of what," she said, sighing. "I'm depressed."

The politics of Downtown Project had a way of bringing even polished guests like my new friend at Catalyst–a well-respected consultant who works with many Fortune 500 companies–to the point of desperate exasperation. Because of the star power of Tony and DTP at the time, many wanted an opportunity to join in on the excitement. But without a direct line to Tony, these guests stood frustrated on the sidelines.

Part of the draw was pure voyeurism. The Tech Cocktail weeks, which focused on the tech community and brought in well-known investors every month, were valuable to those in the community who knew how to take advantage of the situation. Many big names showed up just out of curiosity.

"In the Bay Area, there are so many people they can be meeting. In Vegas, there are not that many start-ups," said Elizabeth Yin, who cofounded the email advertising company LaunchBit, which was acquired by BuySellAds.com in 2014. "Influential people have nowhere else to go and hang out except with you."

LET'S MAKE THIS EPIC

"Can we complete one hundred ninety-two charge cycles in a day?" a young guy wearing a hoodie polled his Project 100 colleagues. "That would give us twenty-eight thousand miles' worth of range."

Project 100 was created to provide an alternative to Uber and Lyft for a select group of downtown Vegas residents. It was named for the one hundred Teslas Tony ordered from Elon Musk in a rapid-fire business deal just after SXSW in 2013.

On this cool September afternoon, the start-up's then ten-person team was meeting in the main floor conference room at Work In Progress, the Downtown Project–owned coworking space on Sixth Street. They were debating how many vehicles to put on the road during the company's beta test.

"What about the range of the Twizy?" another piped up. He

was referring to a small electric car, manufactured by Renault, that looks like a golf cart.

"Assume a lot of our assumptions are wrong," Zach Ware told his team assuredly. "If anything, we should overdo it. If we have capacity issues, it wrecks everything."

"We've come to these numbers from multiple different ways, and we get to the same numbers," a young man wearing cargo shorts and a button-up chimed in.

"I have no doubt about the forty-five vehicles," Zach pushed. "I'd rather not be too conservative. I think the delta of fifteen is too low. My gut says if it's thirty-five or forty-five, go with forty-five and learn from it. I'd rather risk the one-and-a-half million now."

Zach, dressed casually in jeans and a T-shirt, told his team they would revisit the numbers. "We need to create today an ironclad set of membership standards. I'm going to tee this off, and J. J., you can swing," he said, referring to the start-up's in-house attorney, J. J. Todd.

J. J.'s calm demeanor offset his otherwise imposing, nearly seven-foot frame. "Tighten up membership so it doesn't appear that we're offering a service to the public," he began. "The more hoops it takes to get into vehicles, the more likely the NTA [Nevada Transportation Authority] will say, 'You're right: you don't have to follow our guidelines.'"

Zach jumped in: "We can put people on the waiting list, and we can suspend the rules. Gmail did that first for, like, five years. It seemed so exclusive, and that's why Gmail won over Hotmail. And then there's a dialogue that happens: people become accidental advocates of the company."

As Zach spoke, his dog milled around the room; outside the window, I caught sight of a young man buzzing by the Work in Progress office in a Twizy.

"Maybe we don't publish the criteria," Zach continued. "We're an invitation-only club. Do we want to serve everyone? Hell yeah. But we want to control who. We want it to seem special."

J. J. used a legal comparison: "So like Justice Stewart: 'I don't know how to describe hard-core pornography, but I know it when I see it.'"

"We'll be able to make subjective calls," Zach responded. "We're going to file an action in court saying we don't have to go to the NTA."

"Then what?" someone piped up.

"Then we'll all get drunk!" another responded.

"Then we'll get *super* drunk!" Zach added with crescendo.

As Zach held court inside the main-floor conference room, other, smaller teams worked silently upstairs. Along the spiral staircase line stickers bearing start-up logos with pithy names–Zirtual, Whill, iDonethis, Karma–all funded by Downtown Project entities. Like most offices and coworking spaces, the open office plan meant tight quarters. Any phone call would disrupt the entire office, so people took calls in the garage with the Ping-Pong table.

At one of the long, white tables upstairs sat the Rumgr and Wedgies teams, the early Vegas Tech investments cofounded by Zappos engineers.

Sara Hill came out to Vegas to build up Work In Progress. "I was kind of romantic in love with the idea of building a start-up in the community," said Sara, who went on to found the Downtown Project-funded start-up accelerator the Mill. "I'm originally from the Bay Area and moved down to LA. And when I was in LA, which was originally five to six years ago, it was much smaller than it is now. And I loved being a part of that early culture, and 'Let's band together and build this thing up.' The Mill was originally kind of an experiment for us as well, because no other incubators or accelerators were here."

Most Vegas Tech start-ups were not creating world-changing products. They are in the realm of upgrading minor inconveniences, with ideas like a garage sale app, a bowling app, a virtual assistant–the sort of upgrade that Zappos did for American consumers by creating a place for them to buy shoes online. But that is where the demand is coming from. VCs have spoken with their multimillion-dollar investments in consumer apps like Instagram and Snapchat and on-demand delivery services.

In a 2015 article titled "Is Silicon Valley in Another Bubble . . . and What Could Burst It?," *Vanity Fair*'s Nick Bilton captured the state of tech's innovation problem by quoting a comment from Twitter: "SF tech culture is focused on solving one problem: What is my mother no longer doing for me?"

Many of the funded start-ups are service oriented, too, tapping into Las Vegas's core competency of hospitality. There's Moveline, a platform that served as a middleman between movers and customers; cleaning service Maidly; dry cleaning service Mint Locker; virtual assistant Zirtual; and on-demand car service Project 100. The investment in all of these entities plays to the larger Zappos brand. All have modeled their platforms loosely around Zappos ideals (happiness, core values) and its customer service storyline.

People say Tony was still betting on Romotive to deliver real returns, though he publicly expressed optimism for Zirtual.

"Vegas Tech Fund looks [to the outside world] like the last resort for funding," Romotive's founder, Keller Rinaudo, shared with me at an artisanal coffee shop in San Francisco's Mission District after its move, wearing a Sequoia Capital hoodie. He had just fired several employees, which he didn't mention. Romo was a popular toy among the niche tech community, but it didn't have wide enough appeal to spark the kind of sales he and his investors were looking for, so he was working on a pivot. "If we get this product right, we'll change the world!" he yelled to me as we parted ways on Mission Street.

"Change the world" is a phrase that's been so overused in Silicon Valley, it's nearly devoid of meaning. Yet in Keller's case, his new focus was a lot more world changing than Romo the iPhone robot. He didn't disclose any details at the time, but he was raising millions more from investors to develop drones that would deliver lifesaving supplies over Rwandan terrain.

Earlier that day, one of his investors was more measured in his take on the start-up's chances of success: "There are no guarantees in life," Alfred Lin told me straight-faced while sitting at the large cherrywood table in Sequoia's main conference room. Like Tony, Alfred speaks with the air of a Zen Buddhist philosopher.

For all of the Vegas Tech Fund's aggrandizing over ROC, the start-ups that truly focused on ROC found that their ROI suffered as a result. They simply weren't hitting their numbers because they were too focused on facilitating serendipity. Ticket Cake, the online ticketing service, pumped a lot of time and resources into a weekly podcast, called Downtown Podcast, its contribution to ROC. In addition to the podcast, the Ticket Cake cofounders attended all of the community events and frequently took coffee meetings with visitors seeking investment from Vegas Tech. Their extracurricular ROC activities may have supported the community, but their business suffered, and they shut down in May 2014. Life Is Beautiful did not even choose its homegrown start-up to ticket its event. "I blew through two hundred thousand dollars, and I don't think that I can ask Tony for anything more," Ticket Cake cofounder Dylan Jorgensen told me as we walked along Fremont Street after the grand opening of the Hydrant

Club, Downtown Project's membership-only dog park founded by Silicon Valley veteran Cathy Brooks.

After Ticket Cake shut down, he put all of his energy into the podcast, and his cofounder Jacqueline Jensen took a job with a tech company outside the perimeters of the Downtown Project's llama. The way Jacqueline explained it, the shift in thinking was almost like a deprogramming. "My boss couldn't believe that we did all of that stuff for free," she said. "But when you're in it, that's just what you do." The cofounders had started Ticket Cake in Salt Lake City, which is where they met Andy White.

The first two years were exciting, before there were any failures. In addition to the Ogden, many founders lived on what they called "start-up block"–a row of houses that became their start-up community–together on Eighth Street, which fostered a sense of camaraderie.

One of the first start-ups to move to Vegas was Elizabeth Yin's LaunchBit. Her connection was that her cofounder Jennifer Chin (maiden name Hsieh) was Tony's cousin. Elizabeth grew up in Silicon Valley during the dot-com boom and worked at LinkExchange when she was in high school. "It was so exciting, and they were doing all kinds of things and could eat all the pizza they wanted," she recounted. "It was just a dream. I knew from that day on that I wanted to start a company." The Vegas Tech Fund invested $500,000 in a round of funding, along with other investors.

With time, the fund started investing in larger companies and joining in rounds with other investors. It got in on a venture and Series B round with a fast-growing and promising start-up called Banjo. The social media company is based in the Bay Area but agreed to open a Las Vegas office. ROC was no longer a requirement: the Vegas Tech Fund had to start making more sophisticated bets. There's OrderWithMe (later re-branded WithMe), a team from China, which at first wanted to help small businesses source better products in bulk, and now wants to create the retail store of the future.

With so many investments–around sixty or seventy by early 2014–the Vegas Tech Fund was strained in its ability to offer guidance and follow-on funding to its companies. By contrast, Sequoia's multibillion-dollar fund makes only a few deals a year, and has storied companies such as Google and Apple in its portfolio. Alfred Lin credits the eventual dissolution of companies such as Zirtual and Moveline to Vegas Tech Fund's overstretched resources. Tony and Fred Mossler presumably spend only about 1 percent of their time on Vegas Tech, leaving the mentoring to Zach Ware, Andy White, and the other Vegas Tech Fund partner, a Zappos employee named Will Young. But there was hardly any mentoring, and Zach and Will had full-time jobs. Andy was the only full-time employee, and he spent most of his time on deals.

Vegas Tech Fund also relied heavily on the chance that collisions and serendipity would facilitate relationships. But living in the same building as their investors manifested differently for the young start-up founders, who, when things weren't going well, actually did their best to *avoid* their benefactors in the Ogden or out at the bars. For that sort of situation to be successful, there would need to be a high degree of psychological safety–and even then, unusually confident and emotionally intelligent founders.

There were others who moved to Vegas to get in on the excitement even without funding, like Indian-American entrepreneur Hartej Singh Sawhney. He and his Israeli-Argentine cofounder are developing a POS (point-of-sale) system based in the block chain, a platform for all transactions of the digital currency Bitcoin, called Zuldi. They saw Vegas, with all of its bars and restaurants, as the ideal market to test their product; so they rented a place in the Ogden to take advantage of the investors who came in every month during Tech Cocktail week.

The two partners found out about Tony's Downtown Project through their lawyer, who was representing DTP companies in his portfolio, and the two partners booked a trip to check it out. "We got a hotel for cheap at the Circus Circus for twenty-six dollars a night, and we rented a car. They messed something up, so they ended up giving us a convertible Camaro. We would spend the days talking to restaurant owners and restaurant GMs, showing them our app that's designed for servers to do ordering and payments. While we were doing that, we just felt like, 'Holy shit, this city is so good for us.'"

Hartej says one of the best parts of living in the Ogden is that you "get to live like kings" in Vegas as compared with New York or San Francisco. It's easy to get by on $1,000 a month. "I have a word for it," he told me. "Everyone lives like fortythousandaires."

SENSATION WHITE

Sensation, a rave at MGM Grand where everyone dresses in white, drew thousands of revelers for its event in October 2013, including Tony and his posse.

"You don't realize you're sacrificing yourself until later," a longtime employee who has worked with Tony since Venture Frogs confessed to me on the stadium floor. Like many of those in Tony's world, she acclimated herself to fit his preferences. She's more conservative than most in his ecosystem, yet somehow he convinced her to attend the rave that evening.

Tony walked up to us wearing all white and had silver-painted hair. "You two are cut from the same cloth," he told us, placing his hands on our shoulders and giving us both a hug.

Maggie was there too, sort of like a fish out of water and dressed in the most conservative option for white rave attire. The scene seemed most suited for the VFA fellows who had tagged along. I wore a white dress with white fishnet tights and a platinum wig. Tony told me that I should dye my dark hair blond.

Keeping up with the grueling pace of work and partying is the most difficult thing for most in Tony's world. It's a pace that Fred, who gave up a good relationship with his first family (his first marriage failed) for Tony and Zappos, has taken on as a requirement for his job. One time, a group was on its way to the Electric Daisy Carnival. As one reveler recalled, everyone pregamed pretty hard while on the bus en route to the event, forcing Fred to take a taxi straight back home when they were a mile away from the festival gates.

Tony views work and play as inextricably linked, and expects that those closest to him will also embrace that ethos. The night before delivering a keynote at the Cosmopolitan hotel, for example, he hung out at magician David Copperfield's warehouse with a small group until three in the morning. He runs on a few hours of sleep a night and believes that the best ideas and connections come the more he exposes himself to the world. Steven Johnson's 2010 book *Where Good Ideas Come From* informed his thinking around cross-pollination of ideas; and although his keynote about engineering chance encounters, or collisions, is good marketing, he also genuinely believes in the concept and molds his life around potential encounters with new and interesting people.

For those in Tony's inner circle, there's a bent toward extremes at the expense of taking care of one's well-being. "You just don't want to let him down," Life Is Beautiful founder Rehan Choudhry explained.

Yet even so, that sort of dedication can be reversed in a single day. In an environment where loyalty is rewarded beyond anything else, even employees who have worked with Tony for a decade found that a single disagreement could lead to them losing all their power and influence with him.

ZAPPONIANS GONE WILD

Inside the Smith Center for the Performing Arts, a new world-class auditorium on Grand Central Parkway about a mile from the Zappos headquarters, the energy was high, even frantic. It was a week before Thanksgiving, and Zappos was hosting its 2013 Q4 All-Hands meeting, the last one before the rush of the holiday season. The theme was "Gone Wild!" and the stage was decorated as an animal kingdom. Many of the 1,500 Zapponians dressed up in animal costumes and raver gear. "It looks like an anime convention!" my friend said as we walked in.

Quarterly All-Hands are a signature Zappos event and a long-standing tradition that employees look forward to throughout the year. It's designed to be a spectacle that inspires awe like an Apple keynote with the grandeur of a TED conference. Each All-Hands highlights one of the Ten Core Values, and the emotional crescendo always involves a heartwarming customer service story. Once the mood has hit its peak, employees are invited to the stage to share why they love working for Zappos. Inevitably, one Zapponian's public expression of gratitude for his colleagues' acceptance sparks a domino effect, and the stage is lined with a row of so-called corporate misfits, all with brightly colored hair, tattoos, and piercings.

On this rainy and cold November afternoon, Tony spent a significant portion of the three-hour-long meeting talking about the company's move to self-organization. "Darwin said that the species that survive are not the strongest or most intelligent, but the most adaptable to change," he said, looking out into the crowd. "I believe the same is with companies. We must adapt, or we'll die." He cited the fact that most Fortune 500 companies from the last half century are no longer around today. The way to prevent that from happening with Zappos, he said, is to kill bureaucracy and develop a new system for doing things. The company will no longer have traditional managers; everyone will be his or her own boss.

Tony invited up the company's human resources lead to stand between him and Fred. Tears welled up in her eyes as she shared her experience using Holacracy: "I've learned to relinquish power, and it's been so hard, but now I know that people like me for me, and not just because I'm their boss. For the first time, we've been able to process tensions in a healthy way." In Holacracy speak, "processing tensions" is the equivalent of working through conflict.

Many Zappos employees joined the company as call center workers and then worked their way up–a testament to the uniqueness of the company. In most call centers, such a progression is long, painful, and largely out of reach. This fact alone is why so many Zapponians are devout Tony followers: he offered them an opportunity that is rare to find elsewhere. A requirement for the job is to possess a zany, overly enthusiastic attitude on the phones with customers. Paired with the company's overall focus on being happy, it's difficult and uncomfortable for employees to express negative emotions. So suddenly asking them to engage in conflict regularly is a radical move. The *Holacracy Constitution* outlines a very specific set of rules and ways of operating, down to governing who can speak and when in meetings. The idea is to give everyone a voice in the name of innovation, rather than allowing the dominant personalities to determine the company's strategy. That is, if the engineering-inspired system operates as it should.

The cadence of the All-Hands is very meticulously planned out. Soon after the HR director's tearful account, the mood changed: pop music came out of the speakers, and employees dressed in Ranger costumes descended upon the stage. A screen with the reality TV show *Fear Factor* logo lit up, and what appeared to be visiting zoologists pushed large plastic boxes filled with tarantulas into the center. "Who's going to jump in here for a two-hundred-fifty-dollar Zappos gift card?" the announcer taunted, voice rising. The crowd went wild, and scattered hands shot up throughout the auditorium. The announcer selected a woman dressed in a leopard costume to complete the dare. She emerged unscathed and $250 richer.

At the close of the event, guests rushed through the pouring rain to the happy hour next door in the Discovery Children's Museum. Bartenders served drinks throughout the winding playhouses and insect exhibits, which Zapponians brought to the dance floor as they twerked to the electronic music group Major Lazer's "Bubble Butt." Although the company was ostensibly moving to an equal playing field through Holacracy, Tony paid tribute to Arun Rajan, the company's outgoing longtime CTO, in a grand gesture mimicking *The Lion King*, with employees dressed in animal costumes bowing down to Arun to the song "Circle of Life." (The CTO was heading to One Kings Lane, an online retailer that sells home decor, based in San Francisco. At the time One King's Lane was valued at near $1 billion.) The performance was a nod to the shadow power structure and affirmed that some employees are still more important than others.

Across town, at a nondescript warehouse studio in the Arts District, the founder of the messaging platform Nomic was setting up his Hail Mary pitch for Tony. The event, titled "Who Is Downtown?" was guised as an art exhibition featuring a collection of professional photographs of residents, including a number of Downtown Project employees. Nomic even hired a former Zappos PR manager to convince Tony to attend. He showed up at the very end with two female Zappos employees on his arms. But it was to no avail.

Later that week, Henry Kang couldn't understand why Tony wouldn't invest in Nomic, which was experimenting with using its platform to connect locals to small business owners–in theory, a messaging app that cared about the community; but it had not yet proven out its idea, yet nonetheless earned enough users to attract an investor. "They are the *essence* of ROC," Henry said out of anger one afternoon at a nearby deli, pounding the table with his hand. Henry spent years on Wall Street, in private equity and as a venture capitalist, so he understood how the industry works. "If DTP doesn't invest in them, I won't believe in the message." He deeply wanted to believe in the higher purpose Tony was showcasing through his *Delivering Happiness* and Downtown Project messaging. Henry was working hard to live out similar values in his own life. He was one of the few who opened their doors to me during my couch-surfing adventure. I was grateful to have met Henry.

WHISKEY AROUND THE FIRE
WITH THE BURNERS

When I shared with Tony that it was nearly impossible to couch surf in the community–virtually no one wanted to host a journalist– he said that I could live in another DTP-owned crash pad until the end of the year.

In moving to the Eighth Street Apartments, I was transported to a community of Burners: Burning Man attendees who have adopted the festival's Ten Principles as a way of life all year round. In an empty parking lot across from Atomic Liquors, Scotte Cohen was building a massive art installation that would soon go up in flames–literally. Another Burner by the name of "Flash" Hopkins, who is considered the "Mafia Don" of Burning Man, and his friends from San Francisco's storied Cacophony Society were touring a mosaic spaceship to educate the downtown community about the artistic process. And across the courtyard from my apartment was another idealist, Downtown Project's director of imagination Professor Gould. The Dancetronauts lived there too; they performed as often as they could and volunteered their time with Downtown Project's monthly arts festival.

Back in September, after Burning Man, Tony took the Dancetronauts on a tour of Zappos, and invited the group's leader to watch his keynote. Zappos and Downtown Project tours are requirements for anyone who wants to meet with Tony. The Dancetronauts told me that they were promised a large white factory in the Arts District as their warehouse; but it went to hardware start-up Factorli instead. Months after uprooting and moving to Vegas, the Dancetronauts realized that they likely would never receive funding, at least in the way they expected. "My people hardly lift a finger anymore," one of the Dancetronauts told me hastily in the Beat one morning, referring to the free labor he became accustomed to asking his employees for these days.

Scotte received some funding from DTP and raised $15,000 through a crowdfunding campaign to bankroll his Life Cube art installation project.

"Today is going to be a *great* day!" Scotte sang most every morning from his balcony to anyone who would listen. We all lived in an open-style courtyard, and saw one another's comings and goings. At night, the Burners would gather around the fire pit and drink whiskey. They shared with me stories about the Cacophony Society and how its members held a mock tea party on the Golden Gate Bridge. The society is essentially the Theater of the Absurd. Burning Man's cofounder, Larry Harvey, was an early Cacophony Society member, and moved its annual effigy burning from the San Francisco Bay to the Nevada desert, which became what is now Burning Man.

One night Larry was passing through Las Vegas and joined the group; he wanted to see how Tony was bringing Burning Man to downtown Vegas. "It's like he's violating the church," Larry remarked as everyone enjoyed drinks in the courtyard behind the Gold Spike. He was referring to Tony's decision to strip the Gold Spike of its slot machines and turn it into a bar with oversized games like giant Jenga. He was impressed with what he saw, which is a lot coming from a man who founded the most extravagant art festival in the world.

"I was so depressed when I first got here," one of the female Burners confessed, turning to me. "I thought, 'Is this all there is?' There's no way we can stay for two months." She was referring to the sparse downtown connected to the janky (in other words, cheap and tacky by appearance) Fremont East Experience. It was hard to live surrounded by so much homelessness, with no grocery store and few restaurant options.

"Oh, that's so normal–we all go through that cycle," a young woman associated with Downtown Project chimed in. "This is a hard place to live."

"But then," the Burner continued, "we went to the elementary school, Ninth Bridge, and started working with the kids, showing them the spaceship and building things with them. Once we started creating, things got better."

The young woman nodded. I only half believed it, but nodded anyway.

Scotte knew Tony from the dot-com era and had gotten lucky twice, too. When he saw Tony at a conference, he walked up to him and gave his pitch. He wanted to build a massive cube-like structure out of wood (the size of a building) and invite locals to treat it as a blank canvas. Anyone could paint on the structure for free, and everyone was encouraged to write down their dreams on wish sticks and place them inside of the cube. Eventually the structure would go up in flames, sending everyone's dreams up to the sky. It was an idea that he had prototyped at Burning Man. Tony was interested in giving Scotte a blank canvas to quite literally play with fire.

The Life Cube Burn turned into a bigger ordeal than expected. Instead of planning on a week or two of festivities leading up to the Burn, there were two months of festivities around the installation.

"We are doing this for sixty-nine days. This is nuts! This is lucidity!" Scotte told me later. "And I had absolutely no idea what I was doing." But he figured it out and pulled off the impossible. He attracted thousands of Las Vegans and inspired many of them to pursue their passions in the process.

For Tony's part, he liked everything about the Life Cube. Every day that he was in town, he'd bring visitors over to the Life Cube, ask Scotte to tell his story, and instruct his guests to write down their wishes on the wish sticks.

A week before the Burn, when everything was reaching a fever pitch, Scotte got a call from Tony's risk manager and was asked to sit down with Downtown Project's head of operations. He was told that everything had spun out of control, and they were shutting it all down, gating up the cube, until the day of the Burn.

"I wanted this to be Woodstock!" he recounted later. "And then they're shutting it down."

It was a manifestation of what happened over and over again: Tony would invite people and tell them that they had license to pursue their dreams, saying the sky's the limit, without doing any due diligence.

Scotte responded to the shutdown by emailing photos of a man painting the Life Cube by the minute for hours to Todd Kessler of RGG, his point person at DTP. At eleven thirty that night, Todd showed up outside his door at the Eighth Street Apartments.

"Okay, okay, we get it," he told Scotte. "We can leave the Life Cube open. But no music."

HOLACRACY TRAINING IN THE LEARNING VILLAGE

Early the next morning, I walked past the mosaic spaceship in the Learning Village and into the double-wide trailer on the far end of the courtyard. Inside was an uninspiring grey room with a sole string of colorful streamers left over from a party. Two folding tables in the back had breakfast items–boxed cold cereal, mini muffins, watered-down coffee–and about forty Zappos and Downtown Project employees had organized themselves around circular tables for Holacracy training. Each had a massive five-inch thick three-ring binder filled with a Holacracy rule book, along with personalized laminated blue spiral notebooks titled the *Holacracy Constitution*. The book read like a cross between an actual constitution and a religious text, with statements that sounded a lot like "Thou shalt not . . ." and other directives from biblical text.

Sitting at the far back table were Fred Mossler, Andrew Donner the real estate manager, and other male Zappos and Downtown Project executives. Amanda Slavin of CatalystCreativ was also in the room, as were employees of tech start-ups, including Project 100. Tony's master plan was to roll out Holacracy within his entire ecosystem, and that included the start-ups.

"What in a legacy hierarchy would seem psychopathic?" HolacracyOne founder Brian Robertson boomed from the front of the room. He was sporting a lime-green T-shirt, and, with his balding hairline, looked older than his thirty-five years.

"Deviating from the rules," someone piped up.

"Challenging your leaders," said another.

"What are your favorite games?" Brian asked the group.

Fred, who is the second-largest investor in Downtown Project (he told me he's put down somewhere in the "high seven-figure, low eight-figure" range), said flatly from the back table, "Monopoly. Risk."

"Clue," said a Zapponian wearing a hoodie.

"Good," Brian responded. "And those games are only fun when we play by the rules, right?"

The room looked at him blankly and then nodded.

"Think of it as rules for anarchy," Brian added.

"At Zappos, there's so much implicit stuff you're supposed to do because it's part of the culture," said a young woman wearing jeans and tall black boots. "But where do we put it?"

"Our team does the parades," a Zappos recruiter chimed in. "But what if some of us don't do parades? Is it a domain, role, policy?" (Within Holacracy, "roles" and "accountabilities" are defined more narrowly, whereas a "domain" can encompass multiple roles. A "policy" grants or limits authority within a domain.)

"Policy is really hard because the definition of a normal policy has nothing to do with what we have going on here," the young woman responded.

Tony jumped in: "In general, have a bias against domains."

"You want to leave people as much freedom as you can," added Brian. "If you really need a domain, use it. Be careful with it–it's a big hammer."

In coming months, Zappos managers would engage in what could be called "the great land grab." Essentially what happened is that employees claimed domains early on so that they would have job security. Zappos managers were the first to be trained in Holacracy and quick to claim domains to protect their power as managers and to ensure that they didn't lose their jobs in the "managerless" system. One perceived weakness in Holacracy is that it doesn't have a system in place for compensation or promotions. "Brian sold us an incomplete system," Maggie Hsu concluded. Initially on board, she became one of HolacracyOne's biggest detractors.

For a company that hinges its entire reputation and bottom line on serving the customer, Holacracy–which is internally focused–is a curious choice for Zappos.

Brian asked everyone to stand in a large circle based upon

one's knowledge of the *Holacracy Constitution* and then to move into mock "tactical" and "governance" meetings. He likens the system to applying iOS software design to an organization.

Zappos's chief of staff, Jamie Naughton, was in the pilot group. "In the beginning, you feel that the human element is lost completely," she told me. "I remember sitting in meetings and wanting to scream at the founder of Holacracy, 'You don't get it! You don't get it at all!' He said, 'You've got to trust the process.' And I thought, 'This sucks.' You just have to wait your turn to speak your opinion." Over time, Zapponians described the greatest benefits of Holacracy as its conflict-resolution process and being forced to provide solutions to anything they opposed. But mostly, learning the verbiage and adopting the rules was burdensome.

Employees complained of being treated like children, something that Brian didn't even realize he affirmed when he described Holacracy this way: "Imagine a child. You want to guide them to what's right, but you can't do everything for them." He described "the great shift" as not needing to ask for permission anymore.

PIXEL PARTY

"Are you going to Tony's party tonight?" a Downtown Project employee asked me during one of the breaks in training. It was Tony's fortieth birthday. By then, I had been in Vegas for close to five months. I had heard a rumor of a surprise party but hadn't looked into it further. The DTP employee encouraged me to reach out to Tony's longtime time "ninja" (assistant) Liz Gregersen, and she forwarded me the invitation. There were instructions that all guests had to get a minor tattoo called a "pixel" in order to obtain a wristband and attend. "To enter the party, you must receive 1 pixel of a tattoo, meaning a single tattoo needle dipped in ink," Fred Mossler and Andrew Donner wrote in the e-vite. "There will be NO admittance into the party without at least a prick of a needle. . . . If you do not want to receive a prick of a needle, we completely understand and hold no misgivings about you not wanting to attend."

Black Spade Tattoo is on Carson Avenue, parallel to Fremont. By the time I arrived, Michael Cornthwaite and his wife, Jennifer, were there, and the video team from Fremont East Studios had arrived to document the event.

After the tattoo artist marked me with a small blue dot, he handed me a wristband with the words "We are all pixels" etched into it.

Some got creative, placing the tattoo under their tongues, behind their ears, at the tip of their index fingers. I chose to place the tattoo on my hip. By the end of the day, a hundred people shared the same mark. "This is all for you, Tony," one Downtown Project employee said, smiling into the camera. A local reporter caught wind of the party and sparked a minor national news story, with a piece in the online tech publication *Gizmodo* by Alissa Walker titled, "Zappos Isn't a Cult? All Tony Hsieh's Friends Got Matching Tattoos."

That evening, I walked over to the Inspire Theatre, which was built to rival other Las Vegas entertainment venues and showcase everything from burlesque to TED talks, with the Dancetronauts, who were decked out in their white spacesuits and ready to perform. We showed our wristbands to the bouncer and made our way inside. Just inside the door stood a table filled with glow sticks, neon glasses, LED necklaces; the dress code was rave attire, and everyone was in costume. Even the most unadventurous Zappos employee wore a purple wig.

Servers walked around with trays of fernet and gourmet food, and guests mingled. I walked up to Michael, who was standing near the cherrywood-paneled bar. Inspire Theater was one of the many DTP-funded projects that he owned and oversaw. But receiving money from Tony and carrying out the execution were two different things. Inspire had been boarded up for months and endured repeated construction delays as part of the renovation. Tonight was the first time it opened to the public.

"Our last construction workers literally just walked out the door," he told me, putting his hand on his forehead in mock exhaustion. (No doubt, though, the project had taken its toll on him.) "This place isn't finished, but I had to open it in time for Tony's birthday."

Upstairs there was a more industrial space–cement walls, exposed electrical wiring–some of it intentional and some simply unfinished. Over in the box seats was a llama on a leash; guests took turns taking photos with it. (Tech Cocktail founders Frank Gruber and Jen Consalvo even had a llama at their Hawaiian island wedding, which Tony attended, a month earlier.)

Inspire Theater was originally a big part of Tony's vision. On his speaking circuit, Tony told audiences that Inspire Theatre would have 24/7 TED Talks streaming so that you could watch them "on your way to work, over lunch, or whenever." Former TEDMED curator Lisa Shufro attempted to get this vision off the ground, but it quickly proved too expensive. Downtown Project had not considered all of the operating costs. In theory, it was a great idea.

The evening involved a performance by the magic duo Penn & Teller, raunchy burlesque, and plenty of fernet. By the early hours of the morning, guests were dancing on tables and breakdancing on the floor. Everyone was there: Zappos and DTP leadership and employees, Tony's parents, former girlfriends, and a new blond girlfriend with a raspy voice who worked at the Cosmopolitan. But Alfred was not there; at least, I noticed that he had declined on the e-vite and I did not see him that night.

The next morning, I walked into Eat. While I was sitting in a corner booth wearing my sunglasses, Chef Natalie Young walked over. Her story is legendary now. In the very first year and three months of operating, she paid back her loan and earned recognition as running one of the best restaurants in Vegas. "People ask me if I drank the Kool-Aid," she said, resting her shoulder on the corner of the booth. An internal softness offsets her otherwise tough exterior, like the tattoos all around her arms. "And I say, 'Yes, I did, and it tastes *real* good,' she sighed. 'And I just keep thinking, 'We're all so lucky.'"

Later that week, I had an interview with Tony before flying home for the holidays. It was a seven thirty a.m. car ride to his doctor's appointment. Tony arrived at seven thirty on the dot–he is never late. (Former Zappos employee Robbe Richman once said that Tony's punctuality is one of his best traits: he doesn't view his time as more valuable than anyone else's.) When I arrived at the Ogden that morning, Tony's personal driver, Steve Moroney, nicknamed Steve-O, was nowhere to be found in the loading dock. Tony seemed genuinely perplexed, and we walked down the parking ramp and onto the street. He couldn't reach Steve-O and asked me if I knew of anyone with a car. I didn't have many friends, much less anyone I felt I could call at that hour. We started wandering toward the Beat and then down Fremont Street. The neighborhood felt like a ghost town. I had been worried about my questions for our interview–the first one in months–and now I felt the pressure to make a car appear by the time we finished our loop and got back to the parking garage. Ride-sharing services such as Uber and Lyft had not yet come to Vegas, and a taxi could take up to fifteen or twenty minutes to arrive at our location. Zach Ware was working to solve this very problem but Project 100 had not yet launched.

I realized that Tony didn't have any solutions, so I decided to try calling a couple that lived in the Ogden whose daughters I babysat occasionally. As we approached the parking garage, the husband ran out and handed me a set of keys. Steve-O was also parked at the loading dock. I thanked my friend, who was wearing his pajamas, and Steve-O apologized. "This has literally happened maybe once before," he told me later.

As we drove past Henderson, I shared that when I first moved to Vegas, I applied to be a seasonal Zappos call center representative. The process involved first taking a basic online test and submitting a brief Skype video. Passing that, I was invited to the company's Henderson office for a lightning Q&A round with other call center employees—the company's equivalent of speed dating and culture vetting. As part of the process, I was asked to fill out a worksheet asking me to rate on a scale of 1 to 10 how lucky I thought I was. Having read about this exact interview question in many news stories about Zappos, I knew enough not to select too high a number (which would indicate that I didn't think I needed to work too hard), so I circled 7.

"Unfortunately, I didn't make the cut," I explained to Tony. I had moved out to Vegas to write a book about his experiments with Zappos and DTP, and saw my work as immersion journalism. I was continually seeking out opportunities to do "gonzo journalism," so to speak, and thought that landing a seasonal job at the Zappos call center would be a shoo-in—not to mention a great way to learn about the culture. I was willing to stay over the holidays and work the graveyard shift, whatever it took.

"Did you look at the statistics?" he asked without looking up from his computer. He reminded me that it's "harder to get into Zappos than get into Harvard," something the company uses in its marketing.

"You know," I responded, "I don't think I'm zany enough." He acknowledged my response and went back to work. Later, I wondered if he ensured that Zappos *didn't* hire me.

At the airport that afternoon, I ran into his dad, Richard, who was en route back to San Jose. Tony spends Thanksgiving with his family but always does Christmas with friends.

After I returned to Minnesota to spend time with family over the holidays, it struck me that Zappos's experiment with Holacracy would make for an interesting news story. I had moved to Vegas to cover DTP without realizing that Zappos was on the precipice of so much internal evolution. I reached out to my friend Lauren Brown from *Business Insider*, the one who'd encouraged me to come out to Vegas in the first place, to get her thoughts. She suggested I write up something quick for the online news site *Quartz*, a digital news site that launched in 2012 under Atlantic Media, where she was now working. It ended up going viral, hitting more than one hundred thousand views after Christmas and sparking dozens of international news stories. Las Vegas Mayor Carolyn Goodman was right: Tony's effect is electrifying.

- YEAR 3 -

THE GREAT EXODUS

On January 1, 2014, VFA fellow Ovik Banerjee tweeted out to his 537 followers: "Vegas friends, anyone want to give a ride to a wayward Indian from the airport at 9 pm tonight?" The twenty-four-year-old's Twitter feed shows no response from friends. A few days later, his body was found outside his downtown apartment. It hadn't even been a year since the first Downtown Project suicide, of Jody Sherman.

Hours after Ovik's death, DTPers gathered for a meeting in Tony's apartment, where its leaders shared the news. DTP also asked Tech Cocktail not to write an article about Ovik's suicide, but it did anyway, insisting that Ovik was an important part of the community.

That week, thousands of tourists were descending upon Las Vegas for the annual Consumer Electronics Show (CES). It was a week where Downtown Project was supposed to shine, hosting events at the newly opened Inspire Theatre and Container Park for the tech community around the world. The DTP show went on, but the week was traumatic, especially for the other young VFA grads.

Tech reporter Alissa Walker ventured downtown and sensed

that something was off. "I could very tangibly feel that something was wrong," she reported for *Gizmodo*. The young reporter also described the feeling of meeting Tony as "meeting Oz in his Emerald City." Tony would often ask visitors from the media to meet him and his deputies serendipitously, not committing to a time or location.

Her description was particularly poignant that week. After Ovik's suicide, Tony stayed behind the scenes. When the community was looking to its leader for guidance, he stepped back behind the curtain, like Oz. Downtown Project brought in someone to handle grief counseling, but Tony never publicly addressed it. Rather, he stood by his decision to remove "community" from Downtown Project's mission. He later explained that "community" implied that his for-profit entity would be taking on responsibilities that it never intended to handle. Downtown Project employees were instructed to stop using the acronym ROC as well.

Ovik had been trying to get Tony's attention for a while. In her story, "The Downtown Project Suicides: Can the Pursuit of Happiness Kill You?" journalist Nellie Bowles reported that a source said Ovik had felt uncomfortable trying to skirt city zoning codes while operating elements of the Learning Village. There were others like Ovik who were trying to reach Tony, but in an echo chamber of "yes," he didn't seem to believe that anything was truly wrong. Tony shared with *ReCode* his email to Ovik from August 2013, which he later forwarded to me. The points (problems and suggested solutions) that Ovik highlighted in his email are in bold:

hi ovik -

thanks for the detailed feedback. I've cc'd XXXXX and XXXXX so they can follow up on the parts related to XXXXX and XXXXX.

a few points:

- dtp culture/values is not meant to be the same as zappos culture/values. at zappos, it took us 5 years to really figure out and solidify our culture and values, and we had a lot of people issues and turnover during the early years at zappos. hopefully it will take us less than 5 years at dtp, but it's still a process and while it may be painful and unsettling in the short term, fred and i are confident about the long-term outcome because we've done this before and know what to expect. we do hope to move faster at dtp than we did at zappos, but it's still a process and will take time.

- i do think that once we get holacracy up and running (which itself will take about 6–12 months, even at zappos) then many of the issues such as communication, accountability, inability for tensions to be processed, etc. will be addressed. It's hard to appreciate the underlying work that goes into it at this time, just like when constructing a building most of the time is spent on invisible infrastructure stuff and you don't see all the finishes and pretty stuff until the last few weeks of a 2-year construction project.

Problem 1) Lack of Culture, Mission, and Core Values.

Solution 1) Make this a priority. You've talked so many times about the importance of getting the culture right and everything else falling into place. Let's get the culture right at DTP.

this is a priority, but it's also a process and when dealing with a city it's a lot trickier than with a company. at zappos, we can choose who we hire and fire. you can't choose who lives or works downtown, and each business dtp invests in will have a different culture and set of values which dtp needs to somehow integrate with. at zappos we can say we won't work with anyone (including vendors) who doesn't match or respect our values. we can't be as black and white with dtp.

Problem 2) Lack of communication/connectivity

Solution 2) Monthly internal lowdown that occurs regardless of who can attend. Potentially two a month, one as an informational update/market feedback session. The other as a place to talk about problems/criticisms. If information isn't communicated properly, rumors fill in the gaps. It is a natural progression.

like any other idea, you are more than welcome to start implementing this if this is something you are passionate about. feel free to connect with XXXXX for support and ideas on this.

Problem 3) Lack of accountability at both employee and manager levels

Solution 3) Establish those feedback protocols. Even if people are doing things that have never been done before, goals can be set and progress can be measured. It will be different for every employee/manager, but make that a part of the work relationship.

this is something that we believe will be addressed with holacracy over time, but it's a process and definitely a work in progress. in the meantime, i would encourage each employee to just meet regularly with his/her manager to accomplish the above.

Ovik had presciently pinpointed all of the problems with Downtown Project and why so many felt disappointed. It took longer for these elements to percolate through the entire organization before they raised alarm to those outside of it–to people like me, who were living within the ecosystem and could gauge how things were going by the energy but didn't know the specifics of what was really going on.

He pointed out how Downtown Project didn't have a cohesive vision. Ultimately, that was what fissured the entire project. Tony has said publicly many times that if he were to build Zappos all over again, he would create core values from day one. That sort of conviction is what attracted young and impressionable entrepreneurs like the cofounders of Buffer, a social media management tool.

Yet that sort of conviction did not seem to exist within Tony anymore and with his Downtown Project. As part of an exercise to identify personal core values, employees were given a worksheet where they were asked to circle their ten top values. In a meeting before the sheet was handed out to the group, Tony questioned whether "Integrity" belonged on the list–he didn't see it as a value. A DTPer recalls how when the meeting ended Maggie Hsu walked out and said she couldn't believe what had just happened. (When I asked Maggie about it later, she said that Tony gave her an intellectual explanation for why he saw the word "integrity" differently. He views it as a "meta value," she said, which encompasses multiple values. So essentially, he didn't believe "integrity" belonged on the list due to a technicality.)

After Maggie was troubled by Tony's description of integrity, he emailed her this explanation: "When I lead the core values discovery exercises, one of the things I say as they think of their values is that integrity is not a value, and that there is no judgment in values, the power comes from the alignment of whatever values you choose to align behind, not from the values themselves. . . . People usually associate integrity with morals, but I think of it as consistency between what you say and what you do."

Yet Tony didn't seem to be standing by his stated values, namely community. His originally-stated values are the reason that people like Ovik were so excited initially to enter Tony's sphere.

The young VFA fellows had a clearer sense of vision than most anyone else in the ecosystem. Rob Solomon, who started out by working with Don Welch on the small business team and then went on to hold a key financial position within DTP, articulated his purpose with clarity. He was interested in the global economic ramifications of the project. He was passionate about how private money could activate a city in the way that government and tax-payer dollars cannot. "If this could help one other city change something, it would be worth it," he told me. I've never heard his superiors speak with that kind of conviction or vision.

Downtown Project would not have been what it was without the idealism and youthful energy of its VFA fellows, who, during the first year, made up nearly half the seventeen-person core team. Another Vegas fellow, Jude Stanion, organized a confer-ence around Holacracy in downtown Vegas just to understand its nuances better. With cold emails and simply taking the steps necessary to pull together the event, Jude attracted international companies, Harvard Business School professor Ethan Bernstein, and others in order to "Hack Holacracy." He was among those who were forced to operate within its system, and he already felt its limitations. Instead of responding as his superiors did–trying to bypass its limitations, and operate within a shadow power structure, ignoring its rules–Jude genuinely wanted to understand the system itself, despite his skepticism. If everyone within DTP had been so open-minded and thoughtful as Ovik, Jude, Rob, and the other VFA fellows, its outcome surely would have been different. In ways DTP over-relied on its VFA fellows, which frustrated entrepreneurs who wanted to work with more experienced practitioners. More guidance was needed all around.

VFA founder Andrew Yang came out to Vegas for Ovik's memorial. He and I spoke on the phone a few weeks after that, because I was writing a story about his new book, *Smart People Should Build Things: How to Restore Our Culture of Achievement, Build a Path for Entrepreneurs, and Create New Jobs in America.* We had a candid conversation about the dark side of entrepreneurship. Yang didn't place any blame on anyone–but he stopped sending VFA fellows out to Vegas after that.

In addition to grief counselors, Tony pointed to Australian entrepreneur Mark Rowland, whom he had recruited and invested $2.6 million in to create ROCeteer (a wordplay on ROC, and pronounced "rocketeer"), which was a support team for entrepreneurs, with a focus on positive psychology. Dr. Zubin Damania also played a key role in supporting the community after Ovik's death. Turntable Health, his Downtown Project–funded health clinic with a focus on integrative and preventative medicine, had just opened in December, which created a safe space for the VFA fellows.

Business, too, marched on. The number of tech investments continued to climb at a rapid clip. DTP tour guides tallied 7,000 tours in 2013 and were moving full speed ahead. Tony and his

Downtown Project had been profiled 240 times in the past six months.

Surprisingly, Downtown Project announced that Rehan Choudhry would no longer be CEO of Life Is Beautiful; real estate director Andrew Donner would be taking over. Life Is Beautiful had drawn a huge crowd, but it was operating in the red–which was the expectation, as festivals take years to become profitable. Although Andrew didn't have any experience planning large-scale events, Tony thought he might be able to cut costs. One day Rehan was a celebrity, the next, he was ousted.

Millie Chou, Zappos's longtime general counsel, moved over to DTP. "They need me," she told me in passing days before she took her new job, sharing that she was leaving Zappos on a Friday and starting at DTP on Monday. There was a revolving door between Zappos and DTP for Tony's most valued employees.

In a Q&A after a Tech Cocktail talk, Banjo's founder, Damien Patton, spoke candidly about the state of the market. "The talent pool is very shallow here. God dang, it's hard. It's not just about bodies, it's about the right team." He also warned founders not to get distracted by the partying lifestyle. "Focus, focus, focus! Do what you came here to do. Shit–if you don't, you're going to lose." Damien shared how he went from being homeless, to bootstrapping a start-up, to raising millions of dollars. (A year later, by 2015, Banjo had raised more than $100 million.)

DTP publicly reinforced the fact that it no longer stood for community. "We're not a charity," Tony emphasized. "We are not here to fix the homelessness problem." That led to a whirlwind of local press, including a *Las Vegas Sun* article titled, "Zappos CEO on Downtown Project: People Expected Us to Do What Local Government Should Have Been Doing." DTP's new messaging highlighted a focus on "3 Cs: connectedness, colearning, and collisions." The original mission had been completely hollowed out not even two years into the project.

Let's be honest: there is nothing exciting about connectedness, colearning, and collisions. You can't really oppose those words, but you certainly don't feel inspired to rally around them in the way you'd rally around the idea of creating "the most community-focused city in the world" or even "the fire capital of the world"–at least that's interesting, and there is a clearer way to measure progress.

During that time I met with former Zappos call center worker Owen Carver who had started with the company in San Francisco and moved with his team to Las Vegas. He shared that he was always confused by Tony's leadership. His boss avoided confrontation to the degree where Owen finally decided to voice his concerns by submitting a message about company leadership through Zappos.com's customer feedback icon on the website. The commentary quickly made its way to management, but he wasn't given any good answers. Perplexed, Owen, today a young entrepreneur and philanthropist who would go on to run for local office in Las Vegas, finally concluded that his boss didn't want to take a stand: "When you stand for nothing, it's easy not to have anything to criticize." Eventually Tony placed a copy of the book *The Right To Protest* on Owen's desk. But it wasn't satisfying because he didn't know what to do with it, and Tony never brought it up.

The lack of leadership at DTP was begetting a culture of apathy.

Michael Cornthwaite, who had opened a restaurant, bar, and coffee shop in Container Park, pulled out of the park that spring. He said it wasn't because of sales. "Downtown Project has taken on a life of its own," he told me over a shot of fernet on the rooftop of Inspire Theatre. "I don't know that they have a culture.

Zappos's success was always about culture, so why didn't those same rules apply at Downtown Project? Culture should have been number one."

Of all of his Tony-funded properties, Michael was most proud of Tokyo 365, a hidden members-only underground bar inside the Inspire Theatre, and the Scullery, a wine bar that would soon open inside the Ogden. On the other side of the building, Wild, a gluten-free pizza restaurant, was closing. Tony bought out Miki Agrawal for an undisclosed sum, and one day copies of her book *Do Cool Sh*t: Quit Your Day Job, Start Your Own Business, and Live Happily Ever After*–for which he had written the forward and described Wild as a key part of his Downtown Project–disappeared from the windowsills.

It's no secret: LinkedIn has always classified DTP as a real estate company. But now a lot of people found themselves scratching their heads: How could they have missed something so obvious?

Dreams were secondary to the primary goal: profit. ROC was secondary to ROI–despite the fact that so many had been told not to worry. The actions spoke for themselves. A lot of it was due to more scrutiny from Michael Downs, a former director of operations at the Bellagio who was tasked with creating order in the house at DTP, along with Tony's longtime lawyer, Millie Chou. There were subtle signs that, in hindsight, some can point back to that spring: expense reports scrutinized more closely, delays on project launches. But the culture of shooting bullets was so engrained that the correction blindsided them.

To be sure, Tony expects a return on his investment. The fissure and pain point for so many was the reality that started to crystalize, which was much different from what he sold on his speaking circuit and the significant focus on ROC in the messaging. In fact, there was no mention of ROI. The uniqueness of Tony's sales pitch led many to uproot their lives with the expectation of a runway and support, even if he promised it vaguely on a handshake deal. It was a once-in-a-lifetime opportunity, like winning the lottery. Then, with hardly any warning, many were left in the dark and tossed aside like broken dolls.

The vagueness around the terms of the deals is the biggest contention point. It seemed that the lack of clarity was used as a recruitment tool–loose promises that don't need to be assured until success is likely or proven out. Ironically, Holacracy is all about clarity, and that wasn't working for DTP either.

DREAMS CAST UP IN FLAMES

The pilgrimage to the Life Cube Burn in March 2014 was just like the walk to see the Man burn on the playa, but on a smaller scale. Thousands of Las Vegans showed up: all the Burners were there; Flash and his posse even came back to see it. During the pilgrimage on the Burning Man playa, someone yelled out, "We're going to church!" and it felt the same today. In the middle of the Llama Lot on Fremont between Ninth and Tenth Streets was Scotte Cohen's brainchild: a massive 24-by-24-foot wooden structure with painted artwork on the sides. Over the past two months, hundreds of members of the community had been doing the painting. Many loved the nightly parties, with dancers and bohemians and artists.

On the side of the Life Cube structure were index cards for people to write their dreams. One evening, I made the pilgrimage to the Life Cube with former Cirque du Soleil performer-turned-motivational speaker Vital Germaine who'd just published a book,

Flying Without a Net: The True Story of a Boy Who Defies All Odds and Runs Away with Cirque du Soleil. I wrote down and dropped my wish into the Life Cube.

Scotte devoted his life to art after having made a sizable fortune in tech during the dot-com boom. He first created his idea in the desert playa. "I believe in the power of intention, of writing things down," he told me. "I started doing that ten years ago, and it's amazing what has happened." Like many seasoned Silicon Valley entrepreneurs, he has a level of consistent enthusiasm that is hard to match. That intense belief is what carried him through. The number of obstacles to bring the Life Cube Project into existence were enormous: beyond funding and navigating the politics of Downtown Project, there was negotiating with the city about how to safely light a massive structure with thousands of people surrounding it–accounting for all the minute factors such as the direction of the wind and how to manage debris.

In the weeks leading up to the event, neighbors complained that there was a growing open-air festival every night, which is part of what led to the threat of shutting down the entire operation in the final days before the Burn. "There's a reason that Burning Man is limited to a week," my friend observed. "You can't have such chaos for more than that. The Life Cube shouldn't have been a two-month thing." Anarchy is exciting at first, then quickly overwhelming.

At the Burn, I ran into members of my Burning Man camp: Vegas burlesque and street dancers, club promoters, and DJs who operated in the heart of the city's entertainment scene. I also saw Henry Kang near the stage; he was looking for Fred Mossler. For all of his criticism of Downtown Project, he still wanted a place inside the tribe. I also believe he genuinely liked Fred and Tony, and could uniquely support their vision.

As dusk fell, in a grand gesture led by Mayor Carolyn Goodman, Tony was given the match to light the cord and set the entire cube on fire. Revelers watched in awe as the cube went up in flames; the warmth of the heat and the process of watching the structure collapse to the ground were mesmerizing. The last piece of the entire structure that was left standing was the most iconic part of the whole installation: a painting of a woman who was holding her dreams in her hands.

It was a cathartic moment for a community increasingly on edge. In the weeks leading up to the Burn, I met with Scotte and a former conductor of the acclaimed Cleveland Orchestra at the high tables at the Gold Spike. We were exploring ways to collaborate for the Life Cube, and the conductor shared that he had pitched Downtown Project on a spiritual center. "There's no place for people to go. No church, no Alcoholics Anonymous or Al-Anon. And it doesn't have to be religious. People just need a place to *go* and to be able to express themselves."

The Brooklyn writer Jay Dixit, who is non-religious and progressive in his views, lamented the same thing. "These people need a church," he shared with me after pitching Tony in the Gold Spike. Another early Tony disciple who moved back to New York feeling uninspired told me pointedly, "There needs to be a higher order."

The idea of creating "the most community-focused large city in the world" implies collaboration and relationships–but without the word *community*, the intentions behind Downtown Project are ambiguous. There was no unity around the mission. The culture at Downtown Project quickly became fraught with infighting, negative energy, and politics–ironic for a CEO whose platform is company culture. Soon Zappos's culture would struggle, too, under the weight of Holacracy. The dogma and new order would eventually bring disruption to both companies.

The founder of Holacracy says that it "takes about five years" for a company to adopt its system, but this is based on little data. HolacracyOne had barely been around for five years, so it was hard to know how it would stand the test of time. Meanwhile, Zappos and Downtown Project have reportedly paid upwards of a million dollars for Brian's services, and that's not including capital from other start-ups in Tony's ecosystem.

"Have you ever looked into the HolacracyOne IP?" a former Zappos manager asked me at the Gold Spike after the Life Cube Burn. In 2007 Brian filed a patent application with the US Patent and Trademark Office around the double-linked circle design, parts of which he drew from Sociocracy. He titled his patent, "Method for Structuring and Controlling an Organization." The Supreme Court ruled that it's not possible to patent human systems design, which appears to have made his patent obsolete. But Brian still could continue to promote Holacracy as a closed-source system, meaning that companies had to purchase his consulting services in order to adopt the system.

As we were talking, Tony passed through our circle with a tray of fernet shots that he was distributing to the forty-some people who were standing on his side of the bar. Jenn Lim, who would normally be at an event like this, was visibly absent; I think she was celebrating the International Day of Happiness at the United Nations.

"Why aren't they open-source?" the former Zappos manager pressed. Open-source systems, like Matt Mullenweg's WordPress software and the Hyperloop speed train proposed by Tesla's Elon Musk, are created with the intention of being iterated upon in order to create the best possible solutions, sourcing ideas from talent around the world. Critics suggest that the closed-system design of Holacracy indicated that Brian was not interested in suggestions or feedback to the model, even though it had not yet proven out its utility.

With pressure from the Sociocracy and greater organizational development community, Brian made Holacracy open-source a year later, in spring 2015, just before he published his book. In the way that Neil Strauss's *The Game* is designed like a Bible, the *Holacracy* guidebook (subtitled *The New Management System for a Rapidly Changing World*) looks like a tome underneath its book jacket, with its silver lettering juxtaposed on glowing yellow hardcover.

The day after the Life Cube Burn, Keith Ferrazzi, the author of *Never Eat Alone: And Other Secrets to Success, One Relationship at a Time*, gave a talk in the Learning Village focused on the benefits of tribalism. I recognized him from Tony's Burning Man camp; he was the one who renewed his vows in front of the Temple on the playa.

"If we're not part of a tribe, then we die," said Keith, dressed casually and comfortable under the bright stage lights. "The heart and soul of Tony's being is tribal. When a place like Downtown Project offers a well like that, we long for it."

He explained that generosity is the key to social connection. So is acting as if you belong: "Meet someone at their social style, mirror them. Make them feel you're a part of their tribe." Anthropologically, this makes sense. I remembered how during my second visit to Vegas, Tony asked me why I chose to wear a suit jacket. "You don't look like you live here," he told me outside of DCR, implying that I needed to change my style in order to fit in with the downtown community.

Simon Sinek, another thinker in the realm of self-help/ organizational design, who makes his living via TED Talks, other speaking fees, book sales, and CEO endorsements, struck at similar themes when he gave a talk in the Learning Village a few months earlier. "Hiring someone is akin to adopting a child," he told the packed double-wide trailer. "Leaders that make people feel safe instill trust within an organization. If someone is afraid of losing their job, they just feel fear. There's a reason people aren't afraid at Southwest Airlines." For all the incoming messaging and guest speakers, both Zappos and Downtown Project were both moving in the direction of fear.

After the Life Cube Burn, Scotte, then running on adrenaline and very little sleep, stayed behind shoveling the ashes into the predawn hours. The parking lot was completely deserted, when a man emerged wearing a casino worker's uniform.

"You know, you're real!" he yelled over to Scotte, walking toward him. "I was there tonight. You didn't charge anything for tickets. There were no wristbands. You didn't sell anything. And now you're the one cleaning up. That never happens here." Then the man slowly walked back into the early-morning light.

Scotte told me later, reflecting on that moment, "Vegas is a town of lost souls and broken toys."

I got the chills when he said that. I knew he was right. Everyone is desperately searching for something here.

LIVING WITH THE ZAPPONIANS

By spring 2014, I had moved into the Gold Spike, the de facto corporate housing for Zapponians who rented rooms in the hotel, located one block from the Zappos HQ, essentially in its backyard. Although the Gold Spike resembles a dormitory and is not a very comfortable living environment, I was determined to stick with my investigation. I wanted to see how everything would play out. Financially, I was funding the project myself, so I made it work by traveling home to stay with family in Minneapolis for a few weeks or months at a time to save money, and then returning to Vegas for longer stretches. I more or less repeated this cycle for three years, sometimes living in New York where I still maintained and sublet my Brooklyn apartment. By spring 2014 I realized that Tony would not be funding this project so I searched for other solutions–once even pitching early Zappos investor Erik Moore a vision of creating a board of advisors and stakeholders, but I never heard back from him. Jenn Lim described the *Delivering Happiness* book process as a start-up; I, too, saw my book as a start-up. I think that's what Tony had in mind when he asked me to write the real story. He was inviting me to walk the entrepreneurial path along with everyone else.

I chose to live at the Gold Spike for its affordable rent (around $500 a month). The building included a communal kitchen and laundry room, and was made up mostly of call center workers but also contractors and those in other departments. One evening in the laundry room, a female employee on the tech side confessed, "Morale is lower now than it was in Henderson. True, bad at Zappos is better than most companies, but it's not as high. We feel that Tony is forcing downtown upon us, and, quite frankly, not all of us want to hang out downtown. There's also Holacracy, which is being forced upon us, and Supercloud, which is moving from Zappos's coding to Amazon systems. We feel we're becoming Amazon. With all those things, it's wearing."

The company was going through something of a tech exodus, which started with CTO Arun Rajan's departure. Some employees went to Project 100 and other tech start-ups downtown; others went to San Francisco. "If you can get paid so much more, why not?" she said.

A computer programmer expressed a similar sentiment as we watched a speed dating session hosted by Maggie Hsu in the

Gold Spike one Saturday afternoon. As she rung the cowbell for everyone to switch seats, the employee shared with me that many in the tech department believe they're not getting paid well because the salaries are a social experiment on Tony's part to see how low he can pay them and still have them be happy. Culture has long been pitched as the differentiating factor at Zappos and a justification for its lower salaries, but now more companies compete on culture and perks. The programmer ended up leaving soon thereafter to take a job with Google.

Yet for many, Zappos is still a dream job. One employee shared with me that he's the first in his family to not go to jail and really make it.

My neighbor at the Gold Spike invited me to visit the Zappos campus one evening, where we found some free snacks and took the elevator up to the top floor to check out the view. Back in his three-hundred-square-foot apartment (sans kitchen), he remarked on the convenience of the situation. "I'm living the Zappos dream, huh?"

HOLACRACY, FERNET, AND ROCK 'N' ROLL

A surprisingly empty *Delivering Happiness* bus sat outside the Ogden in the hour leading up to the Zappos Q2 All-Hands in March 2014. The bus, with its signature winky face, is easy to spot. Steve-O, Tony's driver since 2010, welcomed me aboard and offered me a drink.

"Vodka tonic, Grey Goose, Red Bull, PBR?" he said in quick succession. He was wearing his usual uniform of jeans, a T-shirt, and a fedora, and looks like Aerosmith's Steven Tyler. Before he started working for Tony, he drove tour buses for celebrities such as Etta James, Snoop Dogg, and once, even Britney Spears. He's as hospitable as anyone in Tony's world and serves as his de facto bodyguard.

The *Delivering Happiness* bus has seen many seasons of revelers. Inside it's just like other tour buses, with inward-facing leather-cushioned seats lining the windows. Next to the kitchen and facing toward the front of the bus is a single elevated seat with a table, which is where Tony usually sits with his laptop as everyone else converses in the area in front of him.

Past the kitchen, which is always stocked with plenty of fernet, are stacked sleeping shelves, and in the very back, a U-shaped leather couch that can fit several people. The bus is how Tony transports his posse everywhere, whether on road trips with close friends along Route 66 or to give a tour through an airplane graveyard in the Mojave desert. He likes to say that he values experiences more than things, and the bus is living proof of the fact.

If it's a smaller group, Steve-O will drive a nondescript black car. He says that in all of these years, he's never seen Tony get angry. He also sees the aftermath from the wildest nights. During a car ride shortly after Tony's fortieth birthday, he shared this with me: "Even after he drinks–last night he was hammered–he's on. And he doesn't forget anything."

One of the Zappos tour guides with bright rainbow hair joined us on the bus. Heidy Stamper is one of Tony's raver friends and has known him for the better part of a decade. Tony pitched her and her husband on moving to downtown Vegas back in 2011, and they got a place on the twentieth floor of the Ogden. They're immersed in rave culture and live out its PLUR ethos as much as hard-core

Burners live out their Ten Principles and Zapponians live out the Ten Core Values. When Downtown Project failed to find its moral compass, she was among those most affected by its teetering.

"I want to see the *heart* come back into Downtown Project," she told me from her Airstream trailer one afternoon. "That's what was stripped away." The ostensible mission of Downtown Project is what convinced her to support it, and she became one of its most important PR vehicles as a member of its hospitality team. She would later help bring PeaceLove Studios to downtown Vegas, a community focused on mental health awareness through creative expression.

"Well, I guess it's just us," Steve-O said, pouring another drink and offering it to us. He turned left onto Sixth Street and merged onto the highway ramp leading to the Las Vegas Strip. This particular All-Hands was at the Hard Rock Hotel & Casino. Steve-O parked the bus in the back of the hotel, and we entered through a side door. Inside we were greeted by a sea of Zapponians with their blue lanyards and a select few Downtown Project employees. We both recognized Tony's date for the event: the wispy blonde who worked at the Cosmopolitan.

This All-Hands followed the same formula as the rest: an opening video (in the spirit of the theme, Tony and Fred Mossler posed as washed-out musicians backstage), a series of heart-warming customer service stories, outside guests who spoke to the company's current strategy (HolacracyOne's Brian Robertson), and others who inspired awe (performances by a magician and the Nevada ballet). Additionally, Zappos brought in a surprise guest on this March afternoon: Nick Swinmurn, its founder. It had been years since he appeared onstage.

In an awkward Q&A, a Zappos employee wearing pajamas asked a series of company origin questions of Tony, Nick, and

Fred, who were sitting next to one another onstage. The inter-viewer asked Fred how he would describe his current duties under his title "no title," to which he responded, "It's a wonderful life." Under the pressure of the situation, Nick said that he was an "ideas guy," downplaying his critical influence on Zappos's success over his seven years with the company.

The event also included a Q&A with the top four Zappos executives–a homogenous group and a visual reminder that Zappos was not as progressive as it sought to be. One Zapponian who works in the call center raised her hand and spoke into the microphone effusively, "Tony, how do you stay so humble? You don't seem like most CEOs." He responded by saying that he uses humility as a strategy: "There's research that Jim Collins points out in *Good to Great* that says companies with humble leaders tend to survive the longest."

Another Zapponian expressed safety concerns, citing that the traffic intersection near the new campus has some of the highest accident rates. "Can we reopen the skybridge?" she asked, refer-ring to the aboveground walkway that Tony had closed in order to facilitate more serendipity through the front entrance. "That's the first I've heard of it; I'll look into it," Tony responded. Zappos would later cite the reopening of the skybridge as an example of employees successfully vetoing the CEO's opinion through Holacracy.

Tony closed the All-Hands with an impassioned plea for ev-eryone to fully embrace Holacracy, generously using the word *super*. "I'm super excited for what's ahead for us," he concluded.

Nate Boyd from Nomic leaned over to me. "What Tony's saying isn't reflecting what's really going on upstairs," he said.

With a boom of closing music, everyone flooded through the ca-sino and into Vanity nightclub. Guests got wristbands for two free drinks. I ran into my neighbors from the Gold Spike who worked for Zappos U (short for Zappos University, which indoctrinates employees into the company culture and practices) and others who were contracting with the tech team. Zappos was in the midst of a shift moving its technical infrastructure to Amazon's, which it called Supercloud. As the company's tech team worked on the Supercloud migration, contracted workers kept the site running.

Zappos happy hours are important cultural events. For the most part, employees aren't afraid to party hard in front of their superiors. "If every CEO operated like Tony, the world would be a different place," Steve-O told me. "Growing up, my mom sat me and my buddies down when I was in ninth grade and said we could smoke pot, as long as we kept it inside the house. That changed everything. It's the same thing at Zappos. If people realize, 'Wow, I can do three shots at work?' Then they don't want to go crazy."

RED PILL, BLUE PILL

"You take the red pill–you stay in Wonderland, and I show you how deep the rabbit hole goes. Remember, all I'm offering is the truth–nothing more."

Henry paused the movie clip on the screen and turned to the rest of us. "That's Morpheus from *The Matrix*," he explained. "He's asking Neo whether he wants to see outside the Matrix, or stay asleep." He then handed everyone two jelly beans, one red and one blue. "Think very carefully about which one you want to choose. I won't judge you either way." Despite what Henry said, I had a feeling he might if I chose the blue jelly bean.

A small group of people attended Henry's talk on "Zen and the Art of Unreasonable Happiness" at the Window, the new learning and coworking space at the Ogden and across the street from the Gold Spike. The space, filled with bookshelves and decorated with artwork evoking Greek goddesses, was intended to be an alternative to the blank gray trailers in the Learning Village.

Maggie Hsu was in attendance on behalf of Downtown Project. Henry explained to everyone that the movie has become an analogy for the Zen life, choosing to not be constrained by society's rules and expectations.

In Vegas and especially among Burners, evoking *The Matrix* is a common theme. The former Zappos manager that I met after the Life Cube Burn was running his own red pill/blue pill test, asking for willing participants to engage in the experiment with him. It's something on which he did a beta test at Burning Man. A Downtown Project employee joked, "If I got a hundred dollars for every time I hear someone talk about the red pill and the blue pill, I'd be a millionaire."

Henry's mission is to share Zen philosophy with others and especially with Tony. (Later, he took a position at the late Zen philosopher Alan Watts's mountain center in California.) When I first moved to Vegas, Henry insisted that I watch *The Matrix* in order to understand the way of things. The movie evokes the white rabbit from *Alice in Wonderland* and related themes around chaos theory and complex systems design. It ties into the ideas of obliquity–that the best way to achieve a goal in a complex system is by taking an indirect route–and serendipity. The concepts tie into what Tony is aiming for with self-organization; he continues to tell his employees to "trust in Holacracy."

Of course, not everyone does. With the increased turmoil at Downtown Project and within Zappos, more followers have questioned Tony than ever before.

DTP's fast and surprising state of disarray attracted many people who wanted to offer Tony a solution. Henry is one of the folks who are trying to reach Tony with what they believe are the answers to getting Downtown Project back on course–such as doing away with nepotism and refocusing on a higher mission. The Project has become weighed down with a focus on process and politics. For the most part, there are two camps: those who still *believe* and those who never did. In February 2014 *Las Vegas Weekly* asked its readers, "Is Tony Hsieh Downtown's Savior or Conqueror?"

One afternoon, just as I was about to step into yoga at Turntable Health, Downtown Project's director of imagination pulled me aside: "It's easy to criticize from your couch," Professor Gould said, alluding to the media and the increasing number of dissenters in the community. "You've got to follow your North Star." A few months later, he would join the dissenters with a very public statement. But this afternoon, he was still a believer.

Over by the yoga studio sat one of the cofounders of Ticket Cake, which was in the process of shutting down. "We started out in our garage and got nearly a million dollars in sales first before we ever approached Downtown Project," she explained, referring to its origin in Salt Lake City. "I have no idea why people wait until they get funding before they start doing stuff." Before moving to Vegas, the team paid itself $400 a month out of their revenue for six months before officially getting funding. Their company blew through the $200,000 for a few reasons, including the fact that downtown Vegas–which was supposed to be a core market–was not producing enough events for the company to provide services. They attempted to seek out potential buyers to explore an acquihire, to no avail. Inspired by the wave of "fail parties" in tech ecosystems around the country, which are designed to celebrate a start-up's life even though it failed, they decided to host one in their Ogden apartment to celebrate their successes and close that chapter. The concept of fail parties was inspired by well-known Boulder, Colorado–based investor Brad Feld, who has sparked the national discussion around entrepreneurship and mental health.

Inside the yoga studio, we joined the VFA fellow who worked alongside Andy White of the Vegas Tech Fund, Laura Berk. She has seen many of the start-up failures and was transitioning into a new role with ROCeteer, the consultancy designed to coach and mentor start-up founders. She had been close with Ovik, and the organization's purpose hit close to home for her.

Zubin and his clinic increasingly played an integral role as the community grieved over the loss of friends, their start-ups (and by extension, identities), and coming to terms with the fact that their idealistic beliefs about this place didn't square with reality. Turntable Health ran on a preventative care model, partnering with a progressive health entity called Iora Health, and focused on integrative health: primary care; counseling services; yoga, cardio, and other classes; and cooking lessons. Juxtaposed against the heavy investment in bars and restaurants, Turntable Health is one of the healthiest additions to the community.

Seeking a respite from the 24/7 party culture of Vegas, I got a membership at Turntable Health and started going there regularly. Almost a year into my commitment to gonzo journalism, living in an unstable community had started to take a toll on me, too. It was hard to know who to trust and particularly difficult to make friends with anyone in the ecosystem as a journalist–in all fairness, they didn't know if they could trust me, either. Because of the high levels of uncertainty and ambiguity all around, everyone was constantly on edge. I didn't realize how much the suicides and the lack of empathic responses had affected me until one afternoon when I was meeting with my health coach, sitting on a plastic chair in a room with a blank TV screen.

"This place, it's just not . . ." I said as tears rolled down my cheeks.

My health coach walked over. "Not . . . delivering happiness?" Her maternal instincts kicked in, and she gave me a hug.

I shook my head. "Not at all." I was affected by the culture as much as anyone else. Although I felt like I was on the outside, DTP, in a way, had also become one of my tribes.

Positive psychology will tell you that contentedness comes from within, but environmental factors also play a factor. Many in the community sought out the counseling services and classes to lead healthier lives but were torn between that and the culture of partying.

Zubin's clinic is the antithesis of bars such as the Gold Spike, which is dark and hardly has any sunlight. The space features floor-to-ceiling windows and a modern design. A receptionist sits on a high table with a laptop next to a stainless-steel kitchen with tea and other offerings for guests. The clinic also doesn't take insurance; instead it's a monthly subscription.

But even for its accessibility not everyone in the community takes advantage of it. Many simply couldn't justify spending $80 every month on top of health insurance. Zappos employees saw the membership as more of a luxury than a necessity. There was a time when I went off health insurance for a few months so that I could focus solely on researching for my book, and during that time, Turntable Health was the entirety of my health care budget. That wasn't the wisest decision I ever made, but it was a calculated risk.

One afternoon, I was the only one in a dance kickboxing class led by one of the physicians who also happens to be a former Coyote Ugly Saloon dancer (like in the movie). When Zubin hired her, he asked jokingly if she could be a backup dancer for his rap videos as ZDoggMD. It must have been a funny sight for anyone who glanced in the room to see a physician eight months pregnant giving a private dance class set to rap music. That moment encapsulated the sort of space that Zubin is seeking to create, one where people don't take themselves too seriously.

KARMA CHIEFS

"High five!" Coach raised her hand to mine as I walked into the Gold Spike after dance kickboxing at Turntable. She was hosting after-hours trivia for Zappos employees. I asked her what kind of blue drink she was drinking, and she told me it was a Hpnotiq, so I went to the bar and ordered the same. Coach, a petite black woman in her sixties, wore her usual uniform of a jersey and backward baseball hat. She started working at Zappos in the call center and eventually became the company's life coach. It was her idea to order a second throne with a crown and scepter for the Zappos campus. "Everyone deserves to be royalty," she says.

After the night at Drink N' Drag with Coach to celebrate her birthday, she shared with me the poignant moment that inspired her loyalty to Tony and Zappos. Following a training session at Tony's Southern Highland's mansion, someone asked where she completed her higher education, and she said she didn't. "I felt awful and judged in that moment," she said. "Then I saw Tony in the driveway, and he noticed I was upset. He said, 'Why not just say that you have a degree in life?' That changed everything for me." Like Chef Natalie, who says that she went to the School of Hard Knocks to anyone who asks, Coach now wears her background on her sleeve with pride. Her role at Zappos is to help employees reach their goals both inside and outside of work—whether it be losing weight or getting a promotion. (Although Holacracy doesn't have promotions, so that would now mean taking on a new role or domain.)

"What exchange is Amazon traded on?" Coach asked the group of trivia players, in her upbeat voice (NASDAQ). For some Zappos employees, Amazon is a looming entity, whose presence they sometimes need to be reminded exists. The cultures couldn't be more different: Amazon is known for bureaucracy and command and control, exactly the sort of thing that Zappos is trying to get away from. It's a mystery to many as to why Jeff Bezos is content with Tony's experiments and the zany office culture. Tony says that as long as they continue to hit their financial plan, they can continue to operate as they want.

Sitting up at the Gold Spike bar were two Zappos employees. One, in the pilot group for Holacracy, shared that he believed the system was adopted out of fear that bureaucracy could stunt growth for the company over time. "It will involve at lot of growing pains," he said presciently, taking a sip of his Moscow Mule. The company was currently going through "the great land grab," where managers were trying to take as many domains as possible.

One of Tony's right-hand staffers confided to me, "Holacracy is tough for people who have been in a bureaucracy for a long time. It's easier for people who are younger because they don't know anything else." Everyone has two titles, one that's outward facing (and for the purposes of Amazon, which is a public company and needs to know that its subsidiaries are managed properly), and others that are internally facing. "It's hard to navigate and find out who does charity stuff if that person's title is 'karma chief,'" she continued before excusing herself to go judge a karaoke contest across the street.

• • •

By summer 2014, Downtown Project employees were quietly starting to let go of their leases and move out of the perimeters inside the llama. Start-ups were beginning to max out on their funding, without proof of future revenue to justify additional funding. Zapponians were not happy with the move to Holacracy, and the company entered one of its most difficult seasons. Some aired their frustrations on Glassdoor, a careers site where employees can leave reviews anonymously, complaining of an atmosphere like a college campus, where being in the "in crowd" gets you a promotion.

Another longtime Downtown Project evangelist who was deeply questioning Tony's message decided to take a sabbatical. Over drinks inside the Ogden, she told me that she was soon departing for a cross-country train ride to clear her thoughts. "Giving a tour through Tony's apartment is like giving a tour in North Korea," she lamented. "It's like how they fill their hotels with people, and then they disappear once the tour is over. That's how I feel, and I can't do it anymore."

Prompted by that conversation, I decided that it was time for me to leave too. I had to get to Silicon Valley to talk to Alfred Lin and Nick Swinmurn and find out exactly how this whole happiness movement began.

"HOW HAPPY ARE YOU, ON A SCALE OF 1 TO 10?"

"The harder you work, the more money you make!" the instructor yelled to us. His voice boomed through the microphone, and he looked like he could be in the military.

I was about to throw up. The man with a shaved head to my

right was a machine. Ke$ha's "Crazy Kids" blasted over the loud-speakers in a high-ceilinged, bright-blue gym called Dethrone Basecamp in Silicon Valley, just across the street from the Burlingame Caltrain station.

"You can do it!" Nick Swinmurn turned to me and kept spinning, faster and faster.

I wanted to know more about the origin of the *Delivering Happiness* story, so I met Zappos's forgotten founder in his element. Nick moved back to California after he left Zappos in 2006. He started a couple other ventures, such as a T-shirt company, but most didn't take off. In 2009, the same year that Amazon bought Zappos for $1.2 billion, he created the clothing line Dethrone Royalty. He then launched Dethrone Basecamp, inspired by the UFC chain of gyms.

"Let's go!" he yelled back at me. After a few minutes on the assault bike, it was back on the ground for intervals: weights, planks, sprints. Everyone else in the gym looked like they had done this before. On a screen, the minutes counted down for each interval.

After investing in the Burlingame location, Nick opened up gyms in San Francisco, Santa Monica, and West Hollywood. He also opened a gym in Vegas, which is now closed. He mostly keeps his Zappos past separate from his new life. "Did you know Nick is the founder of Zappos?" I asked a young woman after the class. She didn't.

"It was just a previous job–I can't spend the rest of my life thinking about the inner workings of Zappos," he told me later.

But he still has something to say about his role in the company's history. After Tony's *Delivering Happiness* came out, friends encouraged him to go public and share his side of the story. "It's just too much work," he explained.

Over dinner the evening before the Zappos All-Hands, Tony asked Nick how happy he was, on a scale of 1 to 10. Nick told him an 8. The next day, as they sat in the front row before the stage at the Hard Rock, Nick leaned over to Tony, "You know, I've been thinking about this, and I think I'm a nine. I'm really happy right now." Tony had told Nick he was a 7. But to a lot of people in downtown Vegas, Tony doesn't seem all that happy.

"But then I realized," Nick told me as we walked around Burlingame, "that Tony had somehow gotten me to think about that stupid number all night."

When Zappos first launched, Tony and Alfred stayed on the sidelines as the company's investors. But once the site started gaining momentum, Tony stepped in and joined its operations full-time. After he decided to really double down on the company, Nick asked Tony to take over the CEO job following a meeting with potential investors during which he realized that Tony was doing most of the talking. He stayed with the company until it hit $370 million in gross sales.

He's moved on. His gyms are well respected, and he lives and works in a utopian part of Silicon Valley. In addition to the gym, he started a small marketing agency called Slake. But there are elements of the larger story that he still wants to rectify.

"Just so you know," Nick yelled to me as I walked to the Caltrain. "Alfred saved Zappos!"

After visiting Vegas for the All-Hands and taking the Downtown Project tour, Nick invited Tony and Fred to visit Burlingame to check out his gym; both declined. Alfred, who says he views Tony as a brother, has had similar experiences: "You have to meet Tony on his terms."

Negotiating the spoken and unspoken terms of any situation is an art and passion of Tony's. He's a gifted game theorist and poker player. There is always a maneuver to be made, a chess piece to be moved. Failure doesn't occur to him as much as: "With the new set of conditions, how do you create something from that?" He would also prefer to manipulate the outcome in an oblique way than face conflict head-on. Most of the time, it's hard to know what he's really thinking.

That's why hiring strictly by culture fit suits his personality: there's less conflict when everyone has "opted in" and abides by the same doctrine. That's also part of his draw to Holacracy. "When you have rules in place, then you can point to the rules," Maggie Hsu explained. "Tony's conflict averse; that's not a secret to anyone." Throughout the years, he's delegated many difficult conversations to Alfred, Andrew Donner, Millie Chou, Mimi Pham, and a host of other "bad cops" in his inner circle.

In describing the culture at LinkExchange, Tony says that he and Alfred basically hired all their friends until they "ran out of friends," which is when the culture got bad. The friends all had similar tastes: they enjoyed going to Taco Bell together, going to movies, going to raves–and they shared similar beliefs around self-organization (less management). Tony once told me that the word "leader" makes him cringe. He is a visionary and a delegator of ideas, but he prefers to stay apart from the actual process. However, managing with little oversight can leave employees confused and, sometimes, operating in a perpetual state of ambiguity.

To understand another piece of the *Delivering Happiness* story and make better sense of Holacracy, I found Alfred, too, in his element on Sand Hill Road, in Menlo Park, California.

"Tony always wanted work and play in the same place," Alfred explained, mentioning the goal of nirvana. He said that Sequoia managing partner Mike Moritz, now his colleague, always said that "Zappos is a lot more like a social experiment," and Tony didn't take it that well. "I've always been a little concerned that he has the tendency to want to go to zero and build it up again."

Like some others who are skeptical of the revolutionary aspect of Holacracy, Alfred remarked that he doesn't think Holacracy really changes the management system. "You're just replacing one hierarchy with another hierarchy. You're not getting rid of management. It's a different form," he said. "The best part of being an investment firm is that you don't really manage anyone. The companies you invest in should be self-managing."

Since leaving Zappos just after the sale to Amazon, Alfred has worked with many of the leading innovators in the world, including the founders of Airbnb, the hospitality start-up valued at several billion dollars (he sits on Airbnb's board). He described to me the shared trait among all successful entrepreneurs: having a chip on their shoulder, something to prove that goes very deep. "I've never met someone who is really well adjusted who is an entrepreneur."

ZAPPOS LABS

My next destination was San Francisco to locate Will Young, the founder of Zappos Labs, the company's research-and-development arm, who has worked closely with Tony for years. He was also one of the partners in the Vegas Tech Fund. Will certainly had more clues to offer.

Zappos Labs is located just off Market Street, in the heart of one of the nicer neighborhoods in the city's tech center. It occupies a single office on a nondescript floor, next to what could be a paper company, or a dentist's office. It feels counterintuitive to walk into such a normal space after spending time inside the company's zany headquarters in Las Vegas.

When I arrived at five thirty on a weekday afternoon, the handful of employees who occupied the small office were all drinking red wine at their desks. In Vegas, it would be fernet or Grey Goose, but the tradition stands nonetheless.

Will greeted me at the door. He's a tall, charismatic Asian man whose job it is to come up with creative new ways to brand Zappos through social media. He pulled out his phone and showed me an Instagram campaign he was working on. Many ideas have failed. So, too, have start-ups that he's advised as a partner in the Vegas Tech Fund. Some are doing well. From the way he described it, everything sounded more like a gamble than a strategy.

"I got really lucky," he told me. "I had no experience, but Tony brought me on anyway." He has the luxury of dealing from afar, both literally and figuratively; and when you're afar, failure doesn't feel so acute. Like John Bunch and others, Will has accumulated enough loyalty with Tony that he will always have a place in the ecosystem. He recounted the story of how they met.

"Everyone has their Tony story, of course," he began. "But this one is legendary. A bunch of guys and I used to play poker in San Francisco, and one time Tony was literally walking outside and came upstairs and joined us to play poker." It was before Tony had sparked a happiness movement, and they had no idea who he was–although he was wearing his usual Zappos T-shirt. They learned that Tony had played in the *World Series of Poker*.

Like Andy White, Fred Mossler, and Zach Ware, Will subscribes closely to Tony's belief system. He is a major piece of the Holacracy implementation, and, like others in the ecosystem, he is also vague about what exactly he does. (With job titles such as serendipity sorcerer, no title II, pixie of positivity, and speaker of the house, it's hard to know what people actually do.) One of Will's stated goals is to bring more transparency to the company's new internal structure, inspired by Buffer, a VTF-funded start-up that is focused on radical transparency. But for the most part, Zappos employees feel that despite the transparency, there is still a phantom operating system cloaked in ambiguity. For example, when Maggie Hsu got tired of Las Vegas, she arranged with Tony to become an advisor and moved to San Francisco to work out of the Zappos Labs office–a rare sort of perk afforded only to those in his inner circle.

There are few who speak up to Tony, but Alexis Gonzales-Black, the other Holacracy implementation lead, whom I met at the Gold Spike pool, is one of them. "I've told him, 'You know, the human race is flawed,'" she said to me later that day at a wine bar near Fisherman's Wharf in San Francisco. "'Have you ever thought maybe you're wrong?'" She was in town for a HolacracyOne coaching training session.

"There's definitely a boys' club," she said while taking a sip of her carafe of wine. Before joining Zappos, she was a recruiter for Teach for America in Las Vegas, which is ranked the worst public education system in the country. Alexis joined Zappos as a college recruiter in May 2012. Many of Zappos's employees are young college graduates; they're easier to train and acclimatize to the culture without any prior working experience. After a number of conversations that led to his $10,000 donation to her campaign for a seat on the Nevada State Board of Education, Alexis joined the Holacracy implementation team.

Alexis is attracted to Holacracy because she believes that less bureaucracy within companies will have a spillover effect into the education space. "People think it's hardest for managers to let go of duties," she said. "No, it's hard for people not used to having responsibility to step up. They talk to me, and I say, 'Go for it. You now have the tools to tap into that power.'"

For all of its grandiosity, for some the system provides Tony a way to compensate for his own shortcomings. "Tony's a terrible manager," Romotive founder Keller Rinaudo told me bluntly at an artisanal coffee shop at Tenth and Mission, echoing a sentiment others have expressed openly. In the same breath, he described Tony's leadership (and subsequent following) as "religious."

Michael said something similar over drinks at his New Orleans–inspired bar inside the Ogden. "I know why Tony's doing this whole thing [Holacracy]. He doesn't want to manage people. He likes the luxury of being able to keep the friendship part separate from the management part." By making friends and family a core part of his financial ecosystem, Tony doesn't want to be responsible for how things play out.

Still, Keller was optimistic about how everything would play out over time in downtown Vegas. "This will be successful," he said resolutely. "It's all the real estate. That's where the money is coming from. It's not going to be tech, education, whatever–you could look at that as just branding. Tech will not be a big part of this; nothing is successful."

Keller's onetime girlfriend Jen McCabe is the former Romotive employee who opted to stay in Las Vegas. She pitched Tony on a hardware incubator that she named Factorli, and he gave her $10 million. For a time, she was also a member of the Vegas Tech Fund. In a story for *ReCode*, journalist Nellie Bowles recounts how Jen launched her investing career with VTF:

> "Next thing I know, I had an email from Tony: "Here's your single sign-off. Here's the papers we use. Here's your salary,'"

McCabe said. "It was just, 'Pick who you like'–so I started investing." She invested in six companies in six weeks. Within four months, she had invested in twenty-four. The average investment was $100,000. Then she thought of Factorli. Hsieh liked the idea of a factory that was based in the United States and would serve a gamut of clients, from ambitious crowd-funded start-ups to larger companies doing prototyping ahead of big projects. Fashion tech start-ups like Flint and Tinder would benefit from Factorli. She closed the $10 million Series A round on Valentine's Day 2014.

Factorli launched that spring but shut down abruptly months later, not long after my conversation with Keller. It was a prime example of the fickleness of things, and the lack of oversight and due diligence within DTP. Before Factorli closed, Jen was a real believer; her journey to Vegas was like a vision quest. "Who sees a city and says, this can be a start-up? It is the craziest kind of risk. And Tony is not using that kind of drive to build a rocket or go to the moon," she said during an impassioned talk in the double-wide trailer, evoking Elon Musk. "He's using it to build things downtown."

While in San Francisco, I stayed with a friend and her fiancé who worked for Google and SurveyMonkey, respectively, and were deeply entrenched in Silicon Valley culture. They hadn't been following Tony and Downtown Project until I shared with them what I had been up to the past year. "People don't really talk about Tony Hsieh or Zappos here," they explained. "There's too much other stuff to keep track of."

A few weeks later, they were the ones to send me the *Pando-Daily* story announcing yet another Downtown Project suicide. Bolt Barber's Matt Berman, whom I had spent a morning with at the Beat coffeehouse when he spoke excitedly about DTP, had gone missing. Reporter Paul Carr couldn't confirm details.

"What is happening to all of Tony's followers?!" my friend who did PR for Google asked me. Having worked with Google executives to carefully craft Google's image, she could also see that this was a PR disaster.

No one else reached out to me with the news. As with the other suicides, Downtown Project worked to keep it quiet, though it loomed within the undercurrent of the ecosystem. I didn't know how to process Matt's suicide. It hardly felt real because no one talked about it. There was no outward mourning the loss of another member of the community.

The tragedies and failures within Downtown Project were not Tony's only concerns. The culture at Zappos was also suffering. An engineer named Chase Adams wrote a departing manifesto criticizing Zappos leadership, Holacracy, and its execution, which spread quickly throughout the company. He later shared with me his manifesto:

> I am an idealist. However, everything I say from this point on is a critical review based on a place created for idealists. I would hope Walt Disney would have welcomed the same feedback in his organization.

Lack of Vision, Direction & A Captain

In GlassFrog*, our purpose is stated as: "To inspire the world by showing it's possible to simultaneously deliver happiness to

---

* GlassFrog is software for companies that use Holacracy, and another revenue stream for HolacracyOne.

customers, employees, community, vendors, and shareholders in a long-term, sustainable way."

If I rewrote this, it would say: "Make everyone happy for forever."

Same thing, yet it sounds way less plausible because it's not filled with words. This is not a purpose statement.

If we step back and look at the first half of our purpose statement in a holistic, short-term view, is this even happening? If you take a snapshot of the past 6 months, have we shown this to be sustainable in a short period such as that?

I believe we've proven we can make customers happy for a while, but employees' happiness is at an all-time low (primarily non-CLT roles). I believe we've disenfranchised the community with a lofty vision statement at the inception of this responsibility. What's worse, it doesn't seem like it's for Zappos or the community, but to profit an individual.

Zappos, as any Enterprise level e-commerce "Service company that sells shoes," is a large, unwieldy ship. A ship the size of the *Titanic*. A ship that size requires precision, constant thought.

It feels like there are ten people at the helm, and none of the ten is our CEO, Tony Hsieh.

All the while, the rest of us are in one of three states:

- Trying with all of our might to make this place better the ways we want to see it better to no avail
- Apathetic to the point of "working from home" without producing
- Outdoing each other as culture fits on core values such as "Create Fun and a Little Weird" or "Build a Team and Family Spirit" to be considered model Zapponians

There is more to the manifesto, but that's the gist of it. Tony and Fred Mossler caught wind of it and invited Chase to sit down with them at Container Park. After that meeting, Chase decided to turn down his job offer from WalmartLabs, the R&D and technology arm of the company, and stay at Zappos. He even updated his manifesto. But a few months later, he took the WalmartLabs position after all.

While Tony was working hard at creating a system so that he could take on less responsibility, what his employees really needed was a leader.

THE "DIRTY THIRTY"

"I'm going to speak on behalf of all of us!" David Gould said resolutely as he passed two employees crying in the stairwell in Downtown Project's brand-new headquarters on Carson Avenue. It was an unlikely show of passion for the Midwestern college professor. Only months earlier, he'd spoken about following a North Star. But things were different today. Much had changed, including the fact that Tony had yet to follow through on his promise to deliver $50,000 to support a college entrepreneurship class that Professor Gould had developed as an exchange with Downtown Project. The students began their projects, but didn't have the resources to finish the class, so they returned to Iowa disappointed.

Mark Rowland, the soon-to-be-named CEO of Downtown Project, tried to stop Professor Gould before he reached Maggie Hsu. But the professor was set on his mission. He gave her a piece of paper and said that it would soon be public. The *Las Vegas Weekly* printed his Op-Ed:

Dear Tony,

We met in the fall of 2010, when your "Delivering Happiness" book tour stopped by my University of Iowa class. I could never have imagined how dramatically that hot August afternoon would change the course of my life. I have retold the story many times of how the students spontaneously followed you out of the classroom that day. Exactly three years later, I left my home, and position at the university, to follow you as well.

The decision to join the Downtown Project's $350 million revitalization effort was based on three core beliefs:

1. The project was engaged in a fascinating "social experiment."
2. The project offered a unique opportunity, to not only make a meaningful difference in Downtown Las Vegas, but also enrich the lives of people living in cities around the world.
3. It was led by a generous spirit.

I was not alone. Some 400–600 people pilgrimage to Las Vegas each month to walk your 19-block footprint, and ponder the ideal that simply focusing on ROI (Return on Investment) is not enough. You claimed that the city of the future would require equal attention on ROC (Return on Community), and I intuitively knew you were right. Though I have come to understand the formidable challenges inherent in transforming a city, the story you crafted was not only visionary, but attainable.

So what happened?

Artist Donovan Fitzgerald's work at the Window. (*Emily Wilson*)

Tomorrow, many of the people who merged their voices with yours will find themselves without a job. While their names have yet to be revealed, the disillusioned expressions I conjure up are keeping me awake tonight. This group will undoubtedly include numerous young adults, who have not yet found your good fortune. As they have naively purchased homes and started families, this decision will impact them greatly.

"Business is business" will be the defense from those you have charged with delivering the sad news. But we have not experienced a string of tough breaks or bad luck. Rather, this is a collage of decadence, greed, and missing leadership. While some squandered the opportunity to "dent the universe," others never cared about doing so in the first place. There were heroes among us, however, and it is for them that my soul weeps.

My heart also goes out to those whose jobs are spared. While that might seem a bit ridiculous, they will surely expend energy trying to understand the secret of why they were kept and others let go. In the end, the only thing they will know for sure is that their leaders lied to them in order to hurt their friends.

While reason might conclude that I should wait to either identify a new job, or collect my severance pay, I am compelled to tender my resignation instead. Compensation was never my primary concern. Doing meaningful work, however, is.

When artist Donovan Fitzgerald began depicting the ideal American city on the cement pillars at the Window, he made the unique choice of shunning physical structures in favor of three female characters. Noting my surprise, Donovan explained that while buildings rise and fall, great cities each require the same principles: Truth, Goodness, and Beauty. "The women," he clarified, "are meant to represent each." I remember staring at the figures for some time before requesting one addition. "What is it?" Donovan asked. "A North Star," I replied, "so that we don't lose our way."

I wish you health and happiness.

Warmly,
David L. Gould

September 29, 2014, was the day that Downtown Project laid off a third of its staff. They called themselves the "Dirty Thirty." It became a viral news story, thanks to the professor's Op-Ed in *Las Vegas Weekly* and a story by the tech news site *ReCode* on the heels of a multi-part series about Downtown Project.

Ron Corso, the owner of 11th Street Records, had a planned meeting with his DTP contact, Ashton Allen, that morning. He walked into the headquarters to find people crying. "Not to get metaphysical, but I walked into the office, and there was something with the energy," he recalled. Ashton told him what was happening and said he would be right back. He returned wide eyed from a meeting with Don Welch and broke the news: "Me too."

Ron couldn't believe it. "All the people who actually have a passion were the ones who were cut out." He observed that DTP was filled with people who probably were great students but didn't possess real creative genius. However, in order to build a place where software developers want to live, you need to have that creative edge borne from passion. "Software developers want to be around artists," he said. "But artists don't want to be around software developers."

At a Downtown Project All-Hands at Inspire Theatre a month earlier, Tony had made it clear that he didn't want to hold as much responsibility and said there would be a new leadership team of six. Downtown Project employees left the meeting still unclear about who exactly was now the point person, though it seemed to be Tony's longtime attorney, Millie Chou. The ambiguity around the situation put employees on edge; they felt that information was being withheld. Noticeably absent among the six was Mark Rowland, who would be named CEO a few months later. One thing was clear to many: Tony had lost interest in his Downtown Project.

"It's just like his LinkExchange story," Michael Cornthwaite told me while sitting in the black leather seats in DCR. "He'd wake up and hit the snooze button several times. Start something, then get bored. It's fun to fall in love over and over again."

During the All-Hands, one of the Downtown Project tour guides pulled aside one of the six, VFA fellow Rob Solomon, who oversaw finances for the fund. "How much exactly do we have left, would you say?" she asked him, sensing that something was amiss.

"Let's just say we have around $349 million," he responded

with a laugh. The VFA fellow was more of the public face: the real money managers were Andrew Donner (real estate), Chrissie Yim (Tony's personal accountant), Don Welch (small business), Zach Ware (tech), and, on some level, Millie Chou (legal). In the 1990s, Tony convinced Millie to return her signing bonus with a white-shoe law firm to work at Venture Frogs. "Somehow Tony helps you know what you really want," she once shared with me on the *Delivering Happiness* bus.

At the All-Hands, Tony presented the then close to one hundred employees with the company's five-year plan, which showed a trajectory of shooting bullets in year two and paring back in year three. It was the first time employees had ever seen it.

When I asked Andrew how much he had invested in real estate, he essentially admitted that the $200 million was gone but would not reveal just how much had been spent or how much was left. "There has never been a limitation or a restriction," he explained. "If it makes sense to buy, we were empowered to go do it. There was never a black-and-white line to me." Andrew operated largely outside the bounds of DTP, so when I asked him about Holacracy, he begged off the question. (Later he described DTP as a company with "a lot of immaturity.")

Yet Holacracy was blamed as a major reason for the sudden chaos and disruption. The day of the layoffs, Maggie Hsu said joyously, "I can't wait to tell Brian we don't need his services anymore!" The former McKinsey consultant was one of Holacracy-One's harshest critics, citing a command-and-control operation. "I will say on the record that HolacracyOne is a terrible company," she told me later at Downtown Project's new grocery store, the Market. "They sold us an incomplete package."

Maggie was among the six who made the decision about the layoffs. She said they chose to eliminate people who "had already fulfilled the purpose of their role." In their assessment, that included the tour guides, the members of the rock group Rabbit tasked with creating a vibrant music scene, the general manager of the Gold Spike, and the Ticket Cake cofounder who took on a new role as a collision scientist. The TEDMED curator arranged to work for the Life Is Beautiful festival. When Lisa Shufro pitched Tony on her plan for bringing the 24/7 TED talks to Inspire and building out the education series, he said it was a "no-brainer"–the same sort of thing that he'd told Jen McCabe, the founder of the $10 million hardware start-up Factorli. It turns out that Downtown Project had made some gross underestimations about costs to carry out some of its core projects. Stripped down, the new budget and focus were clear: real estate and small business, the traditional sort of private revitalization project you can find in cities around the world–not the "four-minute-mile for cities" formula that Tony had originally pitched in his keynote.

There were rumblings of a change in strategy in the weeks before the All-Hands. One member of the Dirty Thirty struggled with panic attacks during this time, sensing that there was going to be a major shift.

"*I* know that *you* know what *you* know," someone taunted Maggie in the Ogden elevator the day before the layoffs.

Maggie refused to answer questions about the layoffs, directing me to HR, and insisted that Holacracy was still in place–when, in fact, the Holacracy circle had been abolished, and no one was using it anymore. Downtown Project has been shrouded in secrecy, and its own employees don't even know what's going on, with the veneer that it is an open system.

One of the Dirty Thirty, also a close friend of Tony's, texted him the morning of the layoffs: "Am I going to be fired?" Tony said he didn't know; he was getting the list that morning–but it's unclear if that was the case. It was particularly painful for all of them because they were all "culture fits," and many were friends of Tony's. Of course, he would find a place for the people he wanted to stay around; a select few would handle special projects for him (become community investments), to give them more time in the interim.

Tony had lost his footing with the undertaking that was intended to showcase one of his grandest visions for the world (revitalizing cities)–ironically, by the very means (Holacracy) to which he was pursuing his other grand vision (self-organizing companies, which would feed into the first vision). There appeared to be no real PR strategy in response. There was an onslaught of negative headlines–" 'Bloodletting' at Downtown Project With Massive Layoffs," "Another Shoe Drops in Las Vegas," "Why Las Vegas Needed a Lot More Than Tony Hsieh's Cult of Personality"–countered by a few pieces in defense of DTP, including a *Medium* post by a Cincinnati-based urban planner titled, "The Long Hard Slog of Community Revitalization (and How Media Fails Us): A Close Observer's Perspective on the Downtown Project, Las Vegas."

The entire response was reactionary: Tony posted an Evernote saying that he was, in fact, never the CEO of Downtown Project. (A member of the six, Michael Downs, maintains that Tony is the CEO.)

People had a difficult time describing the company's organization structure even still.

When the news broke, I was in Cambridge, Massachusetts, visiting Professor Ethan Bernstein at Harvard Business School. He studies self-organizing companies and had spent some time with the Holacracy teams at Zappos and Downtown Project. "You walk into Zappos, and Tony's not the boss per se, but then you see his office, and it overlooks the entire campus," he said from his office, overlooking the courtyard. "And then you walk into his apartment, and it overlooks everything. It's sort of his kingdom."

It felt appropriate to be at Harvard, which is where Zappos really started. It's where Tony and Alfred met. Their partnership is what would meaningfully lead his businesses to high valuations and exits. The absence of Alfred is felt at Zappos and at Downtown Project. Perhaps this whole mess at DTP never would have happened if Alfred had been there. Perhaps he'd have guided the expenses better, chosen people who managed money better, to allocate the funds. It's hard to know.

Across the city, I visited Ministry of Supply, a men's fashion tech start-up. Its president was a former Zappos employee. As with Flint and Tinder, Downtown Project took notice when Ministry of Supply set a new Kickstarter record and invested seed money into the operation. Ministry of Supply had planned to coordinate 3-D printing work with Factorli until the incubator closed. "Everything can't just be charity," Ministry of Supply cofounder Aman Advani said from the company offices in downtown Boston. Also like Flint and Tinder, they arranged to engage in the subscription model, visiting Vegas every couple weeks. "All the start-ups can't just bleed money. There has to be a path to profitability and a sustainable business model."

Aman, an MIT grad who has studied organizational design, also gave me his analysis on Holacracy at Zappos. He believes it's intended to be a "shock to the system," and then sent me a Harvard case study that highlighted his point. "It serves two purposes," he told me. "One is to organize around a new normal, and two is to create a new sense of energy."

On the heels of the Downtown Project layoffs, Zach fired Andy White, citing a change in strategy focused on doubling down on its portfolio companies rather than on a stream of new ones. Although Zach was still involved in the Vegas Tech Fund even as he worked to build Shift, he distanced himself from Downtown Project in subsequent months.

There was also pressure on the small businesses. Since early 2014, Don had begun pressuring Sarah Nisperos to come up with a new business model for Coterie, extending beyond ROC. By the end of the year, deeply in the red, the boutique clothing shop closed. But the constraints and pressures of building a business in downtown Las Vegas were real. Tony asked Sarah to open up her shop in a low foot traffic area in four weeks so that he could attract other recruits. With little time to perform market research, she did, and emphasized to Tony and Don Welch that it would likely take five years to become profitable. She wasn't given the chance to see it through, at least in downtown Las Vegas; Coterie lasted two years. Sarah went on a yoga retreat and moved to LA to open up a shop there. Meanwhile, a flower shop in the John E. Carson Building owned by Zappos Holacracy implementation lead John Bunch also closed after a few short months. I met with him in December and asked how things were going; he said they were fine. Bud & Vine closed a week later.

That's the nature of failure in downtown Vegas, an offshoot of how failure is in Silicon Valley: there's a pretense around success. You're crushing it, until you're not. After that, I didn't know what to believe from John about how Holacracy was going at Zappos anymore.

Not that anyone would blame John or others for their closed businesses: for the opportunity, they all took on significant risk opening brick-and-mortar shops in an area that is fraught with homelessness and low foot traffic, especially after the mass exodus beginning in 2014. There was also a limited amount of housing downtown, one of the biggest barriers to growth. For John, the timing was especially unfortunate: he opened Bud & Vine just as Downtown Project began to fissure and many of its core customers moved out to the suburbs. One of the bright spots downtown is Container Park, which draws families in a way that the area never has before, but they mostly stay within the park.

In the weeks following the Dirty Thirty layoffs, the mood downtown was increasingly low energy and uninspired. The most depressing thing for many was realizing that the vision they'd bought into and wanted to believe in so deeply–the one that justified their time and energy investments, and their decision to follow Tony at his word–did not seem to exist anymore.

What Professor Gould wrote in *Las Vegas Weekly* seemed to be a reflection of what the community wanted to say but no one felt the courage to say.

Tony's high school friend Janice Lopez pushed him on it after it happened. "I recommend you reach out to him instead of ignore it," she pleaded.

Still, after everything, Tony found a place for those Dirty Thirty members he wanted to keep around.

"Oh yeah, I'm drinking the Kool-Aid," Heidy Stamper told me one afternoon. She had been let go but remained in the ecosystem. "It's called fernet."

She reflected on the ambiguity around the situation and how she blamed herself for not really having clarity on what Tony's role was. She emphasized how much she valued their friendship and nostalgically recounted a trip to Belgium and Ibiza last summer with Tony. It was a once-in-a-lifetime trip for her and her husband to partake in Tomorrowland, one of the largest raves in the world. Even then, Tony was on email most of the time, and the entire trip was a whirlwind: everyone was sleep deprived, running on adrenaline, going from rave to hotel room to rave. "He's a Sagittarius, so he has a level of control he wants to maintain," Heidy explained. "It's really hard for him to really relinquish control of so many things he's taken control of." Although Tony could delegate a lot of things, he chooses to remain involved in the intimate details of decisions, which is why his in-box is always so full.

I brought up the idea of how a lot of people now jokingly called DTP a cult. She decided to look it up on her phone and read it aloud:

Cult

noun

1. a system of religious veneration and devotion directed toward a particular figure or object.

Heidy continued reading the other definitions and then her voice trailed off with the very last one:

"a cult of personality surrounding the leaders."
obsession with, fixation on, mania for, passion for, idolization of, devotion to, worship of, veneration of

"None of this has anything to do with religion," she concluded. "So I don't think it makes sense for me to be in a cult." Cult of personality aside, Heidy was one of the kindest people I had ever met. Especially given the delicate nature of the social order in downtown Las Vegas, I appreciated that she took the risk befriending a journalist. I hoped that we could remain friends after my book came out. And who was I to judge? I was here, too, just like everyone else.

At the Zappos Q4 2014 All-Hands, Tony walked out onto the stage visibly nervous. He hadn't addressed the layoffs at DTP or the recent news (Professor Gould's resignation letter and *ReCode*'s "The Downtown Project Suicides: Can the Pursuit of Happiness Kill You?"). Several employees left the All-Hands early, making a subtle statement against their CEO.

Jonathan Jenkins, who'd moved his start-up OrderWithMe (now rebranded WithMe) from China to Vegas, told *ReCode* that he wanted to start a church. He viewed what was happening in downtown Las Vegas as reflective of what in China they call "face." Everyone is always trying to put on a good face and covering up their struggles. He felt it leads only to more pain.

AIRSTREAM PARK

"Maybe I could live in the hostel?" Tony asked for an opinion from the female confidantes who joined him on a walk around downtown. One of them was his high school friend Janice Lopez; the other was Andy White's wife, Oksana. Around the same time as the layoffs, Downtown Project learned that Ogden residents would either have to buy their properties or move out as their leases expired. It was an opportunistic move by the property owner, who appeared to be capitalizing on Tony's presence downtown. Most of his followers did not have several hundred thousand dollars to purchase their apartments. Tony decided he needed to find a new communal living space.

Back in San Francisco, at 1000 Van Ness, Tony, his father, Richard, and their friends owned 20 percent of the building and controlled 40 percent of the property's board seats, giving them sway over all major decisions. But here at the Ogden, Tony and his deputies did not hold as much influence.

The women deterred him from moving into the hostel, saying that living in that environment would not be worth the potential benefits.

"What about the Gold Spike?" he countered, again in all seriousness. "I could live on the top floor."

The women shook their heads. "You'll have no privacy."

The Gold Spike, while better than before, is not a high-end property. Its rooms are decorated with Ikea furniture, and its halls are frequently scented with weed. Guests are given earplugs because it's difficult to sleep with the echoes from the Fremont Experience drifting through the flimsy windows and the pulsing bass from downstairs making its way all the way up to the top floors.

More affordable than the Strip, the Gold Spike draws a certain crowd. A few times I met men in the elevators who were in the city to report to court over drug charges. Another time I met a young Asian woman holding a huge box full of costumes for raving. It's not uncommon to run into Zapponians who are high on marijuana in the kitchen. In other words, it's like a college dormitory. Gold Spike was an appropriate space to videotape the *The Real World Las Vegas* in 2015, which Downtown Project commissioned to increase the venue's revenue and attract publicity–but an unlikely place for its CEO to live.

They reconvened on the twenty-third floor of the Ogden. Janice walked over to the balcony and looked over downtown. Tony had hired her to join the construction team for Downtown Project. Her eyes locked on the parking lot where Downtown Project kept a number of Airstreams. The idea was to eventually transform the trailers into an Airstream hotel, bypassing the need and time to construct an actual building. Tony believed that micro-apartments and tiny-house living were the best ways to increase the density of the area quickly. It was the same philosophy behind Container Park: opening a number of businesses in shipping containers bypassed the need for an actual brick-and-mortar location.

"What if we move into Airstream Park?" Janice asked Tony. She had a background in architecture and was equally fascinated with the idea of small living.

He looked up from his laptop, intrigued. "On the *Delivering Happiness* bus tour, I learned I didn't need much stuff."

Over the next few hours, they got out big white sheets of paper and Post-its and started drafting ideas for what living would look like at the park. They made a list of names of people to ask if they wanted to move in for a trial run, which included mostly close friends from Zappos and Downtown Project. By early November 2014, a month after the layoffs, a group of people moved in. Several of the initial guests were part of the Dirty Thirty. Even Andy White and his wife, Oksana, spent time in Airstream Park after he was fired; they spent their evenings around the campfire with Tony and friends.

I once asked Oksana why she liked being part of Tony's growing posse. We were standing in front of the praying mantis as it spit out fire, and then followed Tony to the Work in Progress garage where the founder of LiveSpark, a pyrotechnic company funded by Downtown Project, performed a fire show. The group included a random amalgamation of people: Tony's raver friends, the rock band OK Go, early Zappos investors. "I fought it at first," she said. "But then I realized: look at all the cool things I get to do!"

The Airstream Park brought unexpected fresh energy and enthusiasm to a community and restored some degree of belief in Tony's vision. It also had an element of magic to it: the entrance was through the *Alice in Wonderland*– and *Delivering Happiness*–themed school buses and under a tunnel of colorful twinkle lights. The ground is covered in fake grass, and mist sprays out as you walk through. Just inside is a communal area around a bonfire and a massive screen for movies that play most nights. Behind the sitting area is a kitchen with a stocked bar. It was an exciting place to live in that moment in time. "It was such a difficult time for downtown," Janice told me. "We needed something to distract us."

From afar, though, it also looked like a way for Tony to escape the public eye during a time when the glare of the media and disdain from residents were particularly high. Airstream Park is located at the edge of downtown, east of the core businesses. It's located next to the Bunkhouse Saloon, adjacent to 11th Street Records, and across the street from the independent bookstore the Writer's Block, all backed by Downtown Project. Its entrance is hidden and guarded by security.

On the eve of Tony's forty-first birthday, friends and friends of friends gathered around the bonfire. Some trickled in from fashion incubator Stitch Factory's ugly sweater party, others from the *Downtown Podcast*, the show put on by Ticket Cake founder Dylan Jorgensen, whose early mission with the show was to change people's perceptions of downtown Las Vegas. As it neared midnight, Tony passed around shots of fernet. In Asian culture 12/12 is considered a lucky number and an auspicious birth date. This year's celebration would be much more low key than the last.

"The group of people he hangs out with keeps getting younger and younger," a close friend confided. "It's like, where are the adults here?" Some of the happiest times in Tony's life were in college–his first brush with real freedom after living under his parents' domain. Ever since then, it has seemed like he's been trying to bottle up that feeling. During a fireside chat in the Learning Village one evening in fall 2013, Tony said he views himself as forever in his twenties.

For all of its early excitement, Airstream Park eventually became weighed down by politics and unwelcome guests. Some started retreating to their apartments elsewhere downtown, and Janice, equally frustrated, moved outside the ecosystem to work for another start-up in Texas.

Alexis, the Zappos Holacracy implementation lead, decided it was time to leave Airstream Park when she returned home from a business trip and realized that taking out the clothes from her suitcase would overwhelm her tiny home. "Then there's moments like lugging my laundry across the park as a group is sitting by the campfire, singing, 'I want to be a billionaire,' right outside Tony's Airstream, and that's just awkward."

One resident, who didn't know many people going in, said that at first it was difficult to conform to the group's norms, but over time it got easier. A year later, he was asked to leave the park along with several others under the guise of construction work.

Tony doubled down on living at Airstream Park. He retained his main unit on the twenty-third floor of the Ogden and transferred the lease for the other two apartments to Maren Kate Donovan, the founder of Zirtual, in the final months before her start-up folded.

But Heidy Stamper points out that while Tony spends most of his time at the park, "he sleeps wherever it's comfortable. That's why he has a place in Juhl," a downtown residential building just blocks from the Graceland Wedding Chapel. "That's why he has a place at the Ogden. That's why he has a place on Shadow Lane. And that's why he has a place in Southern Highlands." When Heidy visited his mansion in Southern Highlands, she couldn't believe he hadn't been there for a year and a half. The place was frozen in time.

Although I stayed out of the media onslaught that fall around DTP, I published a feature-length story for *Quartz* a few weeks later that looked more at the Zappos side of things, titled, "Holacracy at Zappos: It's Either the Future of Management or a Social Experiment Gone Awry." It was the first time that I had weighed in with my observations from spending significant time in downtown Las Vegas. I was concerned about how it might affect my access, but it felt important to publish because there was high interest around Tony's experiment with Holacracy and self-organization.

THE RULES DON'T EXIST

On a bright afternoon in late April 2015, Tyler Williams, also known as Zappos's "Fungineer," and other employees played tetherball in the courtyard, a large open space easily accessible from the corner of Las Vegas Boulevard and Stewart Avenue. The company's headquarters are situated next door to the Mob Museum, the city's ode to its history of organized crime brought to life by former mob attorney Mayor Oscar Goodman.

Inside the corporate lobby is a mosaic framing the words "Part of the Zappos Family." Behind the front desk sits one of the company's long-time staffers, a man who appeared to be in his sixties. He and his wife, who leads the call center, have worked for Zappos for years. In a few days, both of them would leave the company, being among the 210 Zapponians, or 14 percent of the organization, who decided to take a buyout offer.

At the end of March, Tony sent out a companywide email explaining that in order for the Holacracy implementation to work, the company had to take a "rip the Band-Aid" approach, citing the strain of operating in two worlds. He wrote that Zappos would "begin the process of breaking down our legacy silo'ed structure/circles of merchandising, finance, tech, marketing, and other functions and create self-organizing and self-managing business-centric circles instead by starting to fund this new model." Managers who were in good standing would receive their salaries until the end of 2015 but had to find other roles: "To be clear, managers were absolutely necessary and valuable to the growth of Zappos over the years under our previous structure," he wrote.

He gave employees the option to take a buyout offer of three months' severance pay plus an additional month's pay for each year worked beyond four years, with the deadline of one month to decide. He also required all employees weighing the offer to read *Reinventing Organizations: A Guide to Creating Organizations Inspired by the Next Stage in Human Consciousness*, a book by a new management thinker, Frederic Laloux, about self-organization. The book hits on similar themes as Dave Logan's *Tribal Leadership*, describing the different levels of consciousness of a company. But instead of stages 1 through 5, *Reinventing Organizations* starts with "red" and moves up to "teal," the highest level of "consciousness" for an organization. Next to "Holacracy," "teal" became the new buzzword on campus.

At an All-Hands, the Belgium-based author gave a prerecorded talk on a large screen, wishing the Zapponians luck on their journey to teal. I couldn't help but think that Laloux evoked Big Brother in that moment. After Laloux's message, David Allen of *Getting Things Done: The Art of Stress-Free Productivity* fame, and a Holacracy adopter, spoke. Allen, known for his consultancy that claims to hack productivity, spoke in broad platitudes promoting Holacracy's strongpoints. Both he and Brian Robertson had found a way to mutually support each other's systems, just as Tony had been able to promote the management gospels of Simon Sinek,

David Logan, and Brian. In this world of high-level thought leadership, mutual endorsements are increasingly common.

"Teal is the goal, Holacracy is the means," Holacracy lead John Bunch explained to me. Even though teal was intended to provide the spirit to the organization, it still felt a bit soulless. How could self-organization be anchoring?

For all of the forthcoming changes ahead at Zappos, the courtyard that afternoon was surprisingly calm. There was no sense of urgency. Inside the elevators, which are lined with video games such as Tetris on its walls, were taped posters that asked employees to write down their reasons for either staying or going. I walked up to a Zapponian appropriately dressed in a teal shirt and asked him if he was leaving. He said no, but the numbers were high. "It's like every other person. Every day, we're getting an email from someone explaining why they're leaving." Between him and the group of four Zapponians who had joined us, it was fifty-fifty among those who were staying and going.

"Just five days until we're in bed with teal!" a Zapponian posted on his Facebook page leading up to the April 30 deadline.

Zappos has long been a darling in the press, in part thanks to advertising agency MullenLowe for the company's feel-good publicity stunts and Tony's strategy of always asking employees during meetings, "Will that get us in the news?" The public was now watching his experiment closely, and for a company accustomed to controlling the message, Zappos was suddenly in a more vulnerable position.

I continued reporting on Zappos for *Quartz* to advance the story and the conversation. A number of news outlets picked up a story I ran publishing Tony's original offer email–something that a *Fast Company* journalist tipped me off on and I tracked down from a Zappos employee–and others that I wrote subsequently on the topic (such as: "Zappos Is Offering To Pay Even More Employees To Leave"). I was always somewhat worried that my stories would jeopardize my access. And maybe they did, but I'm not sure how everything would have panned out if I had never published anything. By then, the Zappos PR team was well aware of my presence, but I don't think I was their number one concern.

PandoDaily's Paul Carr wrote the most critical pieces. That summer, he published a widely circulated story, "A Holacracy of Dunces," comparing what was going on inside the walls of Zappos and within Downtown Project to *Lord of the Flies*. When I asked John Bunch how the press affected him, he brushed it off as something that he hardly pays attention to, yet he plays a key role in the company's Brand Aura circle, whose mission is to elevate the Zappos brand. While rolling out Holacracy, he and Alexis also created a consultancy to support HolacracyOne indirectly, called Thoughtful Org Partners, marketing their experiences supporting Zappos's rollout with news stories about Holacracy.

Beyond Holacracy and teal ("the letter and spirit of the law," Tony told employees while standing in front of the backdrop of an ancient scroll), the company was undergoing other experiments, such as testing out an "Uber-like" surge pay system in the call center, which was supposed to allow flexible scheduling and pay employees more when the call volume was high. However, call center director Rob Siefker later told me that the experiment was never fully realized.

By the May 2015 Q2 All-Hands, there was finally a break in the tension. The offer takers had made their decisions. Alexis was among those to announce her departure (citing personal reasons), as was company chief technology officer Brent Cromley (who moved to the Bay Area with his wife, Millie Chou, who also chose to leave Downtown Project but remains on its board).

Some left because the offer was simply too good to refuse, others because of Holacracy, but for most, it was some combination of both. Coach left to start her own company, a longtime MC for the All-Hands left to become a comedian in Mexico, and another guy from marketing left to take a job in Korea. Unlike other offers, this gave employees the opportunity to return to Zappos, which is part of what made it so attractive. Zappos lost some of its best talent through the buyout.

In addition to "the offer," another, more lucrative offer was made to another subset of employees: the engineers who were working on the Supercloud migration to the Amazon infrastructure. In order to convince them to finish the project, they were given an extension until January 1, 2016, to make a decision.

The theme of the May 2015 All-Hands was "Reinventing Zappos." The meeting opened with a movie of a guy learning to ride a bike in Amsterdam that is engineered so it moves in the opposite direction as expected. For example, when you try to turn right, the bike moves left. Tyler Williams invited Zapponians to try out the bike onstage and then told everyone that the bike would be in the courtyard all week. "Anyone who manages to ride a hundred feet gets a prize." When I visited campus that week, one of the security guards looked at me confused and then started laughing. "I've been watching that guy," he said, pointing to a Zappos employee. "He just can't seem to ride that bike!"

As Tony took the stage, his hands were shaking. He shared that employees had asked for his resignation and that the last six weeks had been some of his most difficult. On the screen, an image of the book *Delivering Happiness* came up, something that he promotes occasionally during All-Hands to encourage employees to read it. He remarked that he had reread his book over the last few weeks, which brought him back to his roots.

After a series of customer service hero stories, Zapponians welcomed others onto the stage to share anything on their mind. At the very end, a guy with a hoodie jogged up to the stage. "I don't know what everyone's saying about your resignation and taking the offer and all that," he said. "But I'm in it to win it!"

ELECTRIC DAISY CARNIVAL

"This is going to be the hottest Electric Daisy Carnival on record," Heidy Stamper, Tony's raver friend with the rainbow hair, warned me. At 100 degrees, you could easily fry an egg on the sidewalk. Yet four hundred thousand revelers from around the United States and beyond were gathering this weekend at the Las Vegas Motor Speedway for one of the largest raves in the world. It is also one of Tony's favorite events of the year.

To prepare for the event, Heidy invited me into her Ogden apartment and showed me her abundant closet full of costumes from raves past. Her husband, Chad, also the consummate raver, showed me his planned outfit for the night, white sheepskin pants and a rainbow-colored top. The couple has traveled with Tony on many adventures, including to Sensation at the MGM Grand, Tomorrowland in Europe, and multiple shows by famed Japanese-American DJ Steve Aoki around the world. They are immersed in the culture and live and breathe PLUR. Through them, I understood better why Tony was so attracted to the culture. Heidy and Chad embodied it, too. For example, when I first moved to the Gold Spike in spring 2014, they lent me a mattress, bed frame, and a few other items. Chad even spent a few hours setting everything up.

The night of EDC, everyone gathered in Airstream Park before the event. Walking under the mist and twinkle lights, I saw Tony's pet llama Marley walking around as guests mingled. Tony was near the common area, talking to Emily Jillette, wife of Penn & Teller's Penn Jillette. When he introduced us, he said something about LinkExchange, indicating a deeper connection between his Vegas and San Francisco circles. There were a host of other people in the common area, many of whom I had never seen before, such as some former Zappos employees and others who were opening businesses in the area. The number of people who come into Tony's circle is constantly expanding, and it's rare to ever see him alone.

On the bus, I saw more of the usual crowd, including Maggie Hsu and other young Downtown Project and Zappos employees, some of whom had moved to other cities on the West Coast. Jenn Lim was there again, one of the few remnants, if the only, from Tony's raving days of his twenties.

I made my way to the back of the bus, where a young woman dressed as a leopard gifted me a bracelet to upgrade my costume, and a young man showed me the secret PLUR handshake. They were ingratiated into the tribe and its norms. When I asked Tony earlier about joining the group, he asked, "What kind of access do you have?" I shared that it wasn't VIP, and he said something about no cell phone service and relying on serendipity, just like Burning Man. EDC is a sacred space for him.

The bus ride to the Motor Speedway was filled with calm chatter as trance and electronic dance music playing through the speakers. Tony's date that weekend was wearing an outfit that appeared to be made of black pleather (artificial leather), something that video game heroine Lara Croft or Trinity from *The Matrix* would wear. Once, during a Q&A session with Qualifyor founder Kacy Qua, whose education start-up was funded by Tony (and then later shut down), he mentioned that of any character from a movie, he would most like to spend the day with Trinity. His dates caught on to this about him, and played up to characters for events like this.

Tony sat on the high chair checking emails on his laptop when a young Zappos buyer who was launching a fashion line called Melonhopper walked over to him and shared a story about accidently sitting in the men's section at an outdoor spa in Asia, where she was recently on a business sourcing trip for fabrics. The young woman, Lauren Randall, is a spitfire and the type that Tony likes to have around him. Her clothing brand is a take on *Kawaii* culture. The clothes are all pastel and high necked, and her models usually have pastel-colored hair and pale skin. Tony introduces her by saying, "Meet my friend, she's twelve."

After we arrived, Steve-O took a head count outside the bus, giving everyone clear instructions to meet either by the bus in the park at two in the morning or at this bus at two thirty. Tony stayed on this schedule all three nights of the event. Some, like Heidy and Chad, joined him every night, but most could handle only one or two at most.

Inside the event stood massive neon structures: multiple stages, a Ferris wheel, and colorful floodlights everywhere. As we descended into the arena and to the Buddha in the Neon Garden, we were greeted by a sea of ravers–most in their twenties and some even younger, though there were people of all ages in attendance. Electric Daisy Carnival is one of the largest and most commercialized raves in the world, owned by EDM entertainment mogul Pasquale Rotella. The group immediately started breaking off. Tony was on his cell phone at the bus inside the arena, trying to reach a friend he wanted to meet up with.

I followed Heidy, Chad, and their friends to one of the main stages. On the screen above it were words being spoken by a computerized female voice over the music. "We are all on this planet together . . . But *who* engineered us?" and other existential messages. It felt like Aldous Huxley's *Brave New World*, the book that captures the feeling of utopia/dystopia that emerges when a culture pursues pleasure at all costs.

The Zappos employee whom I'd gone to Sensation White with explained to me that the massive raves in Europe are sometimes called group therapy, "because that's exactly what they are." It's something that Tony wrote about in his book–how he's not typically the spiritual type, but raving gave him that overwhelming sense of spirituality:

> The entire room felt like one massive, united tribe of thousands of people, and the DJ was the tribal leader of the group . . . It was as if the existence of individual consciousness had disappeared and been replaced by a single unifying group consciousness, the same way a flock of birds might seem like a single entity instead of a collection of individual birds . . . I made a note to myself to make sure I never lost sight of the value of a tribe where people truly felt connected and cared about the well-being of one another.

Later that night, we found our way down to another stage. Tony arrived with his date; walking behind them were Anthony D'Onofrio, a founding member of cryptocurrency platform Ethereum, and Brad Johnson, the former Downtown Project employee who manages Airstream Park for Tony. Near the stage stood Janice Lopez, who'd conceptualized Airstream Park, and another early Downtown Project employee whom Tony met at Summit Series.

As everyone began dancing to the music, I saw Tony standing alone, wearing all white and leaning over the metal railing. He was transfixed by the fire displays, the dancers on stilts dressed as trees, and the massive, blinking owl behind the stage. When I asked him if he really enjoys raving or if he does it primarily for the benefits of social cohesion, he responded, "I like to see people experience the emotion of awe."

"Isn't that awesome?" Chad came up to me, pointing at the owl. "Check out that blinking. It looks so real!"

"Yeah, definitely," I responded. "But it's still so . . . manufactured."

The night took us back to the VIP area of the park, where everyone was sitting on the couches on top of the bus. Out of nowhere, a former Downtown Project employee climbed up the side of the vehicle and collapsed, exhausted, onto the roof, next to the group. "I can't believe I found you guys," he said, out of breath. "I was stuck in the Enchanted Forest . . .

"Wait! What the heck is the Enchanted Forest?!"

Everyone burst out laughing. Some members of the tribe that evening were still figuring out what their next step would be after having been laid off by Downtown Project, while others had taken the Zappos offer or left on their own terms. But they still felt protected, in a way, by the invisible walls around Tony's tribe.

The bus pulled in at around three o'clock on Monday morning, with some of the passengers reeling on synthetic drugs and alcohol. Some were in the sleeping cubbies. I remembered that before it became the *Delivering Happiness* bus, it was the tour bus for the Dave Matthews Band. The bus served both entities just as well: there are many parallels between the two.

That night was the third and last time I tried MDMA while in Tony's universe. I took a half dose so that I could still be on my game. But a member of the crew called me out for being too cognizant and alert; I was asking too many questions. Taking a half dose of MDMA seems like a good metaphor for my approach to this entire project: enough to be taken with belief and enough to maintain clarity. I often struggled with balancing the two.

I decided to publish a story about my experience at EDC for *Quartz,* highlighting how rave culture has profoundly affected Tony's business decisions. Under the headline "Zappos CEO Tony Hsieh Believes Rave Culture Holds a Key to Business Strategy," I wrote:

> Those close to him say that the losses and the subsequent press are taxing on him. That's why events like EDC are so important to Hsieh; they remind him of his original motivations . . . In a 2014 interview with *Playboy,* he explained that rave culture introduced him to the "hive switch," where people organize themselves for the greater good, like bees that live together as a unified force. It's a concept that Hsieh has pursued over the years and has elevated with his goal of making Zappos self-organizing.
>
> Jenn Lim, a longtime friend and CEO of Delivering Happiness, a company-culture consultancy that spun off from the eponymous book, met Hsieh during the height of the rave era during the dot-com boom. "There was the convergence of those two things [the rave era and dot-com boom], and that will never happen again," Lim tells *Quartz.* "It definitely was a pivotal time in [Tony's] life and in my life in terms of what I went through in coming across that culture and how it shapes and informs different things . . . There is this greater collective consciousness as a global society. You don't have to call it happiness; it's well-being, purpose, or PLUR."

After more analysis, I concluded the story with a quote from the early Ethereum founding member Anthony D'Onofrio because our conversation shed light on Tony's experiment with Holacracy: "Only around twenty percent of the population actually want to be leaders," he said, weaving through the crowd. "For many people, freedom is being told what to do." He says that he's not citing any hard data, but "an argument could be made based on the way humans have evolved into tribes."

While the issues at Zappos loomed, Tony still saw the value in investing in experiences: going to EDC, and taking a select crew into the Mojave Desert to an airplane graveyard to explore the possibility of bringing one of the airplanes into downtown Vegas. (Meanwhile, the concept for developing an airline at Zappos had yet to be realized.)

That evening, Tony's tribe hung in balance. Who was there was as notable as who wasn't: a lot of former OGs weren't; Fred Mossler wasn't there. Zappos's head of finance, Mike Akrop, and CTO Brent Cromley were both departing. DTP's director of finance Rob Solomon was on his way out. The foundation that Tony was using to build Zappos and Downtown Project–the theory of self-organization–felt like no foundation at all. It was as fluid and unanchored as a drug trip; a night at EDC.

A few weeks earlier, Emanuel Sferios, the founder of the non-profit DanceSafe, which provides booths with information about recreational drugs and test kits at raves, was invited into Airstream Park by one of its residents. He asked Tony if he would appear in his MDMA documentary. "You know who has even more influence than millionaires? Billionaires!" he pitched Tony in front of a small group. Tony said he'd think about it. A few weeks later, he emailed Emanuel and politely declined the opportunity.

If Tony's goal was to re-create the experience of rave culture downtown, the *Las Vegas Weekly* has documented his success with at least one resident with this passage:

> "I feel like I'm on something," the guy told [Container Park manager Doug] McPhail as he took in the park, the kids and parents, the happy vibe all around. "I feel like you gave me some kind of a drug."

Meanwhile, the politics inside Airstream Park had gotten so bad that residents noticed Tony hardly left his trailer anymore. The chaos was palpable and reached a fever pitch as the temperature in Las Vegas rose. One resident who had a new baby walked outside her door to find new livestock–chickens, llamas–on any given morning.

"Airstream Park reflects Tony's vision," an ousted member of his inner circle told me. "That's what he wanted. A bunch of people–kids–that were on hand and he was the Pied Piper of the pack running around. No rules or regulations."

The cascading system failure extended everywhere. Shift shut down that spring after a very brief attempt to fundamentally change the way people move in a city. Although Tony had already provided $10 million in funding, when Zach Ware approached him with his hand out again in fall 2014 for a cash infusion, Tony declined. The start-up's new tagline was "Shift happens"–incidentally, a foreboding statement. Zach gained his weight back over that time, and wrote in a blog post that the start-up nearly killed him. "We were too prideful early on," one of Shift's early employees offered as a diagnosis for its demise. Like many start-ups, its desire to scale too quickly befell the company. For the promise of one hundred Teslas, only twelve of them made it to Las Vegas. Zach told me that those Teslas were eventually sold to various buyers.

The same thing happened to Moveline, which was growing at a rapid clip to around a hundred employees and one day shut down operations completely and moved to Texas for new investors who rebranded the company as OneMove. Moveline couldn't pay its debts, something that fell upon its customers. Elizabeth Yin of LaunchBit had used the service to move back to San Francisco when she joined the accelerator 500 Startups as a VC, but because the company went under, she had to pay twice as much for her moving costs.

Even Downtown Project's "Sorceress" disappeared. Sarah Nisperos and Coterie were once lynchpins of Tony's "City as a Start-up" talk that he used to convince people to move to Vegas. There were other less notable failures, at least in the eyes of the public, that quietly faded away.

"Everything is a façade," a local tech founder observed. "Tony should have purchased the Ogden. When he moved out, every-thing fell apart. There was no core, no central meeting spot."

The local tech founder was right: many failures could be traced to the fact that there wasn't good, affordable housing downtown. When Tony conceptualized Zappos's move, he pitched employees on being able to live within walking distance from work. Most could not afford the Ogden, which now was asking $500,000 for its units, and places like the Gold Spike didn't work for families. (The Gold Spike is hard even for single people, at least as long-term housing.) When I asked Tony what his biggest regret was with Downtown Project, he told me that it was not ensuring there would be enough residential housing.

Entrepreneur Shane Stuart, whose juice bar Grass Roots was funded by Downtown Project, explained to me how hard it can be to attract business without the natural foot traffic, and especially after the Great Exodus, and the discontinuation of Tech Cocktail and Catalyst Weeks. When Grass Roots fell into the red, Downtown Project infused his company with an extra $10,000 to keep it operational.

"Everything can't just disappear at once," he said.

But the juice bar's days were numbered too. A year later, it would no longer exist. I was particularly sad to see Grass Roots go; it was one of the healthiest entities downtown. I used to go there every morning.

PASSAGEWAY TO BIBLICAL EDEN

Eden, Utah, is utopia in its own right. The road winding up to Powder Mountain goes deep within the Ogden Valley. Its majestic beauty fits its name; it resembles biblical Eden.

The beginning of the road is lined with large, white, regal structures: the Mormon Church. The Church serves as both a cultural and economic anchor for Salt Lake City and all of Utah. About halfway up the mountain sits the perch where Summit Series conducts its affairs. The entrepreneurial network bought Powder Mountain in 2013 for $40 million.

I made the pilgrimage to Eden to understand the mind of someone who broke all the rules: Google X engineer Dan Fredinburg, whom I had met at that first Catalyst Week and who trained to climb Mount Everest on Powder Mountain. He never made it back from Everest: Dan was killed in a 2015 avalanche there. Understanding Dan and Summit was a way to better understand Tony and the utopia from which he drew inspiration.

Eden is a place where many of the "dreamers and doers," as they call themselves, find refuge. The *New York Times* used the term "luxury self-actualization set" to describe them. The community includes ten thousand entrepreneurs, artists, and thought leaders from around the world, but a smaller subset attends its events regularly, and an even smaller subset lives in Eden. If things go according to plan, many more will move there over the next couple years as Summit Series builds its city upon the mountain. Its five young male cofounders dream it to be an epicenter for commerce, arts, and politics. They even pitched the White House on making Eden a modern-day Camp David. Their motto is "Make No Small Plans," and they have attracted names such as Virgin founder Richard Branson, Google chairman Eric Schmidt, and actress and philanthropist Sophia Bush into their network.

When I visited in August 2015, the core team was preparing for their annual adventure to Burning Man. They were working on their art cars, including a stretch limousine with a *Back to the Future*-themed hoverboard on its rooftop.

"There's this idea that people have that entrepreneurs are like Ayn Rand's *Atlas Shrugged*, with the world on our shoulders," explained Jeff Rosenthal, one of the Summit cofounders. He was sitting on a broken couch in the Summit HQ overlooking the Ogden Valley. "That's not true. We're doing it because we love it." Rosenthal and his four other cofounders are in their late twenties and early thirties.

That week, a shaman was in residency with the Summit crew. A few weeks earlier, it was a dominatrix. Both fall under the same purview of facilitating radical self-actualization, a deep inner knowing of self. I ran into the shaman in a nearby gathering place when he was coaching a visiting tech founder. The founder alternated between looking the shaman in the eye and glancing down at his phone.

"We all need to go back to where we were in the womb," the shaman Rafael Bejarano said, explaining the spiritual exercise he takes clients through. A Mexican citizen, Bejarano traveled the world and is considered a master sound healer. He seemed to possess a lot of wisdom for his forty-one years. "When we go back into that space, we're in a place with no fear. If we can just get *there* and rewrite our stories, then everything falls into place."

Earlier that morning, one of Summit's real estate managers took me on a tour and brought me up to a high perch on the mountain where the women of Summit were asked to bless the land. I was still an outsider to Summit Series but got the sense that within the community, the female entrepreneurs are more highly respected by their male counterparts than outside its bounds. It's part of what attracted me to the group after first encountering its members during Catalyst Week in Vegas. Many of the men that I met were like Dan Fredinburg and embraced Athena (feminine) qualities. "Everyone who came around Dan said, 'Now I have a great measuring stick for how I want to live my life,'" Jeff Rosenthal explained. I had observed that too in the short time I had known Dan. "There's a level of intimacy," he continued, describing how his friend had transformed in the last few years from an adrenaline junky to a more thoughtful and empathetic human being. "Type A, alpha male, you have this showcase–'*whoa, roar*'–but that's not actually the showcase of masculinity. The real power is when you can have that life and capacity and live that way with complete vulnerability and transparency."

I realized that part of my disappointment around what Downtown Project had become could be traced to that inaugural Catalyst Week. I was under the false impression that Downtown Project was going to be like Summit Series. CatalystCreativ founder Amanda Slavin had curated a group of people with real soul. Inspired, I had high expectations for the Downtown Project community after meeting this principled subset of entrepreneurs who seemed to operate by a different standard. Pseudo-entrepreneurs aside, I could sense that there was real dignity and freedom around the work that many of them do. It even felt magical. But the magic that Amanda pitched me on, which I experienced during those initial five days in November 2012, dissipated quickly. Just like pixie dust or the final sizzling of fireworks at the conclusion of a festival, before everything goes dark.

"How do you feel?" my mountain guide asked me after I had the opportunity to bless the land.

"It's like magic," I responded, looking over the valley.

The space is meant to feel sacred with divine energy. On the Summit grounds and within its community, there is a sense of "pleading to the Gods," a recognition of the influence of a spiritual dimension in provision and success. The entrepreneurial endeavor is so uncertain, with so much left up to chance, that this is one more element to tip the scales in one's favor.

Of course, there are no guarantees in life. Even someone as prepared as Dan Fredinburg–it was his second time on the mountain, after he'd narrowly escaped death the first year–wasn't invincible. Risk taking is glamorized within the Silicon Valley set, but the risks are real.

"There is a component that is Icarus," Jeff said. "Of all of our friends, he was most certain of his immortality. If you could ask Dan how he would have liked to have died, he would have said,

'Closer to the top.'" He then shared a story of how he spent the other weekend in a test plane with a friend doing negative G loops in the air. "If I die like this, it's not going to be surprising, but it would be a tragedy that will affect my loved ones. Putting yourself in these experiences and feeling the edges of life made Dan feel alive, and it makes a lot of us feel alive."

Hardly two weeks after my visit, I learned that the shaman I'd met atop the mountain was killed in friendly fire in Egypt. We had texted because I wanted to know more about what he was beginning to explain to me that day, about stepping into your personal power by going back to your origins. The tech entrepreneur sitting next to me wasn't really listening, but I was.

SHIBARI

"So you could really be suspended from the ceiling?" Lauren Randall, the spitfire Zappos buyer and creator of Melonhopper asked me outside the Griffin on Fremont Street. She was dressed as a fairy princess with bright purple hair. It was Halloween, and she was referring to my Shibari costume. I looked at the gunslinger ties and told her it probably could.

At Burning Man, I met an artist who practices Shibari, the Japanese art of rope bondage. As we searched for a disco spaceship art car in the deep playa, he explained to me the counterintuitive nature of it: "When you're all tied up, that's when you can actually free your mind," he said. It reminded me of something the Ethereum founding member said at EDC, how for most people freedom is being told what to do. He was referring to Holacracy and self-organization generally, based on the way humans have evolved in tribes. But I saw many parallels.

The Shibari artist and I were en route to the celebration of life ceremony for Dan Fredinburg hosted by the Summit community. Dan made a strong impression on me because he operated outside the bounds of normal society. Like Tony, Dan was a master game theorist. He understood how power systems worked, and that solutions, resources, and influence were about just finding a single entry point in. He was able to hack Google's bureaucracy and use its leverage against itself–classic judo strategy–in order to get funding to attempt Mount Everest.

His ceremony in the deep playa was filled with colleagues and other friends from San Francisco and Silicon Valley who were on a range of recreational drugs. For those like Dan, recreational drugs are a way to see the world differently. He and a former Google colleague even pitched a class to the University of California at Berkeley's Haas School of Business that involved taking LSD, citing its influence on visionaries such as Steve Jobs.

The day before Halloween, I'd run into Heidy on the Fremont Street Experience and shared with her my costume idea. She connected me to a man who operated in the underground Vegas bondage community, and he agreed to create the costume. His tribe, I realized, was just an extension and subset of the Burning Man community, which meant it's also closely interconnected to the ethos of Silicon Valley. They share similar views on extreme experimentation.

The bondage community views ultimate freedom as the ability to have clear boundaries and complete submission and complete control, depending upon their preferences. By defining the rules of the game, they could enjoy the game–sort of in the way that Brian Robertson described the rules of Holacracy. I asked the Vegas Shibari artist how they ensure that the power dynamics don't get misplaced or misused in normal life. "Doesn't that just mess with your head over time?" I asked him. "And pose a risk?" He said that it just takes some level of self-awareness to protect the space.

The night took us back to Airstream Park, where Tony was washing dishes in the kitchen and a young woman, Qualifyor founder Kacy Qua, was sitting by the bonfire. She'd worked previously for the X Prize Foundation, whose mission is to fund projects that will "lead to technological breakthroughs that will benefit mankind," founded by entrepreneur Peter Diamandis. After Qualifyor shut down, she focused on consulting with Zappos to onboard the company to Holacracy. Specifically, she was working on the badging process (badges denote skills and compensation). "It's *hard*," she confessed. "I'm speaking to everyone on a high level, and then I realized I was doing it all wrong. They don't care if Zappos changes the world with its new management system. They want to know that they're going to get a paycheck next month, and they want to know how to get a promotion." Holacracy had addressed certain aspects of the system, but not compensation, hiring, and promotions–some of the most essential parts of running a business. (Later, Zappos dropped the badging process.)

Still, Kacy believes that self-organized companies are the future. She shared that she met some young entrepreneurs from the Summit Series community in the Netherlands who were doing Holacracy. "They're *doing* it, and they're excited about it!" She had never heard of Sociocracy or the fact that the system originated in the Netherlands. For her, as for Tony and John Bunch, Holacracy is a high-level experiment.

A Zappos employee who worked in the call center and now worked in tech support expressed to me his opinion that "there's an empathy gap" with Tony and the Holacracy rollout. "He doesn't understand what it's like to worry about making rent or paying bills. He doesn't realize that if two badges have different compensation attached to them, we're not going to choose the lower one just because we want to pursue our passions."

Many employees still see it as a sort of "dance" that they need to do in order to get paid. And they still need to abide by the company's Ten Core Values. "Holacracy has made everything better," a longtime Zappos employee told me on the floor of the Smith Center during an All-Hands. "You can still be fired for a values violation. That might seem cultish, but it's true."

During the happy hour after the 2015 Q4 All-Hands, a young woman paced back and forth on the Smith Center lawn waiting to speak to a guy with blue hair and piercings. He was one of the employees who'd gotten up onstage at the end and thanked everyone for accepting him. Before joining Zappos, he worked as a manager at McDonald's.

"Here's the proposition," she told him finally. "We're doing a video series sort of like *Parks and Rec* that will explain how Holacracy and teal are working out at Zappos. It's part of the Brand Aura circle. And I would love to recruit you to write for us." The two had worked together previously in the call center as seasonal workers and then quickly moved into new positions.

The woman shared with me the moment that she realized she was "all in" with Holacracy. She was visiting a CVS walk-in Minute Clinic, and her doctor seemed rushed and had no bedside manner. "The doctor couldn't even look me in the eye," she recalled. "Then I looked at her and said, 'You didn't go to school for this, did you?' And in that moment, I realized, with Holacracy, with what Zappos is doing, we can free people from this. We can launch a movement and change lives in all professions."

Zappos wants people like this employee: people who are passionate about Holacracy. The company also had to hire more
call center workers to account for the fact that now so many call
center workers want to do other things in the name of Holacracy.

Navigating the minefield of teal and Holacracy is a daily challenge. "This is how we operate: ready, fire, aim!" one Zappos
employee put it. "Everything has always worked in the past. But
what if it doesn't work anymore?"

At the very back high table in the communal area at Airstream
Park one evening, Brian Robertson stood alone, drinking his beverage and taking in the scene. I didn't recognize him under the dark
lights. He told me enthusiastically that HolacracyOne was looking
at clients like Google–the very company that had spearheaded this
sort of flat structure but was now mostly bureaucratic as it has
grown to sixty thousand employees. Entrepreneurially minded
people such as Dan Fredinburg will always find ways around the
system; they don't need rules to free them to do so. But most
operate within the rule systems and need to be reminded of the
"ask forgiveness, not permission" ethos, even in Silicon Valley.

The next day Zappos hosted a "Virgin Disruptors" conference
at its headquarters, and Brian spoke passionately onstage about
the broken bureaucratic systems in corporate America today.
He had lost weight (something that he wrote about for *Medium*)
and looked like the young programmer he once was. There was
a season at his previous company, Ternary Software, where he
pushed the engineers to create software to break into the video
game business, a highly lucrative market. The effort failed, and
instead Brian focused on developing Holacracy.

I imagine that operating within a Holacracy feels a bit like
being inside a video game. At least, that's how it sounds when
people describe it.

REAL RESULTS

"We're not here to take part, we are here to take *over*!" the fitness instructor yelled at us from the front of the gym on the edge of downtown Las Vegas, just past the Arts District.

His words brought me back to the moment inside Dethrone Basecamp in Silicon Valley on the assault bike next to Nick Swinmurn. Both gyms are designed for intervals, boot camp style.

Real Results gym was founded around the time that Downtown Project was formed, but opted not to ask for funding because it wanted creative control and didn't want to be tied to a fifty-fifty partnership indefinitely.

"We started out with donated equipment," one of its cofounders told me. Real Results became one of the most sought-after gyms in Las Vegas, attracting the founder of EDC and other entertainment moguls. There are plenty of customers to be found in a very physical city where cocktail waitresses, performers, and club promoters want to look their best. Its emphasis on positive psychology as its guiding ethos also attracted Fred Mossler, Arun Rajan, and other Zappos employees. You can find them at Real Results at seven o'clock most weekday mornings.

One Saturday morning, I was unknowingly in a circuit group with one of the Holacracy implementation leads. As our instructor yelled, "Time!" and I let my thirty-five-pound disc weight drop from above my head to my side, she immediately called me out. "Come on, keep it over your head until we get to the finish line!" Also in attendance was the former communications director for Downtown Project, who'd left shortly after the mishandled response to the layoffs and management change. She moved out of the Ogden and bought a house with her family a few miles outside the main Fremont East District. In the early days, she was easy to spot at DCR and Gold Spike, with a drink in her hand. "I'm made up of Grey Goose," she joked onstage during one Lowdown.

Downtown Project has long been known for its hard-partying culture, something that still holds true. Even as one of the managers of Real Results spoke at the December 2015 Downtown Lowdown, guests enjoyed alcoholic beverages and the entire Place on 7th venue smelled of weed. But the culture of partying has started to wear on enough people, and Real Results is increasingly a destination for those within the ecosystem.

The gym, located inside a graffiti-painted warehouse just off Charleston Boulevard in the Arts District, is sparse and hardcore, with cement floors and high ceilings. Inside the gym, there is nowhere to hide during the group classes. On the wall are inspirational quotes etched by members of the gym, including this one from a Neil Young song: " 'It's better to burn out than to fade away'–Fred Mossler."

SYNCHRONICITY

Mark Rowland is an unassuming choice to lead Tony's Downtown Project. Mark is from Sydney, Australia, where he sought to create a replica of Zappos. It wasn't the first time someone has attempted to do that: there are Zappos imitations around the world–including Zalando in Berlin, and a host of other companies that have taken their playbook from the Zappos model, not the least of which are Downtown Project-funded start-ups such as Zirtual. But unlike some of the other copycats, Mark decided to email Tony: "I'm going to replicate your company in Australia, just so you know. Cheers." Mark was referring to the launch of his online retailer StyleTread.com, where he gave himself the title "chief happiness officer." To his surprise, Tony emailed him back immediately, suggesting karma as the culprit, as he had previously tried to replicate aspects of restaurant chain Wagamama (where Mark was then CEO of the Australian licensee at the time) years ago. Mark assumed that Tony was referring to his Venture Frogs restaurant at 1000 Van Ness in San Francisco.

Mark invited Tony to Australia, arranging for him to speak at a few different engagements, and later Tony invited Mark to tour his Downtown Project as it was getting off the ground. With Tony's $2.6 million in investment in ROCeteer, Mark moved his family across the world (his wife was convinced of the opportunity after attending Rehan Choudhry's Life Is Beautiful festival in fall 2013). While Mark was securing his visa, he mentored start-up founders via Skype from Australia. He played an integral role in sparking a discussion around mental health after the suicides and shared with me a story about how he contemplated taking his own life for a split second when he was trying to raise a Series B funding round for StyleTread. It came down to the wire, quite literally within hours. His current success is what has given him the platform and courage to speak about the topic. Many entrepreneurs in the DTP ecosystem speak highly of Mark. They all say that in addition to providing excellent business advice, he seems to genuinely care about their well being.

I first met Mark at Inspire Theater, where he was practicing a variation on Tony's keynote address to help evangelize the message. Afterward, we went to the Perch, a restaurant overlooking Container Park. He told me that he is certified in neuro-linguistic programming (NLP), a kind of psychotherapy based on positive psychology. It involves questioning deeply-held, limiting beliefs. He has seen it work miracles.

"When I look at my clock and see 11:11 or something, I know I'm on the right track," Mark explained. "Synchronicity."

In Mark, Tony saw someone who wasn't looking to him to jumpstart his career; he had already built one. Mark had battle scars and the inner knowledge of what it's like to risk it all. Instead of going local, or even national, Tony brought in someone from the farthest corner of the world to lead his revitalization efforts.

After the Downtown Project layoffs, Tony, Fred Mossler and the six decided that they needed to find a point person who could be the face of DTP. Tony no longer wanted to do it. Michael Downs and Millie Chou both immediately took themselves out of the running; being a public persona was not either one's strong suit. No one else in the group wanted to step up, either. Eventually, Tony settled on Mark to lead a new arm of the company, called DTP Ventures. DTP Ventures was a *portion* of Downtown Project; it did not encompass all of its scope. Mark was tasked with improving Downtown Project's image and pushing the venture, which was still deeply in the red, to profitability. Tony also asked him to improve the culture.

"THE PURGE"

On the Monday night before Christmas 2015, a small group gathered around a stone table near the bonfire in Airstream Park. It was primarily the OGs: Zappos's "Fungineer" Tyler Williams, Janice Lopez, Steve-O, Heidy Stamper, Tony's technical advisor Jeanne Markel (who had taken on John Bunch's role of "shadow"), and about a dozen others. They were sitting in lawn chairs around the stone table playing an impassioned game that involved charades.

Instead of holding plastic cups with shots of fernet or other hard liquor, the group was primarily sipping on glasses filled with red wine. "The Purge," as it came to be known, had been successful, and everything was right again inside Airstream Park.

The man who'd been tasked with carrying out the Purge was also in attendance. While driving me home from Real Results earlier that month, Brad Johnson framed it for me as a construction situation, while alluding to it being about something else. "My job is seventy-five percent politics," he explained as we approached Fremont Street. In reality, Tony just wanted the park to be filled with people he trusted again. So he asked Brad, who manages the park, to tell all of the non-culture fits to leave under the guise of construction. (There would be construction—later.)

"There's no one I'd do this for except Tony," he told me. "I have the best job in the world. One day I'm entertaining a Chinese festival executive and other cool people. But, yes, it can be stressful." Two months earlier, during the Life Is Beautiful festival, he managed the park's operations and the demands of its residents at all hours, pausing only to slip away briefly for a flight to Chicago to attend a funeral, and then returning for the remainder of the festival.

To create a greater sense of community after the Purge, Tony arranged for some of his closest friends to stay in crash pads for the month—to give the impression that the park was closer to capacity.

"You guys have to *actually live* in the park most of the time," he told his friends. Many had apartments at the Ogden, Juhl, or Urban Lofts, a group of industrial-style townhouses located downtown, but he wanted to have the real experience of community—going back to the days where Mimi Pham would arrange for breakfast in the mornings when she was in town, and Tony would message the group via Slack in the middle of the night to let them know he was making a batch of soup in the kitchen.

Tony no longer felt captive to his own experiment, hiding out in a tiny Airstream trailer. He emerged more and started spending evenings out by the bonfire again. All of the ousted residents were out by the end of November, and he surrounded himself with his favorite people in the weeks leading up to the holidays. He called it Winter Camp.

After the Purge, one of its former residents showed up at the biweekly jam sessions, open to friends of friends in the park. He had known what was going on but wanted to show that he had no hard feelings. Of course, there was no construction, only different residents in the trailers. He continued to show up to the biweekly sessions. "Still, no construction!" he told me with a laugh.

But more seriously, some of those who were forced out say that it took months to recover psychologically: "One day you're part of a community, the next, you're out."

FURTHER FUTURE

Inside Gold Spike, near the cornhole, Zapponians enjoyed free drinks from the bartender. It was an event to honor "Holiday Helpers" who went above and beyond the call of duty: that is, workers who spent additional hours on the phone beyond what was expected of them. Every holiday season, Zappos has a tradition where all employees are required to spend at least ten hours on the phone to support the influx in call volume. No one is exempt, not even Tony.

The previous week, the company had lost another fifty employees to the Supercloud offer. Between the original offer, the Supercloud offer, and other departures in 2015, attrition climbed to 30 percent. And that didn't include the percentage of tech workers that transitioned to Amazon in lieu of the Supercloud offer. In just twelve months, nearly a third of the company had walked out the door. Tony pointed out that Zappos's annual attrition is around 20 percent, still below average for a call center.

"When people leave, it's like a death," one call center worker wearing glasses and a red zip-up hoodie said, describing the effect of the layoffs and the bond that all the employees shared. "We're all family. We're a tribe, you see," she explained, pulling me aside to hammer the point home. She shared that she was one-quarter Native American and that her tribe in Utah was broken up. "The government said there weren't enough members, so we didn't exist."

Despite all of the departures, which certainly have affected the culture, the call center and Zappos University employees at the party didn't seem to harbor any negativity toward their employer. In fact, they were more excitable than ever. Zappos, it seems, is two separate companies: there's the business operations and tech side of things, and the call center and the softer-touch operations–the culture, the heart of the company.

One young woman sitting near the billiards table shared that what she loved about working at Zappos is that she can "be funny at work and have coworkers laugh at my jokes." She added, "And I can also wear this to work," pointing to the football jersey she was wearing. The woman sitting next to her nodded.

Another woman who'd previously worked at Liberty Mutual Insurance on the East Coast said that her old company prohibited swearing at work, whereas here, she could. "I heard someone say the word *bullshit* during a meeting, and it was so refreshing. It wasn't in an immature way; it was in a human way."

That week, I published a story on *Quartz* that disclosed the Supercloud offer takers, titled "Zappos Has Now Lost 18% of Its Employees to Its Radical Buyout Offer." I walked over to Tony.

"Why didn't you talk about how generous the offer was?" he asked in frustration, swirling his drink. Outside, pop and EDM music pulsed. "So what kind of message does that give to employees? What's the point of treating our employees well? We're damned if we do and damned if we don't." I couldn't tell if he was genuinely angry or if he was trying to see if I'd write another story that would change the conversation in the media.

COO Arun Rajan, who'd returned nine months after his dramatic departure during the (prescient) *Lion King* "Circle of Life" show at the 2013 Q4 All-Hands, said that the buyout was not a layoff. Yet Zappos was trying to get rid of its project managers, many of whom received nice salaries. In advance of the offer deadlines, a select few of them were pulled into a room with Arun and told that they were *highly encouraged* to take the offer.

What ended up happening was that many of Zappos's best employees ended up leaving. That's what usually ends up happening with self-selection: those who have other options or can see beyond the current situation depart a less-than-ideal scenario. Those with few other options stay, and they have become the ones tasked with making Holacracy the human operating system of the future.

During his time back as acting COO (he also worked at DTP as CTO), Arun emailed Zappos employees explaining that the company was in the process of looking for an external COO. Another executive familiar with the recruiting process shared that Zappos contracted with large recruiting firms to bring in a COO. He was hoping that they'd find someone who could diversify the good ol' boys' club. "If you don't have that original thought, not having anyone questioning," the former executive remarked, "a death spiral occurs."

A few weeks later, Arun announced that he would be filling the role. He told me that his return to Zappos was an intentional one: his nine-month hiatus at One Kings Lane revealed to him that the culture at Zappos was unique, as was his ability to have an impact as long as he had Tony's support. He got lucky in that he'd originally joined Zappos as CTO days before the Zappos-Amazon deal went through.

Tony's philosophy is to make a lot of bets, but not with those in his inner circle. Arun's return naturally raised some questions and led employees to ask: *Why would one of its top executives return so quickly?* Zappos is hardly a dot on the radar screen for the global e-commerce giant, but some wondered if Amazon was growing impatient with the company's experiments.

Supercloud, which had been Arun's idea, was taking up significant resources. "Thankfully we had enough people stay around," Arun told me. "But yes, it was absolutely difficult." And ultimately, Tony's decision to make a lot of bets at once–moving downtown, adopting Holacracy–was testing the wherewithal of his employees. "We were trying to figure out how to grow, grow, grow," he told me. But Supercloud put the brakes on the sort of exponential growth that characterized Zappos's earlier years. "You don't have to be growing all the time," Arun said. "[We decided] let's be true to who we are as a brand." Which, he explained, meant investing in longer-term strategies right now.

As the company wrapped up Supercloud, anyone on the tech team who had an innovative and low-cost idea that could push the company forward and rally the troops was rewarded. One of those was Manish Honnatti, an Indian-born engineer who risked his US visa (and in doing so gambled on being deported back to India) by declining a job at a top-tier software company while waiting to hear back from Zappos. He came up with the idea to focus on its best customers (building on the Best Customer Strategy) by creating a platform that would recommend items based on a customer's lifestyle preferences. He named his Holacracy circle "Zappos Zero," alluding to how the company was trying to get back to its roots.

How much slack Amazon is willing to give Zappos is a function of how much slack Wall Street is willing to give Amazon. At the start of 2016, investors were impatient with the company's still-yet-to-be-determined date for when it will deliver on its investment. (Yet over the course of the year, Amazon stock rose significantly.)

"We might as well not do anything good for employees," Tony continued. "We might as well be just like every other company out there. Give people two weeks [before letting them go]. Not treat them well. The thing that has gotten missed in this whole thing is just how generous we have been. Who else does this? Take two weeks, take a month, travel the world, climb a mountain."

When I pointed to the disenchantment that I was hearing from some of Zappos's departed tech employees, he took issue by suggesting that the type of person who would complain is the type of person who would find something negative about any situation. "Say that a forty-year-old minority is told at the end of the Zappos training that they should consider taking three thousand dollars, four thousand dollars, to quit. It has nothing to do with them being a minority, or forty," he said. "But they might interpret it as, 'they need to leave.' You're interpreting the buyout out of context; it's a generous company policy where we give people an opportunity to explore their options. What if we were like most companies? This person who was told they should consider leaving might have been told that their whole lives, and so that's their interpretation. But the headline ends up being, 'Zappos is racist, or doesn't hire older employees.'"

He speaks in sample sizes and control groups. "The group that is reaching out to you is self-selecting." Then he articulated his argument big picture again. "If you look at where the world will be in fifty years, where do we want our world to be? Not treating employees well?"

Moments like these were the ones where I couldn't discern how much he believed what he was saying and how much was PR spin. The line had blurred. One moment I thought I had it all figured out, and then the next he throws a curve ball. The reality is, it was probably some combination of both.

The call center employee from Utah who is one-quarter Native American, walked over again. Tony knew that she was an expert in Chinese cooking and asked her if she had come up with any new recipes recently. This sort of intimate knowledge about his employees is exactly the sort of thing that inspires loyalty.

The way out of the company's current predicament was to double down on culture, and that's exactly what Zappos was trying to do. It had recently created a circle devoted to culture. Part of the culture problem recently, according to one of its head recruiters, was the fact that Zappos had hired an influx of contractors, especially on the tech side. Because they were contractors, they were not required to pass Zappos's culture test.

One of Zappos's longtime recruiters told me, "Tony didn't just say, 'Let's fuck our culture.'" She had been one of the most adamant voices against Holacracy. Short of saying "I told you so," she expressed some regret at watching this experiment unfold.

Zappos's culture is important not just for the company's morale and productivity, but also because it's a means to a healthy line of revenue. In addition to income from tours and speaking gigs (it costs up to $30,000 even to have relatively unknown names from Zappos–i.e., not Tony–speak at events), there's Zappos Insights boot camp, which lets anyone attend three days of Zappos culture boot camp and costs $6,000 per attendee. The company has made its culture as much of its selling point as its core business. And it continues to generate revenue and interest around culture because Tony travels the world to promote the Zappos message.

Earlier that week, while sitting in a Zappos conference room that had its walls painted with an image of the Dalai "Llama" (a llama dressed as the Buddhist monk, in a nod to Tony's obsession with llamas), longtime recruiter and Zappos Insights lead Christa Foley lit up when she recalled a turning point from the All-Hands last summer.

"It was a big moment when Tony said, 'Let's put culture before Holacracy,'" she stated proudly. "I knew that Tony had recommitted." She also acknowledged what many Zapponians now speak about freely: "The joke is that this is a cult."

Yet for all the emphasis around culture and Tony's impassioned arguments around creating a better world with happier employees, sometimes it seemed that he couldn't be more apathetic about the whole thing. In fact, I often wondered if Tony even *believes* in happiness.

KÀ

Just before Valentine's Day in February 2016, Zapponians filed past the slot machines in the MGM Grand on the Las Vegas Strip and into its KÀ Theatre–one of the most stunning venues in the world built for its Cirque du Soleil in-house resident. One of its performers fell to her death in 2014 due to a technical malfunction, but the KÀ show lives on.

Most All-Hands are high energy, this one notwithstanding. After the 1,500 employees took their seats near the stage, the lights dimmed, and a large screen descended with the words "Zappos Q1 All-Hands." There was a feeling of nervous energy, the kind that goes along with uncertainty and spectacle.

Tony stepped onto the stage, wearing a black-and-white Western-style shirt, a rare deviation from his usual uniform.

"That was all they would let us do," he joked about the dramatic descending screen.

After some opening remarks, he walked offstage, and a video depicting the theme of this All-Hands began. It depicted a roundup of Zappos's successful PR campaigns from 2015: a viral marketing campaign around Thanksgiving called Pawlidays, a gift-giving campaign, and city visits around the country where Zapponians perform a good deed and "deliver happiness," a concept that Zappos's ad agency came up with a few years ago and has consistently been successful. The video was an attempt to remind employees of the good news, contrasting it against the wave of negative press in the past year.

All-Hands are rally-the-troops moments, and the event at MGM was a grand gesture to get the company back on point. The emotional appeal was strong, and employees got onstage to rally their coworkers. Lead links, who are de facto managers in Holacracy, from different circles walked onstage and described their purposes.

One employee from the payroll team stood onstage with the image of the Grim Reaper on the screen. He introduced himself as head of compensation. "I'm not the Grim Reaper; don't be afraid," he told the audience, seeking to placate everyone's concerns around the Zappos pay structure, which hadn't been figured out yet–*three years* after the company had adopted Holacracy–and was in an indefinite holding pattern. This meant that the average employee's wages might be frozen for a while, and what's more, Zapponians had little clarity around how much they might be making in the future.

The lack of guidance and answers regarding compensation is a major reason that Maggie Hsu called Holacracy a "bad Shakespearean play" in a white paper: it left the companies to contend themselves with the answers to the most import aspects–indeed, the foundational elements–of a business.

Two young men walked onstage; they had created a circle dedicated to conflict resolution. "With everything happening at Zappos right now, we want people to feel that they have tools to effectively manage tensions," they explained. The way they presented their idea, it felt like being led through group therapy. "Talking about people behind their backs won't get you very far," they summarized. "Being caring and thoughtful and addressing the issues fairly will. If you need help with processing your tensions, come find us."

In his 2015 book *The Happiness Industry: How the Government and Big Business Sold Us Well-Being,* British sociologist William Davies describes an endemic in Western society where corporations have begun to take on the task of managing the emotional well-being of its employees. Transitioning into a knowledge society sparked this change, where workers spend all day at their desks and focus on customer service and human relations more than physical labor. To perform well, employees need to be well mentally. CEOs are now psychologists-in-chief. Davies argues that we've swung too far and that employees mistake their employer's excessive concerns about their happiness as being for any reason other than their productivity.

The lights dimmed in the theater, and Tyler Williams brought out a Tiki torch into the center of the stage. The fire from the light was the only light in the house. A Zapponian walked onstage and began rapping. The young man began with rapping about a tough childhood and hard knocks, and how working for Zappos was his redemption:

He made change all right he eventually he became the change he wanted to see. You see to him this was a culture shock but to them he was a culture fit so to speak and all of a sudden my boy got on his knees and began the ascension to his feet and he stood up . . .

Delivering Happiness was my man's new mission, WoW was his business and business was good. Embracing and driving change in his own little weird ways. Keeping an open mind creativity became . . . an adventure . . .

And while the team was building a family spirit, and y'all know how real family do, doing more with less sometimes with only one point to prove . . . In the pursuit of happiness you got to be passionate and determined and most of all remain humble and you can't lose . . . 'cuz round here being good to people is our culture, the very lifestyle in which we choose.

The crowd started cheering. He rapped about the company as a tribe and asked why his peers weren't content with their pay because we're all just lucky to be here.

The theme of entitlement has resurfaced often at All-Hands in recent years. Some speculate that the perks and everything have become so expected that employees have lost sight of the company's mission. Everything is a spectacle; everything is over the top, so it is continuously difficult to top the previous perks. There is an expectation of grandiosity, to be entertained.

With the crowd riled up, Tony walked back to the center of the stage to deliver the sobering news of the All-Hands: the survey results from *Fortune*'s annual "Best Companies to Work For" list had come in from the company's employees, which revealed more dissatisfaction than any previous year. As the media had been reporting for several months now, employees weren't all that happy with Holacracy. Tony asked reporters in the audience not to share the details, and then went on to share that there will always be something to be angry or frustrated about. He gave the example of the company's move to downtown Las Vegas, which had dropped as a concern. Zappos didn't know if it would make the *Fortune* list this year, which had always been a huge selling point (it didn't).

For Zapponians, there are always changes and surprises under way, like coming back from vacation to discover that there are gender-neutral bathrooms. There is an expectation of change; nothing is fixed.

Every piece of bad news is countered with better news. Tony asked the crowd to answer this question: "What would you do with one extra day?" Then he instructed them to look under their chairs. A few people found a golden ticket. He asked what they'd do with a free day, and one woman yelled, "Go to a hotel for a night without my husband and children!" to hoots and hollers. Tony crescendoed the energy in the room by telling everyone that they had February 29 off.

Tyler joined Tony onstage and told everyone to share the announcement on social media with the hashtag #LeapDay. "We want to petition for a day off for everyone in the US!" he yelled to more hollers.

"But just remember, we want you to use the day well," Tony said. "Actually do something on the list that you created."

With a dramatic dimming of the lights and pop/dance music blasting over the loudspeakers, Tony introduced his father, Richard, who walked onstage in a full-body monkey suit.

"It's the Chinese Year of the Monkey!" he yelled to the crowd. The Chinese New Year had been the previous week, and he was announcing the grand opening of the new Zappos China office.

Many at Zappos aren't familiar with the company's operations in Dongguan, an industrial city just outside of Hong Kong. The office started as a base to develop its private label brand and evolved into a location that also managed workers who would handle the photo imaging for the site. It's relatively easy work that can be done for much cheaper overseas than in the US.

Richard gave a brief overview of the company's China operations, highlighting that "Zappos China has a direct line to Amazon." Then Fred Mossler, Arun Rajan, and Steve Hill, vice president of merchandising, walked onstage in full-body monkey costumes. Later during the All-Hands, they all got onstage to wish a longtime Zappos employee good-bye, and then, as the lights were dimming, pulled out minibottles of fernet and took shots together. Zappos was moving to a Holacracy, a more equal way of working, but the good ol' boys' club, as the former executive described it, would remain–challenging any real attempt at progress.

The second half of the meeting was a surprise performance of *KÀ* by Cirque du Soleil, a coming-of-age story about imperial twins who are on a perilous journey to manifest their destiny. The performance is one of the Cirque du Soleil's most spectacular for its acrobatics, with cast members flying seventy-five feet in the air, and for its pyrotechnics and stage design. Afterward, everyone filed through the casino into Hakkasan nightclub. Zappos happy hours are infamous, but this one topped most: Zapponians were dancing on granite tabletops as the DJ spun EDM and techno lights blared through the room. Janice Lopez was among those dancing on the granite, and she extended her hand to pull me up above the crowd. Next to me was a Zapponian who was a cultural ambassador but had become more jaded about the company's new strategy under Holacracy. Although it was only five in the afternoon, everyone was partying as if it were midnight. The DJ directed the crowd, and they responded. "We work *hard*, play *hard*!" the music pulsed, and everyone threw up their hands in unison.

The night ended in a dizzying haze, with culture leaders passing out taxi vouchers to everyone as they left. Emerging outside of MGM, I texted a Zapponian to see if there was an after party somewhere on the Strip. I had gotten to know the employee while living at the Gold Spike. Our run-ins ("collisions") in the communal kitchen evolved into more substantive conversations.

"Let me tell you a secret," I texted the employee, who works for the tech help desk. "Sometimes I want to be a Zapponian."

"Welcome to the Dark Side," he wrote back.

"Dark Side?" I responded.

"Well, it's a grey area. You know that ;)"

Even then, after all this time, I was still conflicted about what I thought about Tony, Zappos, and Downtown Project. The reason I couldn't figure out where I stood is because Tony holds his intentions close to the chest. I had resigned myself to the fact that I would probably always feel conflicted.

On #LeapDay, two Zapponians, Danielle Kelly and Garrett Miller, got married at Airstream Park to draw attention to how the company had created a paid day off on Leap Day. Tony officiated the ceremony for the couple, who were dressed casually and with tattoos running down their arms, behind an altar bedazzled with Zappos signage and with local news stations in tow. Through that publicity stunt, I realized just how much Tony had come to embody the Zappos brand and how much Zappos was about him. It was difficult to differentiate between the two. Maybe it was the ultimate branding strategy, but I wondered if it really made him all that happy, always being a walking brand.

IS LIFE BEAUTIFUL?

On a brisk February morning, the Zappos lobby was filled with Zapponians and community members alike. It was nine o'clock, and the lobby had mimosas and Bloody Marys, with music pulsing through the open courtyard. The Wendoh Media co-owners were wearing sunglasses and fashionable scarves and coats. Other Zapponians with bright hair walked around sipping the alcoholic drinks before the workday. Several Zapponians peered down from the balconies encircling the courtyard.

As usual, Tyler Williams, who sports a red beard, was standing with the audiovisual team, making sure the sound equipment and speakers were ready. Zappos was live-streaming an art graffiti-off, where artists painted images in the courtyard in a competition. It was the official kickoff and announcement of the dates and bands for Life Is Beautiful 2016.

Years ago, Rehan Choudhry, the Pakistani-American entertainment executive who'd conceptualized the festival, would have been thrilled to experience the atmosphere on the campus that morning: seeing the effect that Life Is Beautiful has had on Zappos and how both Tony and Tyler were betting on Rehan's vision to lift up downtown and Zappos. They started calling Life Is Beautiful a movement, the same way that Delivering Happiness is a movement. The Life Is Beautiful team even created a manifesto, which begins with: "Life Is Beautiful is a movement. We are a soul collective. Among us are dreamers and doers, challengers and compassionates, optimists and outliers. We inspire and transform. . . . So if you've just dropped in, join us. You'll fit right in."

But Rehan wasn't involved in any of that. After the 2014 festival–overseen by Andrew Donner–Tony handed over the festival reins to the Wendoh Media founders Justin Weniger and Ryan Doherty. He invested several million dollars into Wendoh and established a fifty-fifty partnership with the founders to operate the festival and run a few DTP-owned bars and restaurants. Life Is Beautiful has reportedly lost more than $20 million in its first three years, around the amount of its initial investment. However, festivals typically take a few years to hit profitability.

The final separation between Tony and Rehan happened in early 2016. In a LinkedIn post describing the aftermath, Rehan posted graciously, "Be good to each other."

Rehan is now regaining his footing with a new project. He told me that he's working on a hybrid media and events entity called A Beautiful Perspective and that he's raising $3 million; did I know of any investors? I told him that I didn't.

Milling through the crowd that morning were Zappos's resident historian Paco Alvarez, Fred Mossler, and Joey Vanas, who runs another, smaller DTP-funded arts festival in downtown Las Vegas. DTPers were there to live-stream the event with their iPhones. A local pastor was in the Zappos lobby, absorbing the scene. The community rallied around the event. The activation came together in only just a few days: it was a prime example of self-organization working at its best.

Janice Lopez, who had recently returned to Vegas after a short stint at a start-up in Texas, played a key role in the event. When I saw her that week at an artisanal coffee shop next to the Airstream village, Janice spoke about creating an Airstream community in Joshua Tree, a desert campground in the California desert. "What if I could create these communities all over the world?" she posed. Tony gives people a taste of their dream jobs, enough so that it's hard to go back to anything else.

But as journalist Paul Carr pointed out in his feature-length story for *PandoDaily*, "A Holacracy Of Dunces," Tony doesn't always deliver on his promises:

> Ultimately, of course, many of these dreamers would end up leaving Vegas, some unhappily. Each has his or her own story of the moment they realized it was time to go, but there are common themes: Hsieh was brilliant at painting a picture of utopia. But his famed phobia of conflict or confrontation meant he wanted nothing to do with actually negotiating the terms of delivery. For that he would hand things over to a constantly fluxing group of advisers, hangers-on, family members, yes-men, waifs, and strays who would–in some vague way–be responsible for figuring out how to deliver on Hsieh's promises.

As Janice explained to me, "There's a lot of pain. And there are a lot of assumptions from people that Tony would fund them. People take what Tony says at face value. 'He said I should do this,' and so people think that they should."

But Tony sees the ecosystem more than the individuals who make up the ecosystem. "He's looking at everything from this far-off place, from over here," she pointed far to the left. "He's looking at the system, the ecosystem. And that means he's sometimes removed from the human emotion aspect of things in the now moment. He trusts in the *process*. When I ask why certain people are here, certain things, he says he trusts in the *process*."

FROM THE BIBLE BELT TO VEGAS

"Look *happier*!" Melonhopper founder Lauren Randall commanded one of her models. The model was dressed like Barbie, wearing a pastel-colored rainbow wig and copious amounts of makeup. The way she was standing, in Melonhopper clothing, high platform heels, and with bold makeup, there was an edge to her innocence. That's the idea behind Lauren's interpretation of *Kawaii*, the clothing style that originated in Japan.

Lauren grew up in the heart of the Bible Belt in Fayetteville, Arkansas. After graduating from college, she received an offer from a Christian fashion label in Tennessee. Before relocating, she took a detour weekend trip to Las Vegas and never turned back.

Professionally, it has paid off tenfold. Tony is among those who encouraged Lauren to go out on her own and create a clothing line.

"Tony is creating his own universe, so I decided that I want to create my own universe," she told me. "I pitched him the idea to build castles downtown, sort of like the Magic Kingdom, and he told me that I totally should."

When Lauren learned that the Irish singer Enya lives in a castle in Europe, she asked him if they could bring her to Airstream Park. He forwarded the email to a Zappos employee and a partner in Wendoh Media to see if they had any ideas.

Standing in the warehouse studio, which was designed so that there were two sets–including one with a large Victorian-style bathtub, where another model wearing a midriff-bearing pastel two-piece and platforms was sitting inside, surrounded by stuffed animals and Care Bears–Lauren's boyfriend Christian Velazquez took out his iPhone and used Snapchat to capture the scene.

The model Lauren had commanded to look happier cracked a slight smile while still maintaining her resting bitch face. The model is a computer programmer by day, EDM DJ by night, and manager of technical operations/model for Melonhopper. She embodies the feminist undercurrent of the brand Lauren is seeking to create.

"Here, check this out," Lauren walked over to Christian and me, pulling up an Instagram account revealing a woman who was also dressed in *kawaii*. She, too, looked like she belonged in an adult Disneyland. "It's Chrissa Sparkles! She's modeling for us too. Oh God, I love her."

Lauren looked and dressed like her models, in a short skirt, tight pastel crop top, and bright red lipstick. For all of its perceived superfluousness, there is serious money to be made in the *kawaii* fashion market. It's a niche community, but a passionate one: its consumers view *kawaii* as an identity and a lifestyle.

Christian offered a philosophical, high-level explanation for why the market is growing. "This style says something about where our country is headed, with more open-mindedness. We now judge less on what we're wearing. I don't think I'd wear a suit with that fabric," he said, pointing to a shade of light pink in front of us, "but I wouldn't judge a guy who did. The entrepreneurs and small businesses will be the ones to first come out with these new styles. The mass-market companies won't risk it. They'll get there eventually, but first companies like Lauren's need to reach people. And it's amazing: you now reach people in the Bible Belt because they see girls share images of themselves in these kinds of outfits on Instagram. That's how it spreads."

One night while partying with Lauren and Christian, I met one of his friends from Harvard, who'd previously been a pastor and authored a book about interracial faith. Several drinks in and on the rooftop of Commonwealth, overlooking downtown Vegas, he told me why he left the church. "I discovered that I could do more good by being an entrepreneur," he reflected. He was in his early thirties. "There was too much dogma to contend with in the church. As an entrepreneur, you can actually have a real influence."

In Airstream Village after the photo shoot, Lauren introduced me to the cofounder of Kappa Toys, a woman named Lizzy New-some, who is half of a husband-wife team. She was also dressed in *kawaii*. During SXSW in Austin, Tony walked into her toy store, which was in the process of shutting down. He asked if she and her husband wanted to open up a location inside Container Park. Given a lifeline, they immediately said yes.

"Dressing like this is my antidepressant," Lizzy explained. She was wearing a light-pink coat with puffy sleeves. "That's what it comes down to. If I have the worst night but I get to wake up and wear a neon dress, I'm happy."

Lauren nodded. "Most people, especially women, dress for others. With this, it's all about dressing for yourself." At Zappos, Lauren worked on the private label team. Most of the dresses she bought were black: it's what women wanted, and a sure sales bet for the retailer. "When you wear black, it's like you're telling the world, 'Don't look at me. Let me hide.' When you dress like this, people run up to you on the street and ask you to take a picture with them."

"ENTREPRENEUR SCHOOL"

The 9th Bridge School is located at Bridger Avenue and Ninth Street, just a few blocks away from the activity on Fremont Street.

It's Tony's brainchild, but his cousin Connie Yeh realized the vision. It was a multimillion-dollar effort to create the sort of school for the future. The US education system is one of the areas that Tony wants to disrupt. He believes in training people to think for themselves (to be entrepreneurs) rather than memorizing facts–making him part of a much larger movement behind the push for education reform.

Connie was equally passionate about the idea of creating a new system that goes against the status quo. Like her cousin, she grew up in an Asian family that prioritized grades and performance above all else. It led her to the Wharton School and a job on Wall Street, which made her parents happy. But building something from scratch, thanks to Tony's multimillion-dollar investment, has given her an opportunity unlike anything she would have dreamed up herself.

Like many of the tech entrepreneurs, Connie was entrusted with a lot of money and very little oversight. And like her peers within the DTP ecosystem, she is uncomfortable talking about the amount of money and risk involved. "We're handling people's children, people's money," one person integral within the ecosystem confessed. "I'm among those who don't really want to talk about the fact that I've never done this before. For most of us, we've never done these things before. But how do you get experience? You have to start somewhere."

Whenever I asked Tony about this, he gave me the same response. "Uber wasn't created by people who knew the taxi industry," he countered.

The 9th Bridge School is a gated, renovated former church. Its stained-glass windows and church bell reveal the building's origins. Inside the gate and through the courtyard, Connie led me quietly around the first floor. There were windows that showed dark playrooms where infants were sleeping. It looked like an incubator. As we continued down the narrow hall, I saw older children, up to a year or so old.

"Aren't they cute?" she remarked.

She took me into a room near the playground where the children had two special teachers who were passing through Vegas:

it was Dana Albany and Flash, the Burners whom I had lived next to for a season.

"We're teaching the kids to create mosaics," Flash said, his white hair as wild as I remembered it.

The 9th Bridge School started with fifteen children and now has about fifty, from infants to second graders. Originally, the idea was that 9th Bridge would be a place where Zappos employees could send their children to school. However, the private school, which costs several thousand dollars annually, doesn't work for most Zapponians.

Connie led me over to the stairway and up to the second floor. She pointed to a small pulley system with a bucket sitting next to the railing. "Our kids are encouraged to use design thinking, systems thinking, and engineering," she explained. "They decided that a pulley was faster than carrying art supplies up and down the stairs. Everything is designed so that the students have choice," she continued, pointing to a student-created glass elevator like the one from *Willy Wonka & the Chocolate Factory* and a collage depicting *Alice in Wonderland*.

In his keynote, Tony likes to say that 9th Bridge is designed with neuroscience in mind.

"Teaching kids that failure is good," she said, articulating the school's mission. "It's the learning process."

I got to know a set of parents who lived in the Ogden and sent their two children to 9th Bridge, and they were always enthusiastic about it. After Flash and Dana visited, their oldest daughter returned home and proclaimed that she wanted to be an artist. Her mother, an entrepreneur herself, took it to another level and secured a booth at the local arts festival First Friday, so that her daughter could sell canvases of her artwork to passersby. "You gotta start 'em young!"

her mother told me. I imagine the young girl always took home a profit because her canvases sold out every time. I purchased one of them as a Christmas gift for my sister. I also think her mother might have been trying to get Tony's attention.

ATOMIC LIQUORS

Atomic Liquors is the oldest bar downtown. It's on Fremont between Tenth and Ninth Streets, farther east beyond the other establishments and in the middle of the stretches of empty parking lots and bus stations that draw the homeless population. DTP purchased Atomic Liquors and its surrounding land for an inflated $3.48 million in 2014.

The building itself is a dive bar, darkened inside with few windows. It is the sort of place that you go just for the alcohol; there isn't much else to see. Yet it was the heart of Vegas in the golden days of the 1950s and 1960s, when the Rat Pack would perform and then sit on the rooftop and watch the atomic bomb mushroom clouds rise from the Nevada Test Site sixty-five miles northwest of the city. One evening, I sat down with the bar co-owner Kent Johns, and he briefed me on Vegas history: about the golden days, the "atomic cocktails," how Frank Sinatra used to spend a lot of time downtown with showgirls, and how the mob ran the city.

Because of its proximity to Airstream Park, Atomic became Tony's new bar of choice when he moved out of the Ogden. First it was Michael Cornthwaite's DCR, then it was the Gold Spike, and now it was Atomic Liquors that enjoyed the $500 bar tabs.

Tony sat in a booth in the back corner with Tech Cocktail co-founder Frank Gruber and his technical advisor, Jeanne Markel, who shadows him everywhere. Tony ordered a round of drinks and shots for everyone. "I just started a low-carb diet, so I'm going to do tequila," he explained. "I do this about once a year, and I'll lose, like, twelve pounds in about eight weeks."

Frank, whose start-up Tech Cocktail was a primary recruiting tool for Downtown Project and the Vegas Tech Fund, was there to meet with Tony about getting approval to restructure the company so that it could raise outside funding. Tech Cocktail, now rebranded as Tech.Co, has hosted twenty monthly events in Las Vegas, bringing in entrepreneurs from around the country to showcase Downtown Project and give them access to the Vegas Tech Fund. Tech.Co did a significant amount of PR for DTP, and DTP was also a good platform for the Tech.Co brand–a mutual win-win. DTP also benefited from Tech.Co's vast national network. Even while hosting the monthly events in downtown Vegas, Frank and his partner (and now wife), Jen Consalvo, traveled to more than fifty cities around the country to host similar events.

DTP has undoubtedly made life more interesting for the couple, who became parents in late 2015, but they were concerned about getting the sign-off on their paperwork so that they could move forward with pivoting their company to focus on content instead of events.

"We've been to a lot of [start-up] funerals lately; we just don't want one to be our own," Frank told me later. (When I asked whether Tech.Co was profitable, Frank and Jen explained that they spent their investment money, which is what investors expect you to do–"we weren't generating so much revenue so that we could grow." And they did.) They had made the decision to go all-in on Vegas, purchasing a loft and starting a family. Aside from inside Container Park, it's rare to see young parents downtown.

The sort of legal holdup that Frank and Jen were facing was

not uncommon and is a by-product of the rushed and fly-by-the-seat-of-their-pants nature of Downtown Project and its mission to revitalize a city in five years instead of the usual fifteen to twenty. The holdup was around the tax structure, they told me. While each start-up is an individual entity, from a tax standpoint, for Tony everything is interrelated.

"I'm not doing fernet tonight," Frank insisted.

Our shots arrived, and Tony waited for us to down them in unison. The ritual of drinking is something I've never seen him give up.

The night's conversation started innocently enough, but it took a turn after I asked him why he used the *Delivering Happiness* brand to extend to the entirety of the Downtown Project, when entrepreneurship was mostly not a very happy endeavor. In advance of our conversation, I had sent him a talk by conservative columnist David Brooks of the *New York Times* about how there's no rule for suffering in happiness culture. His only response to that email was: "Are there any next-action steps?" (verbiage used in productivity guru David Allen's *Getting Things Done*).

There was a happiness backlash going on in America, and his brand wasn't immune. There's also a subtle backlash emerging around the cult of the entrepreneur. Rand Fishkin, founder of the SEO (search engine optimization) analytics company Moz, is among the entrepreneurs who are demanding more honest conversation about just how difficult it is to build a company. He has a forthcoming book about the topic, with the working title *The Transparent Entrepreneur.* The psychological, emotional, and physical ramifications are often far deeper and more challenging than the media make the entrepreneurial lifestyle out to be. In recent years, as the funding market has become more lucrative and accessible, there has been an influx of entrepreneurs who are "playing house" in Silicon Valley and beyond.

"*Delivering Happiness* is about Zappos," Tony deflected. It was, but Zappos and *Delivering Happiness* were the selling points for the vision. Downtown Project was always about Zappos, and Zappos was all about delivering happiness. It's impossible to unravel the interconnected ecosystem: former Zappos employees are VTF investments, and there is a revolving door between Zappos and Downtown Project.

"If this were a city full of happy people, that would be the best sort of advertisement," a VTF founder once said to me. "But no one's happy here." Another early follower, who worked at a number of tech funds in administrative and related roles, described the early scene as "manufactured." Urbanist Leah Meisterlin, who is an assistant professor of architecture at Columbia University, echoed the sentiment in her report, "Antipublic Urbanism: Las Vegas and the Downtown Project" for *The Avery Review*: "Walking along Fremont, I felt no active excitement, spontaneity, or curiosity, but rather the growth of a scripted narrative and a correspondingly enforced restraint."

We kept sipping our drinks, and the conversation began to feel heavier.

"You never answer anything directly," I said. Frank, wearing jeans and a button-up shirt, nodded in agreement. He had interviewed Tony multiple times onstage for his Tech Cocktail events. Granted, Frank was part of Tony's PR strategy, but it was sometimes frustrating to interview someone who spoke only in marketing sound bites.

We ordered another round of drinks. Tony did offer up one new and interesting piece of information, which was that there was a chance he had spent more than $500 million on the project, though he said he didn't know. The investment vehicle is a function of Amazon stock, and so, as I understood it, whenever the stock rose, the remaining available investment amount rose.

Frank and I started asking him questions that everyone wanted to know the answer to: Is he frustrated that everything hasn't gone as well as he planned? Why didn't he bring in seasoned venture capitalists? Or more mentors?

"There's an interesting study around this thought exercise. Imagine if the Chicago airport was gone, how would you turn the land into a forest? The normal academic answer would be to look at all the species in a forest and transport them from another destination and it'll be a forest," Tony responded. "But it still needs to go through an evolution process in order to get there. Without those initial species existing you'll never get to that final stage. For example, Catalyst Week talks don't exist today. But that doesn't necessarily mean that they shouldn't exist in the future."

"So you really believe in self-organization," I replied.

"I believe in evolution," he said.

"You never give the full truth," I pushed, frustrated with his theoretical responses.

"Are you calling me a liar?" he shot back. "What if something you did based on good intentions was totally misconstrued?" Frank and I looked at each other: it sounded like Tony was about to break down. At a Zappos All-Hands, he once shared that he cries only when he's happy.

Like many trained CEOs, Tony knows how to say a lot without saying anything at all; that is, speaking in PR platitudes without answering the question.

Then he turned the tables on me. "What would *you* do? Why can't you offer an example of a question that I didn't answer? I am not a liar. That is what's the must hurtful."

"It's not anything specific," I replied. Now my voice started to crack. "I know what it means to give up everything with good intentions and be misunderstood." It was too difficult to hold back; tears started falling down my cheeks.

The night evolved from a slotted thirty-minute conversation to two and a half hours of attempting to resolve tensions, and I couldn't stop crying. I was frustrated that this person and the vision he had cast–which I had crafted my life around–was not what it had appeared to be. Cognitively, I knew this much earlier. But what led to the breaking point was finally asking him questions that got to the heart of what felt disingenuous about it. I pressed Tony on why he hired so many inexperienced leaders and why entrepreneurs weren't given more support. Many had uprooted their lives and followed him, expecting the support of an authentic, purpose-driven community, only to be left to fend for themselves. I asked Tony if he could reconcile happiness culture with the fact that entrepreneurship is mostly about suffering. I was not satisfied with his answers.

In his feature about Holacracy for *PandoDaily*, Paul Carr wrote that the only time he nearly cried in his professional career was sitting at a table with the author of *Delivering Happiness*:

> Hsieh arrived at our late-evening meeting surrounded by his usual entourage and clutching a Solo cup filled with happiness. I explained the crisis, entirely of my own making, and asked–begged, really–for him to put our personal disagreements aside in order to ensure my employees [at NSFWCORP] could make rent. I'd repay the loan with interest as soon as our (already committed) funding came in.
>
> It wasn't his answer that brought me close to tears, rather his unwillingness to give one. Instead he suggested we try to close

our new round sooner. Every entrepreneur who has lived the gap from "yes" to cash knows what a punch in the gut that is. Hsieh then invited a member of his entourage into the room and asked me to repeat my tale of woe to him. After I'd humiliated myself for a second time, Hsieh asked the interloper: "What do you think I should do?"

When I shared with one of Tony's deputies what had happened that night, she assured me that it was common. "During our meetings once, I just started crying harder. But it didn't work." Whether it was tears, or sadness manifested as anger, engaging with Tony in earnest brought many to the brink with their emotions.

Later that night, Frank called after I'd arrived back at the Gold Spike. He couldn't believe what had just happened and offered his support. "It's like therapy," he empathized. In that moment, I got a glimpse of what it would have been like to be part of the tribe. "So this is what it could have felt like, to be here with friends."

Lying down on the air mattress in my Gold Spike dorm, the EDM music blaring outside my window, I felt like I was at Burning Man all over again–a reminder that this place still didn't feel like real life. It still felt transient and unanchored. Seeking more stability, the following week I moved into a hotel room in the Gold Spike Oasis.

THE FUNERAL

The next time I saw Tony was a week later, at a funeral, held at another bar downtown. The co-owner of Atomic Liquors died that weekend of complications during gastric bypass surgery. Like many Las Vegans, especially in its nightlife underbelly, Kent

Johns lived hard, and his body showed it. He once took me on his golf cart to help transport cases of liquor to a party in Airstream Park. The surgery was supposed to be a gateway to a new life, but he never woke up to experience it. Kent was just fifty-three.

The funeral was held at Place on 7th, a venue between Ogden Avenue and Fremont Street. While I was standing outside waiting for Lauren Randall and Christian Velazquez, Tony walked up wearing his Zappos T-shirt and jeans uniform. At the same time, Kim Schaefer, the former communications lead for DTP, arrived at the door. She had stopped attending DTP events once she departed the company soon after the Dirty Thirty.

"Group hug," Tony said and hugged us both. I remembered how in the early days of the project, Kim was protective of DTP and called herself Mama Bear.

At Ovik's funeral in 2014, Kim had been angered by the fact that a local journalist was there. She wanted to find a way to get him out. This time she no longer had the same role as DTP's Mama Bear, but I still felt like she might ask me to leave.

Lauren walked up, and she was wearing black. Janice Lopez was there too and spoke to the "polarity of everything in this city. There are the highs and the lows, and nothing in between."

As we walked out, Janice looked at the ceiling. "We were going to put glass fish tanks up there, but it was too expensive," she said in a voice still filled with possibility. She told me that she had decided to travel with Tony and another one of his friends to Necker Island, Richard Branson's private paradise in the British Virgin Islands, in a few weeks. "It's, like, you invest everything in one fell swoop. Where else in the country does this happen?"

I gave her a hug good-bye and then walked over to the bar with Lauren and Christian. We ordered shots in honor of Kent: lemon drops for Lauren and me, and tequila for Christian.

"Kent would tell me that I am beautiful," Lauren said wistfully, referring to the way that Kent didn't have any difficulty telling people exactly what he thought, and dispensed compliments freely. It was a deviation from the hard and sometimes overly cynical Vegas culture, where compliments are just a precursor to a transaction.

Guests mingled at the bar and took shots in his honor, as Kent would have wanted. After the last call at the bar, everyone dispersed back into the streets, which were more alive than when we'd entered the venue. Friday night in Vegas was just beginning.

DELIVERING HAPPINESS

Next door to Twitter's headquarters in the gentrifying Mid-Market District of San Francisco (where the homeless population is still very present and aggressive), is a high-end coworking space. I met Jenn Lim at the front desk, and she led me inside, past security and the Buckminster Fuller dome, similar to the one in Container Park. A few people were sitting inside the dome with their laptops, having a meeting. The Buckminster Fuller dome has become a popular symbol for Silicon Valley: initially it represented potential and innovation; now is an icon for insularity.

"Do you want anything?" she asked, motioning to the beverage station to the right. I wanted to get water but the ionized water machine looked too confusing. Jenn had just returned from TED in Vancouver, British Columbia, with Tony and others. Alfred Lin was there too.

In San Francisco, Jenn gets to fly outside Tony's center of gravity. Like Alfred, Jenn is someone that he's known for years and could trust with the responsibility of managing his image.

She and Tony share many qualities: both are soft-spoken, Asian, hold a tool kit of jargon around happiness, and are mostly approachable.

It's been six years since she first embarked on the bus tour that became the catalyst for her life's work. It came together in a matter of weeks and set the foundation for a career that she never imagined when she was laid off as a consultant during the dot-com boom. Stories like Jenn's are reminders that those who operate in Tony's world long enough often see dividends, sometimes years later. It's a historical precedent that has proven out for several, and is part of the motivation that keeps people around.

"We had to go through several bus drivers before we got to Steve-O," she explained nostalgically, referring to the tour. The bus needed a driver that fit its cheerful image. "We had this Australian guy who would yell 'Fuck!' to other drivers and get road rage, and we're like, 'No!' That's not good for the brand."

After the tour, when Jenn had already been acting as a lead evangelist for *Delivering Happiness*, Tony asked her almost as an afterthought, "You want to be CEO of this, right?"

"And I said, 'Yeah, I thought I was already doing that,'" Jenn explained. "It just seemed natural; an organic process." In Tony's world, that's how people land their jobs: by default.

Jenn has had a hard time figuring out how to make Delivering Happiness a sustainable business. It's been propped up mostly by Tony's speaking engagements and her own gigs, as her speaking fees have also risen over the years.

While Jenn was busy building Delivering Happiness, Zappos created Zappos Insights as a separate anchor to promote Tony and the company culture. Any speaking engagements done on the Zappos campus would go to Insights, and any outside of the campus went to Delivering Happiness. There would always be some tension between Delivering Happiness and Zappos Insights over the years, because in some ways they became two competing entities.

Jenn shared that in early 2016 she laid off more than half of her twenty-five-person staff, paring the group down to ten. The team doesn't have an office space and usually works out of an employee's apartment. She told me that they also own an Airstream just outside the city.

"I did a reassessment and decided to simplify DH," she explained. "I should have done this a long time ago. It's Business 101."

She let go of what she calls variable talent–mostly designers– and now has a core team of business development and sales. "We need to move away from speaking engagements as the primary source of income." The goal is to move toward becoming a sustainable consultancy.

Delivering Happiness has a portfolio of formidable clients, including McDonald's and a sixty-thousand-employee New York health care chain. But the business of happiness can be fickle and difficult to secure over the long term after an initial push. In lean times, happiness initiatives are the ones that are cut. A package with Delivering Happiness costs around $115,000 to $200,000, depending on the client and how long it wants the service.

The word *happiness*–especially today, as the pop psychology revolution has been replaced by a focus on authenticity and vulnerability–doesn't always sit well with companies. One of its most reliable and longtime clients, New York City–based discount clothing retailer Century 21, has incorporated the Delivering Happiness model but replaced the word *happiness* with *flourish*. Interestingly, Delivering Happiness was tasked with correcting the culture at Downtown Project when it took a dip, to no avail.

Jenn dismisses the happiness backlash that William Davies

describes in his book *The Happiness Industry*. Even if "happiness" is getting a more superficial rap in the United States, it's gaining traction around the world.

Jenn's Facebook profile photo proves the fact: her background shows her standing center stage at a venue in Dubai surrounded by a sea of sheiks dressed in white. She gave her Delivering Happiness talk in the United Arab Emirates (UAE) a year ago, and now she's preparing to return. Dubai just announced that it appointed a minister of happiness. "Dubai is Vegas on steroids," she told me.

According to the World Happiness rankings, the UAE is the twenty-eighth happiest country. Dubai, its largest city, is on a mission to become the "happiest city on the planet." The *World Happiness Report*, commissioned by the UN, notes that the Buddhist Kingdom of Bhutan is on a similar mission to become the happiest country in the world. Interestingly, there is a race between one of the world's most consumer-driven societies and a small Buddhist kingdom to be crowned with the title of "happiest." They are taking very different roads to get there.

It's worth noting that the world's happiest man is a Buddhist monk. Scientifically and statistically speaking, that makes sense, since there is enough research pointing to embracing spirituality and Zen-like principles as a key to happiness. Both are gateways to inner peace. Psychologist Jonathan Haidt covers this in his 2006 book, *The Happiness Hypothesis: Finding Modern Truth in Ancient Wisdom* (it also happens to be one of Tony's favorite books).

Some of the most notable and deep-pocketed leaders of the tech world ascribe to Buddhism. Biographer Walter Isaacson wrote of the profound influence of Zen Buddhism on Steve Jobs. Facebook founder Mark Zuckerberg is famously inspired by the religion and philosophy, citing his wife Priscilla Chan's influence.

Among other benefits, spiritual practices have a way of calming the mind, leading to greater productivity.

Arguably, one of the most coveted jobs in America is some fusion of chief executive officer and spiritual leader. Tony embraces this connection. When journalist Max Chafkin said that Zappos strikes him "as not unlike a religious cult," Tony didn't disagree. "There is a lot you can learn from religion," he replied. "This is not just a company. It's like a way of life."

THE EUPHORIA OF FAILURE

PublicUs is not a Downtown Project–funded entity, but it likely wouldn't exist without the influence of DTP. It's on the corner of Fremont Street and Maryland Parkway, two blocks down from the Airstream Park and 11th Street Records. The artisanal coffeehouse and restaurant looks like a place right out of Brooklyn or San Francisco.

I was there to meet Zach Ware, who had moved into the Urban Lofts next door. (He was also spending a lot of time in LA.) He showed up in a blue polo, and it was clear that he was in a better place than the last time I saw him. His receding hairline was greyer, but he looked twenty to thirty pounds lighter. And he seemed genuinely happier.

"I'm a lot more Zen," he explained, sitting down with a cup of hot tea. "Things that got to me years ago no longer get to me. I've been wondering, what have I been doing for the last five years?" His voice still ached with regret over the decisions that he made or could have made to save Shift (formerly Project 100), but it sounded like he'd made peace with the failure.

Vegas Tech Fund rebranded as VTF Capital in a publicity campaign in early 2016. Part of the website rebrand included a description that goes against the very lifestyle that Zach blamed for the dissolution of Shift:

"If you're eating a microwave burrito at your desk at 2 a.m. on a Saturday, you're doing it wrong."

Shift shut down a year ago (around April 1, 2015)–the two-year anniversary of its inception with the Tesla order.

A trip to Miami was when Zach knew that Shift's days were numbered. He flew there for fourteen hours to give a talk on his company. On the plane, he created an Evernote that explored what he'd do if Shift shut down. After his talk, he walked out of the room and threw up. Then he got a text that one of his key engineers was leaving. "I felt gross," he said.

When he got back to his office in Vegas, he knew what he had to do. "You look into the room and see: married, just bought a house, married with kids. There were two options on the table: either do a Hail Mary and see the ship sink with the crew, or make the decision to end the game early enough to cover everyone's salary and give them enough severance so that it wasn't difficult to find a job later. Looking around the room at my employees, that decision was pretty easy."

Still, Zach lamented the decisions that got him there. One was the unfortunate result of what had become a painful reality for the Downtown Project and small businesses: the lack of affordable housing in downtown Vegas. Without people living in the area, there was no target market for the cars. Another decision he regretted was the Project 100 Tesla news story that went viral from SXSW in 2013.

"We should never have released that Tesla story," he said. "No one releases their entire playbook to the world before they've even started building." The article served the story of Downtown Project but created an early handicap for Shift.

"To get huge media attention is very intoxicating," Zach told me in a moment of rare candidness. "Tony will in one breath say, 'Think bigger, dream bigger,' and then turn around and say, 'Where's the profit?' So he's looking to me, and all of us to deliver on those promises. He casts the grand vision, and we have to make it happen.... Tony will undoubtedly look at me in a few years and say, 'Where's the profit?' "

In that moment, I realized that Zach felt the weight of delivering the investment that will make Tony's decision to reinvest his entire windfall from Amazon worth it. In addition to Shift, Zach has had a number of high-profile failures in his portfolio such as Moveline and Zirtual. He's lamented not being more involved with some companies earlier on. But it would have been almost impossible because Tony encouraged them to shoot so many bullets, and he and his colleagues didn't have the experience yet. When Andy White left in fall 2014, VTF Capital had made a hundred investments. As of spring 2016, the fund had made a handful more. Zach and Will have said that it's because they wanted to spend more time with founders, which was true, but it's also because the fund had spent the majority of its money and was now biding time until it could raise more money from LPs, or limited partners: investors who invest in VC funds.

"We're less outward focused, and everything is focused on operations," Zach continued. "The only way that we'll ever invest in the next Facebook or the next Amazon is if we help our investments."

A major liability for Zach, Will, and Andy was always that they did not have a track record yet. Early on, they might have done better branding themselves as angel investors, who do exactly what the term suggests: they write checks, and then disappear. But VTF was a seed and early-stage investment fund, and those are the ones that typically require the most support from investors (especially from investors who are leading the rounds). When companies are raising larger rounds–Series B, C, D, and so forth–the deals are more transactional. A company's earliest and formative years are when it usually needs guidance from seasoned investors.

When Tony and Alfred established Venture Frogs, the two had already successfully sold a company to Microsoft at a high valuation. The stated purpose of their fund was to deliver a return to their investors. VTF placed value on ROC in addition to ROI, so the purpose was different.

Tony and Alfred saw that the highest value they could provide founders was going in the trenches with them. As a result, they saw a high return on a number of their investments: In addition to Zappos, there was Tellme Networks, where Alfred worked as VP of finance, as well as OpenTable, Ask Jeeves, and MongoMusic.

All of Tony's successes were partnerships with Alfred: Link-Exchange, Venture Frogs, and Zappos. (Although Alfred wasn't involved much in Zappos from 2000 to 2005, he was on the board.) There is a unique sort of trust between the two. When Alfred had agreed to join Zappos as CFO after bringing Tellme Networks from a $60 million annual deficit to a profitable company that would sell to Microsoft for $800 million in 2007, Tony didn't tell Alfred that Zappos was currently in a cash crunch too and that its line of credit would drop from $40 million to $30 million by the time he walked into the office. "During that time, we could have completely gone out of business." Of course, Zappos did not. After the Zappos sale, the technology news site *TechCrunch* named Alfred the man "with the Midas touch."

Initially, entrepreneurs liked the fact that their VTF investments were tied to a two-time successful entrepreneur. But soon many discovered that they weren't going to receive advice and support from Tony himself. Some opportunistically found a way, but he was largely inaccessible to many who didn't know how to approach him with that sort of request. He distanced himself from the fund by holding only veto power. Zirtual was among the exceptions where he'd invested personally, so he made time for meetings with Maren Kate Donovan.

Elizabeth Yin from LaunchBit, who took a VC job at well-respected Silicon Valley accelerator 500 Startups after successfully exiting her company (*exiting* is Silicon Valley speak for taking a company public, or being acquired at a desirable valuation), says that the strength of the accelerator is pairing new VCs with seasoned VCs. That is the best way to learn.

Even Elizabeth, whose cofounder was Tony's cousin, did not understand VTF's decision-making process. "Was there a main person? Did all decisions have to go through Tony? I don't know," she told me. "Who actually was in charge of setting that strategy? I don't know. The funny thing is the person who actually decided on us, I think, is Arun, who was the CTO of Zappos at that time."

She speculated that perhaps the specific team is in place because Tony values loyalty more than anything. "Especially for the role that Andy had, anybody would have died to take that role. People would have moved to Vegas; people would have moved anywhere for that role. *Tony could have gotten anybody.*"

VTF Capital has not had any major successes yet, and many brush it off as another one of Tony's experiments. However, there are certainly notable successes–including LaunchBit's sale to BuySellAds.com; garage sale app Rumgr's acquisition by eBay; and bowling app Rolltech's merger with Sports Challenge Network. Yet there is still a lot to be desired within the VTF Capital portfolio of about 100 start-ups. Perhaps time will shift the scales. Andy counters that it takes thirteen years for a company to exit, implying that the real assessment shouldn't be made for eight more years. "All the failures will happen first," he told me. I remembered that in summer 2014, when I asked him about some of the fastest-growing companies in the fund, he confirmed Moveline and Zirtual. Collectively they had several hundred employees and counting. Within weeks, both folded.

Because VTF was so focused on making deals, there was little to no advising on the fund's part. Over the years, the most unsolicited enthusiasm has been for Fred Mossler and his retail expertise. Fashion tech entrepreneurs such as Jake Bronstein from Flint and Tinder (which was purchased by online retailer HuckBerry) believe that their start-ups have benefited from Fred's advice. Although Zach has his critics, Ministry of Supply (later rebranded as Ministry) cofounder Aman Advani has high praise for Zach's influence on his company. Shift's failure no doubt has given Zach the battle scars and insider knowledge to help his portfolio companies avoid a similar fate. In general VTF Capital entrepreneurs say they enjoy working with Will Young, citing the fact that he's good with product development and honest about his weaknesses.

Ever since Romotive moved to San Francisco, it has sort of dropped off everyone's radar. Andy White didn't know anything about the company's pivot after he moved to San Diego from Vegas; and even Will, who is based in San Francisco, confessed that he didn't know anything about how it was doing. Perhaps it's because the company has far surpassed many of the VTF Capital companies, most of which did not or likely will not receive its equivalent in funding, and become a fixture in the San Francisco Bay culture.

Romotive, then Stork, now Zipline, was tackling real-world problems. Keller Rinaudo has raised $43 million from multiple investors, including Yahoo founder Jerry Yang, GV (formerly Google Ventures), and Sequoia Capital, to develop the drones for Rwanda. "I always wanted to create a transformational company," Keller told me. The iPhone robot Romo is now completely discontinued. It's amazing how his team kept things quiet for years as they were changing strategy. "We made that decision about two years ago but stayed quiet about the change of focus."

As for the Ticket Cake founders, two of them dated while they built their company and broke up when it failed. Dylan Jorgensen stayed in downtown Vegas to work on the *Downtown Podcast*, which he airs every Thursday from Inspire Theatre. He moved from the Ogden to a Gold Spike dorm. His partner Jacqueline Jensen traveled as far from Vegas as possible, spending months doing a Hacker Paradise in Bali and then partaking in a Remote Year, where she is traveling to twelve cities with a group of nomads. She became a "community evangelist"–a popular job title in the tech world, typically encompassing public relations and social media–for infographic design app Piktochart.

Zach has transformed his body, which has the power to transform the mind. For that reason, I think that he may genuinely be in a different place; not everything is spin. He even takes his blender with him everywhere to make fruit juices and has stopped drinking alcohol. At least he's practicing what he's publicly advising his entrepreneurs.

One thing is for sure: Zach's relationship with Tony has changed. He chose to have an intermediary between him and

Tony while he was running Shift; it was good for their working relationship and their friendship. Many of Zach's former employees say that they would work with him again.

Zach's experience with public failure gave him more understanding and empathy for other founders, such as Maren Kate Donovan of Zirtual. After her company folded overnight, shocking her four hundred employees, she went through a very brutal media cycle. At the same time Zach realized what an abrupt and likely preventable collapse Zirtual was: "I have zero tolerance for allowing your company to get into a position where you are not in control of its spending," he told me. "It is irresponsible. It is disrespectful to your employees in particular." While Zirtual was sold in a fire sale, Shift had $2 million in the bank when it shut down. Maren wouldn't comment on the value that Andy or Zach brought to her company, but she did tell me that she should have taken Tony's advice from early on. He warned her not to feel the pressure to grow so quickly and succumb to the stress to become a unicorn company.

I reached out to Maren after she wrote a *Medium* post calling out vulnerability as Silicon Valley's biggest problem–I thought she nailed it. Venture capitalist Marc Andreessen once told the *New Yorker* that Silicon Valley is one place where people are "fake happy" all the time. Elizabeth of LaunchBit wrote about this phenomenon in a blog post, "We're *Not* Crushing It."

It seemed to me that the media was tougher on Maren than it would be on a male founder who blew through his money quickly. She conjectured that the male founder would have raised a Series B months ago and there would have been no failure. Tony told her that it's not fair that that's the way the world is. I agree with both of them.

After a romantic breakup, Maren decided to become a nomad,

too, traveling to wherever people would pay her for consulting work. She is really interested in end-of-life care. When I asked her why, she said she was inspired by "everything from the death of my company, to the death of a loved one, and some other personal losses a year before." Her wandering took her to Miami, where she took a job as COO of Roam, a coworking start-up for nomads. Her Twitter feed suggests that she is still recovering from the public failure.

After Jody Sherman's death, Downtown Project's first entrepreneur suicide, there was a moment in time where all the founders were suddenly more honest with one another and banded together. "CEO circles were honestly kind of pointless [before] because everyone was so tight-lipped," said Elizabeth. "From that point on, CEO circles were very productive, people would talk about all their problems, try to help each other out. You really felt community from that point on. As horrible as it sounds, if that hadn't happened, I don't think the community or the CEO circles or the start-ups would have been that tight."

One thing she's learned as a VC is that part of the job is being a shrink. To that end, she said, "Mark Rowland [the Aussie who was brought in to coach start-ups through ROCeteer and raised awareness around entrepreneur mental health after the suicides] is the reason to take Vegas Tech Fund's money." That is the view of entrepreneurs across the board. When I asked Andy why his team didn't provide more mentorship to start-ups, he said that money and mentorship are two different things.

"Increasing the density [of the area] was the priority," Andy told me, still on message.

Because of that directive, the young entrepreneurs who didn't naturally seek out assistance or know how to navigate an ecosystem like this were left to fend for themselves. Those green

entrepreneurs were the most vulnerable to believing they had
to fit an outdated stereotype of what a founder should look and
act like. The all-powerful Silicon Valley myth is what founders
like Maren are trying to chip away at with posts such as: "2016
Is the Year of the Pegasus." Without the myth, founders would
embrace more of the limitations and unique superpowers of their
own humanity.

There is a false narrative in Silicon Valley that entrepreneurs
need to sacrifice their well-being for their companies–Zach is
among those who learned the hard way. One of his partners in
the Vegas Tech ecosystem, Sara Hill, shared with me the same
sentiment one afternoon at PublicUs (which, next to Grass Roots
[RIP] and Zubin's health clinic, is probably the healthiest place
in the Fremont East area). Sara moved to Vegas from California
to develop coworking space Work In Progress, and then the Mill
start-up accelerator. She now manages around a $1 million bud-
get and is working to diversify her classes. "The days of coding
24/7 with Red Bull are over," she told me. (Notably, Tony regards
sleep deprivation and Red Bull as key players in his success, and
subsequent happiness, in *Delivering Happiness*.)

Sara, Zach, Will, and others are working to change the narrative
around what entrepreneurship is. The current narrative around
the young male, John Wayne archetype is societally entrenched,
but many of today's investors and founders are working to level
the playing field, and encourage more diversity of thought.

In many ways Tony reinforces this narrative, but he also does
his part to break it down in others. For example, despite the fact
that Tony maintains a good ol' boys' club at the center of both
Zappos and Downtown Project, he employs a high ratio of women
like Sara Hill to manage important elements of his portfolio and
operations. Females fill the roles of managing all of his personal

wealth (Chrissie Yim), legal matters (Millie Chou), personal and operational risk (Stacie Chang), schedule and personal affairs (Mimi Pham), chief of staff (Jamie Naughton), technical advisor (Jeanne Markel). The key female advisors in his life are more behind the scenes than the men, but they play a crucial role.

While en route to Santa Monica back in 2013, I shared with him a book I was reading, *The Athena Doctrine: How Women (and the Men Who Think Like Them) Will Rule the Future*, about how leadership in the future will increasingly depend upon embracing stereotypically feminine qualities such as communication and connectedness. "You embody a lot of these traits," I told him. He took the book and flipped through a few pages, nodded, and then handed it back.

All of the concepts and the ideas he is putting forward make theoretical sense. Self-organization speaks to what's happening in a networked world, with systems such as the block chain and others being tested and financed. Social networks have unprecedented power: LinkedIn was sold to Microsoft for $26 billion in 2016. Facebook controls incredible amounts of data.

Tony's ability to tap into the future is why so many people were drawn to his vision. It just seems like ego (rooted in the masculine) is really the only thing holding him back from them playing out to the highest degree; from self-organization taking place. People need a leader, but they also need to be empowered. What appears to be happening at both Zappos and Downtown Project is that their leader doesn't want to be a leader, and yet still holds all the power.

"Tony doesn't need to be CEO of Zappos anymore," Alfred pointed out. "He is attached to his baby. When you like seeing your name in lights, it's hard to let go."

He said that Tony's core competency is that he's a creative genius. The aspects of managing the business itself have always been on someone else.

Back to the psychology and euphoria of failure–Sonny Ahuja, another DTP employee, who owned two small businesses, explained to me once the philosophy around failure in Las Vegas. One of his companies, O Face Doughnuts, an artisanal donut shop on Sixth Street, shut down over the holidays in late 2015. Like Zach and many others, he pointed the failure to the absence of healthy foot traffic downtown. Unforeseen factors–such as what happened with the Ogden and the Great Exodus–affected its closure. Healthy foot traffic would include the young hipsters who poured through the streets every month for Tech Cocktail and Catalyst Week. That was the demographic Tony was targeting: the young entrepreneurial set that he met on Powder Mountain or on the festival grounds at Coachella, a large music festival in the California desert. This set wanted to know Tony and his money, but ultimately it didn't want to move to Vegas. Another important demographic that was notably absent were Zapponians–indeed, the reason that everything exists. Gluten-free donuts and $4 coffees are beyond the budget for most call center workers, a miscalculation on DTP's part.

Although friends say the failure crushed him, Sonny's other business, Bin 702 in Container Park (and nearly a block away), which he co-owns with Don Welch, was thriving. Sonny has been in the restaurant business for years, and his cheerful and quirky demeanor doesn't seem to match with the sort of risk that he takes on regularly.

"Vegas loves failure," he said, smiling. It's a rite of passage. To win big, you need to feel the sting of hitting the bottom. With small businesses, as with start-ups in Silicon Valley, failure is a badge of honor. It's proof of having been through the trenches.

Sonny was protected more than others: he placed multiple bets and had previously taken a salary with DTP while he was getting his businesses off the ground. And like every other DTP-funded enterprise, he could walk away from O Face Doughnuts without having to pay back his investors.

There is still a demand for donuts downtown, though. A few months after Sonny's shop closed, another donut chain opened in its place. There was a line out the door on opening day.

NICK'S REDEMPTION

Nick Swinmurn emerged from the back of the restaurant, where he was talking to one of the waiters. He still sported his signature short haircut and goatee and was wearing a brightly colored T-shirt. He had recently opened Nachoria, a manifestation of a dream that he had years ago while he was building Zappos.

"I'm going to create a restaurant that just sells nachos," he told his coworkers at 1000 Van Ness in San Francisco. Zappos was the priority, but it was an idea that he filed away.

In a sense, Zappos was overtaken by Tony's cult of personality. Nick gave away control of the company during that fateful meeting when he handed over the CEO title, and Tony has since rebranded the company in a way that didn't reflect Nick. He took back that control with his Dethrone Basecamp gym and now with this new restaurant in Silicon Valley.

Nachoria is also located Burlingame, only blocks away from his gym. So while Tony and Fred are claiming land in Vegas, Nick is making his own physical mark on Silicon Valley.

He's also seen recognition in other ways. "The other day, my staff saw something on the news," he said pointing to the flat-screen TVs hanging from the ceiling. "It was how this retailer in the South struggled because of Zappos. They even mentioned my name as the founder!" Then he added resolutely: "Zappos will always follow me."

In recent years, he has heard from his initial investors: friends and family who put in the few thousand very early dollars to get the start-up off the ground. "They have said things like, 'Hey, thanks for the opportunity to invest. Because of you, I now have this house,' which is pretty cool," Nick shared. "They invested maybe a few thousand dollars. But it was a big risk; for them, it was all of their savings. In hindsight, it seems like the right bet, but there were no guarantees around Zappos's success."

Although the company was founded in 1999, it sometimes feels like yesterday. That's in part due to the fact that the Zappos story continues to live on in the media, thanks to Tony's branding strategy.

In one of those satisfying moments that reveal the life cycle and karmic power of investment in Silicon Valley, behind our table sat two men, both wearing Sequoia-branded T-shirts. The investment firm that Nick had relied on for his success was now investing back into him, in another way. He didn't have to do the work this time except to create something that he loved with the money he got from the Amazon sale.

When Nick last visited Las Vegas, he went to lunch with Fred Mossler and Tony at Nacho Daddy. Fred told the waitress, "This is all here because of him," pointing at Nick. At first, Nick thought that Fred was referring to his original idea for Shoesite.com, but he was actually referring to Nick's idea for a nachos-focused restaurant. Fred had filed the idea that Nick threw out in conversation at 1000 Van Ness and resurrected it years later. It's funny how ideas work and how they change ownership. Nick didn't hear about the chain until it opened. A very early Zappos employee who has a stake in Nacho Daddy later told Nick that he didn't know if the chain really has a strategy other than throwing money at it. "That's what worked for Tony, right?"

Any seasoned entrepreneur knows that coming up with an idea is the fun part. "All that matters is execution," Michael Cornthwaite once told me over a beer in Container Park. "Ideas are a dime a dozen."

A few months before Nick called Fred in 1999 to see if he wanted to interview for a position at his new company, Shoesite.com, Fred wrote a note to himself with an idea to create an online shoe company. He put it away in a box. Then one day while at his desk at Nordstrom, his phone rang.

"I don't know if you're looking to leave your company, but I have a really great opportunity for you," said the voice on the other line.

RED PILL

When Mark Rowland stepped down from his role as CEO of DTP Ventures in April 2016, he renewed his focus on his job with ROCeteer. His email signature notes, "The Red Pill"–a nod to *The Matrix* and accepting life with clear eyes rather than through a buffered reality. The Red Pill signifies primarily two things: allowing oneself to fully feel life's ups and downs, and accepting the challenge of one's mission without any complaints.

A few days later, he pulled up to the Gold Spike in a red Acura. "Want to get out of downtown?" he asked me.

Although I hadn't been downtown for a while, one day there already felt like a day too long. Despite DTP's investment to date, the homeless population is still high and has gotten cleverer with approaching passersby, like the man who strikes up friendly conversation while walking alongside people and then discloses that he was recently released from a Supermax prison.

Mark turned right onto Fourth Street, between the Gold Spike and the Grand Hotel & Casino, and drove toward the highway interchange that provides roads to the Strip, Salt Lake City, and Los Angeles.

We started talking about Holacracy. "We stopped using the H-word at Downtown Project," he explained. When Mark took over as CEO in early 2015, he and a few others decided that they still wanted to try self-management/organization. By that point, everyone was burned out on Holacracy and blamed the system for the company's challenges. Adopting another new organizational structure felt exhausting. Everyone just wanted to do his or her job and go home at the end of the day.

"It was nearly impossible to even say 'self-management' without drawing up ideas of Holacracy," he said. "Even I don't love Holacracy." Then Mark gave an example: "I'm driving this car and am in charge of where we're going. You can give me suggestions, but ultimately I'll make the decision. It's the same with Holacracy: power is limited to work within the context of the system. You can't go outside of the rules."

The drive on highway 95-S reminded me of a previous drive with a former Zappos manager who's convinced that Holacracy is really an outright attempt to control the masses through subtle brainwashing.

Mark likes the tension-resolution process of Holacracy and believes that it's more effective than typical conflict-resolution processes. But the strict meeting format feels constricting. Tony has compared it to learning another language, and Mark sees it the same way–and like many others, he sees that as imposing and forceful as opposed to an improvement to organizational processes.

As we pulled into a shopping district in Summerlin, one of Las Vegas's nicest neighborhoods, Mark remarked, "Didn't Zappos implement Holacracy before the trial run was even over with?" That was true: even before the trial group offered its okay on the new system, Tony instructed his staffers to go ahead with rolling it out into the entire organization. In fact, Tony said later that he wished he would have just rolled out Holacracy to the entire organization all at the same time. "That way, everyone would start speaking the same language right away," he explained.

Like Maggie Hsu, Mark also had some real criticisms. "Brian is the spiritual leader," Mark explained, referring to Brian Robertson. "He can't say anything off message." We parked, got out, and he shut the door to his Acura. "Did you know that Brian wrote a blog post about how Holacratic companies shouldn't have core values?"

He had just been ousted from his job by Tony and was wearing a *Delivering Happiness* T-shirt. I appreciated all of his leading questions. At least he was willing to engage on the hard topics.

The way that Mark explained it, he presented DTP with a plan of action: basically, either he was out or Michael Downs was out. It sounded like interim CEO was the plan all along. But that wasn't the full story. Later I heard that Mark had been asked to leave. Tony and Fred took him to dinner and asked him how he wanted to go. He had moved his family across the world only to be told to leave. He reminded them that he had a contract with ROCeteer.

Mark is circling back to the role that he came in with; the desire that he had in the first place. Before moving to Vegas, he would

Skype with Downtown Project–funded start-ups beginning at four in the morning Australian time.

And Mark's coaching worked: ROCeteer made life better for the start-ups. Founders and employees of those companies genuinely experienced higher life satisfaction and opened up to Mark about their challenges. However, as soon as he became the lead of DTP Ventures, those same founders and employees saw him differently. They brushed off their problems as temporary and situational and told him that everything was running great. Playing the roles of CEO and psychologist-in-chief is a difficult balance.

Many start-up founders learned the painful lesson that managing one's emotions and life is the key to getting your start-up to run–at least sustainably–for the long term. It can't be the other way around. Even Zach, whose prize was Shift, says it's not worth losing your soul over a start-up.

Well-known Silicon Valley venture capitalist Ben Horowitz wrote about how the unspoken challenge of start-up life is the psychological battle that goes on within. He wrote about the taboo topic on his blog initially and then incorporated his thoughts into a book, *The Hard Thing About Hard Things: Building a Business When There Are No Easy Answers.* That is also Mark's passion: helping founders overcome the psychological battle within. If he can continue to make a dent in this area with DTP-funded companies, it's possible that his long-term impact will be stronger as lead of ROCeteer than as CEO of DTP anyway.

Mark's departure highlights just how concentrated the power is. Even as CEO of DTP Ventures, Mark was still in the dark on things. He once joked with Tony that he couldn't use telepathy to read his mind.

TRAVELING TO HONG KONG
WITH THE MONKEYS

The Monday after Easter, Tony's parents, Richard and Judy Hsieh rode down the escalator into the boarding area for a Cathay Pacific Airways flight to Hong Kong. Both wore their Zappos backpacks, worn from use, and were dressed casually to travel fourteen hours from San Francisco across the Pacific. A handful of Zapponians appeared soon, including the monkeys–minus Tony, who was en route to Richard Branson's Necker Island–and three other male employees. One young Zapponian sported a large Mohawk that stood about ten inches from his head.

The team was headed to the grand opening of the new Zappos China office, as Richard had announced at the previous All-Hands meeting.

Near the terminal, one nonmonkey Zapponian explained his thoughts on Holacracy. He was confused but also interested in where the real power lies. "It's a federal-versus-state issue," he said. "Does the power rest with the GCC [main circle] or in the smaller circles?"

With the buyouts and the reorganization around the work, employees were now concerned with holding enough "people points" (100, to be exact), with fear that they might get sent to "the Beach": aka "no-man's-land," where they need to find new roles. Both employees and circles can fall into a deficit. "Circles can 'fall into a recession' if they don't have enough people points," the Zapponian explained. "I've learned more about economics with Holacracy and people points."

The onboarding process of Holacracy takes up a lot of mental energy–it's essentially a reprogramming–which is why a few hundred opted to leave in the process. Tony often compares it to learning a new sport, or adopting a different language: "Imagine that you're teaching people how to play soccer for the first time, and even the referees are learning it for the first time."

Richard handles international operations and is one of three Hsiehs who have worked for Zappos. Tony's youngest brother David previously worked for the company but departed with the 2008 layoffs. Tony's brother Andy also worked for Zappos and has supported his brother in other ways; for example, launching an app service similar to Postmates, called Lux Delux, in 2013 to serve the downtown Vegas area. However, it appears that Lux Delux has since shut down.

"What do you think of Downtown Project?" I asked Judy Hsieh, who was sitting quietly away from the team in the terminal.

"Don't ask me!" She seemed surprised, throwing up her hands in mock exasperation. Judy said exactly what she meant. I gathered that she didn't really understand all of it. Tony has said throughout the years that she still encourages him to become a doctor or a lawyer; it's still not too late. Even so, she's played an active role in his career; Judy managed the Venture Frogs pan-Asian restaurant in 1000 Van Ness. And she and Richard have embraced the world that Tony has created for himself in their own unique ways–I remember being surprised to see Richard and Judy sporting glowing raver gear to participate in the 2013 Rock 'n' Roll 5K, which went through downtown Las Vegas, after which they climbed onto a high platform to operate the fire-breathing praying mantis that guards Container Park.

Richard and Judy immigrated to the US in the 1970s from Taiwan before having their three sons and brought with them the values of their culture. Veering outside of a guaranteed route to success–such as becoming a doctor or lawyer–is considered a big risk. Tony's book resonated in Asia for that reason: the fact that he goes against the traditional Asian narrative. Underneath the surface of the relatively light language of his business book appears to be a manifesto on Asian culture's obsession with success and the narrow road that it takes to get there. "Bring your whole self to work" is a commentary on Asian culture. In Japan, for example, the entire city essentially wears the same uniform to work. After traveling to Hong Kong, I visited Japan and came to this conclusion about that uniformity: at least they know what to expect. While the ability to wear anything to work at companies such as Zappos can be liberating, that, combined with the high levels of ambiguity, adds a layer of psychological weight.

As we approached the immigration line in the Hong Kong airport, Richard told everyone to bypass the tables and fill out the cards in line instead. "The key is moving through the line. Do your cards in the line," Richard said knowingly and cheerfully, nudging the monkeys and the rest of us along. Fred Mossler and the call center leader traded notes on the destination address and flight numbers, quickly filling out the form as the line continued to move forward.

After we made our way through the line, Richard led the group to the currency exchange and gave a briefing on how much cash to take out. I continued on with the group as we weaved through the airport and onto the flat escalators.

Fred and I began talking about Holacracy and how it would be received in broader Asia. Arun Rajan piped up: "Did you know that Toyota's original 'stop the line' philosophy was the genesis of the Lean movement?" The "Lean" movement, developed by American entrepreneur Eric Ries, is a trend in tech culture that focuses on iteration and failing fast. As Arun pointed out, it's surprising that the genesis for this popular way of organizing work emerged in Japan, where speaking out in any way isn't looked upon favorably. "Stop the line" is exactly as it sounds: anyone in the company can stop the conveyor belt for any reason. That philosophy is also built into Holacracy's DNA: in fact, Brian Robertson opens his book with the metaphor that every button on a plane is important. Just because every other button is off doesn't mean one lit button should be disregarded.

We stepped into the train that would bring us to the central hub outside the airport and Richard joined the conversation. He said something about Chinese e-commerce company Alibaba, but I couldn't catch all of it.

I didn't have time before the trip to secure my visa to enter Dongguan, so I gave Richard a hug and parted ways with the team at the airport. Richard is a lot more open and personable than his son, and it's easy to feel more of a connection to him. We were going to try to conduct an interview at some point between departing San Francisco International Airport and arriving in Hong Kong, but the interview would have to wait.

A few weeks later, Fred announced that he would be leaving Zappos in June 2016. Soon after that, I finally confronted him about the fact that people view him as a yes-man. It was a conversation I had been avoiding for quite some time and held my breath for his response. Amazingly, he didn't seem all that offended. "My views happen to align with Tony," he said. I asked him if he ever disagreed with Tony. He said there was one other time he quit Zappos, back in 2002. It sounded like a dramatic event, and Tony convinced him to come back.

Fred had lost too much with his first family to Zappos, and now, with a new wife and two young children, he has a second chance at a family life. He told me that Tony lives life at a high intensity, and so you have to be equally intense in order to work with him.

When people talk or write about Tony's philosophy around work-life integration, there is generally a positive spin to it. But I now see that (a) it's not just a philosophy, it's a directive to those who work closely with him, and (b) this way of life takes a hard toll on those people, from Fred's first marriage crumbling, to Andrew and Zach being hospitalized after the city hall deal and Zappos campus opening, to the psychological prison that many current and former employees find themselves in.

Somehow, through the marketing of his happiness message, Tony has been able to package his lifestyle and expectations around productivity as something that is light, when it is not. He documents his schedule (more or less) on a public Evernote, something that I once mentioned to a management professor in Michigan while reporting on a story. Her response surprised me: "Can you imagine how that makes his employees feel? If there's a way to shame workers into working more, that must be it."

It was a refreshing take on something that, through the warped lens of Silicon Valley culture, has been rewarded. Silicon Valley culture generally treats transparency as a virtue, which is a curious development that allows start-ups to maximize PR under the veil of transparency.

PROCESSING TENSIONS

Even though Tony and I had reconnected at Kent Johns's funeral, we still had a number of unresolved tensions from our conversation at Atomic Liquors.

He suggested that we resolve the conflict with the Holacracy conflict-resolution process and sent me a link to section 3.2.6 of the *Holacracy Constitution*. We went back and forth on a number of emails that covered no real substantive ground.

Frustrated, I canceled three of our meetings because he had turned scheduled one-to-one meetings into one-to-three and one-to-six meetings. It's a common way that he does business, pulling in multiple people to meetings so that there is always a much larger group by the end than there was at the beginning. But I just felt like a data point in his effort to increase collisions downtown.

One afternoon, I finally had the collision I was looking for. I saw him walking alone by the parking garage across from the Gold Spike between Fourth Street and Las Vegas Boulevard, and ran up to him. "This process is just stripping all of the human emotion out of it. You are choosing to highlight exactly what you want to highlight and avoiding the rest." I didn't believe in Holacracy or his intentions around it, especially after this. It felt like he was trying to prove that he was right more than he was trying to understand.

Two months later, we were still frozen in the same place. "I don't want to be a data point in Tony's experiments," I kept thinking on my fourteen-hour flight back from Hong Kong. By then, I was so angry with him that I could hardly sleep. The Holacracy tension-resolution process was enormously frustrating and going nowhere. The only solace that I found was for two hours watching Aaron Sorkin's 2015 movie about Steve Jobs, where you see more of Jobs's emotions and complex humanity at the very end. I wanted to know that Tony cared more about the people in his social experiments than the data from the social experiment itself. Even after all this time, I was still unsure who this person really was, but I retained hope that he was more empathetic than people gave him credit for.

I emailed Tony and asked if we could just do the Holacracy process in person. He agreed to devote as much time as was needed to process the tensions.

At ten thirty the next morning, I arrived at Airstream Park and, with the go-ahead from the security guard, walked under the canopy with twinkle lights and into the main area near the stage. The llamas were milling around, which made the park smell sort of like a farm. It was mostly empty, except for Ashton Allen sitting on a lawn chair eating lunch. He waved hello.

The door to Tony's Airstream was open, and he was sitting at the table doing work on his laptop. Inside it looked like his and Michael's trailer at Burning Man, but without the coating of playa dust. Everyone in the camp knows that if his door is open or unlocked, you can walk in at any hour. Once you enter the trailer, everything is visible: there's a small seating area up front, with a table and tiny kitchen; a small bathroom and a stand-up shower; and a bed at the far end of the trailer. When Tyler Williams was living in the park, he would join Tony early in the mornings, starting at around four o'clock, to check emails before the day started.

He gave me a hug and apologized for the trailer being so hot. It was only April, but it already felt like August. Being exposed more frequently to the intense heat of the desert sun in the summertime is one of the drawbacks of living in the park. It has sprinklers everywhere that spray water from above and are consistently activated, but that doesn't downplay the fact that it feels like the Middle East.

"So," he said, opening his laptop, "tell me what your tensions are."

I had created a long Evernote on the plane with thoughts, but nothing felt right to begin with. I wanted to ease into the conversation instead. For a second, I held back, but then, as he began typing verbatim everything I said–"You are just manipulating people to moving here, that was your whole strategy all along, using the Neil Strauss game strategy"–it became easier to continue with the next. I started to feel vulnerable sitting there, as he typed every word, not pushing back on any of the statements. Minutes went by, then nearly an hour, then two hours, then three hours.

"Look, I wasn't even mad at you before this," I said, exasperated. I hadn't slept in days and felt vulnerable and exposed. "That's another one. Why would you ever use this Holacracy tension-resolution process at Zappos? It's so much work. I just don't know why you would ever use this at Zappos."

As we got to the end of listing all the tensions I could think of, I felt a sense of relief. This wasn't an interview, but it sort of was, because I asked him questions indirectly through all the things that I shared.

We started going through them one by one. It was a painstakingly slow process.

"I'm really confused about Kona," I said abruptly. I didn't understand why he had invited me on the trip. There was never any clarity around it. In hindsight, I realized I should have probably prepared a pitch for the meeting. Amanda warned me about that.

"I travel with, like, twenty people a year," he continued. "Actually, I tell potential founders or any romantic partners to go on a weekend together. It's an easy way to tell if you can work with that person . . . We survived that weekend, didn't we?" It seemed to be his way of explaining that he didn't have any obligation to explain the purpose of the trip. I now gather that, in the way that potential entrepreneurs are vetted over the course of a few days in Las Vegas, I was also being assessed as a culture fit during that trip. I wanted more answers, but in the moment, that was better than nothing.

THE KINGDOM OF HAPPINESS

My face and shoulders softened. Frank Gruber was right. The meeting a few weeks ago was therapy, and this was an extension of that. I didn't care as much about the nature of the answers as I did that he simply answered my questions honestly.

Throughout the process, we talked through every single tension. He titled the Evernote and up at the top wrote "Governance," and below that "Tensions," and every one was written next to a check box. He gave some of the sections subtitles. So far, there were thirty-six tensions. His next meeting had been canceled, so we continued.

Under "Governance," he created a new set of rules for our relationship. I told him that our email exchanges tended to go in circles, so I wanted to limit email to only the most basic conversations.

"What kind of conversations?" he asked.

"Well, you know, ones that don't require a lot of work," I said, searching for a way to clarify it.

"See, this is the hard part about Holacracy," he responded. "Defining exactly what you mean."

"The thing I don't like about our emails is long back-and-forths when it requires emotional energy."

"So we can't use email when it requires emotional energy?"

"If we're going to define it, yes, I think that works."

He added a bullet under "Governance":

- anything that requires emotional energy to communicate cannot be done by email (but text message should be okay)

We reconvened three days later and concluded with fifty-six tensions. That's when we really got to the heart of the matter.

"Remember when you picked me up from the hospital after Greg Besner's party?" I asked him as I sat down at the table. "I realized that after that event, I placed you in this narrow category of people who would pick me up from the hospital in the middle of the night."

"But don't you think that other people here would pick you up from the hospital? Like Heidy?"

"I don't know," I responded. "So what is going on, at least back here," I continued, pointing to the back of my head, "is that you're supposed to be the person who always comes through. At the last hour, you're supposed to be someone who comes through."

After all this time, all this resistance and through the most unlikely means, I finally caught a glimpse of the person that I'd encountered in the hospital that night. After five hours of a tension-resolution process, I finally believed that Tony did care about the people participating in his social experiments.

It mattered to me, and it mattered because I wanted to know that what he was selling this whole time was actually real and an extension of something for the right reasons. It mattered to a lot of people. Holacracy was a way that Tony could have more control over his relationships. It might not be working all that well at Zappos, but it was working in his personal life. At least on his side of a relationship.

THE ZAPPOS FAMILY PICNIC

The next day was the Zappos Family Picnic at Craig Ranch Regional Park, a stunning area in North Las Vegas. It's about a twenty-minute drive from downtown and is set against the backdrop of mountains and red rock canyon. It's a welcome respite outside of the city: some of the best of Vegas's sprawling outdoors and an idyllic place for the annual picnic.

The party started at eleven on Saturday morning, with employees walking into the park with their spouses and children, many of them wearing the Zappos "Zeehaw" branded T-shirts. Near the entrance to the amphitheater, where a country band was playing, was a stand of fresh strawberries. Another host handed out cowboy hats.

I picked up my wristband and entered through the gates.

Inside the park was a Ferris wheel, a zipline that went over a small man-made lake with bright-blue water, country line dancing, cotton candy stands, and a host of other attractions.

Janice Lopez walked up with her two kids and asked me to take a video of them riding on a mechanical bull in a large blow-up arena. They had just driven in from LA, where she'd started working a new job at an architecture firm. She maintains a place in Vegas. Internal politics are what pushed Janice away, but after experiencing life elsewhere, again she returned and wants to be part of Tony's vision.

"These people work their asses off, and this is their reward," she said resolutely, also resigned to the fact that there is a constant conversation around her high school friend's motives. She sighed, looked over at her kids, who were in line for a ride, and continued. "This was always a long-term bet–all of it." She was referring to Downtown Project and Holacracy and the many experiments in between. "Tony sees the world in fifteen-year increments, not just a few years at a time. And who has the guts to try these kinds of things?"

Janice is one of the best barometers of where Tony's head is at: she has a stake in things but not so much that it clouds her vision. She maintains the balance of being both an insider and an outsider at the same time. So I always took her opinion seriously.

She pulled out her phone. "Tony and the gang is over to the left of the Port-a-Potties, and he says they have fernet." She looked over at her kids, who were busy enjoying the tilt-a-whirl-style ride and still wanted to get tattoos and cotton candy and ride the zipline. Fernet would have to wait. "He wants you to have this, Mom." Her daughter stretched out her hand with a cowboy hat.

We finally ran into the gang when the event was closing. A long-time Zappos employee who has played a key role in the Holacracy rollout was there with her husband. Janice's son ran up to her son, and they linked arms. I recognized most of the group, but Fred wasn't there.

The group of mostly young adults got on the bus outside the park and took their seats. Tony looked out at the kids who were walking alongside their parents and then yelled out to them, "All the kids who want to ride the bus, jump on!" and motioning with his hand.

The Zappos employee and her husband invited me to ride back to Airstream Park with them. "You know that Tony does Holacracy with everyone, right? All of his personal relationships have purpose statements. We're friends, but when we meet, he wants to dive into agenda items. It's his language." She continued, "He wins you over. And then you forget what you were mad about. With a lot of people here, that's what happens: he just wins them over." She later explained that she meant Tony wins you over with logic. I understood that cognitively, especially after having gone through that process. But weeks later, I found that I was still unsettled because logic doesn't account for empathy. The Holacratic system offers a host of loopholes around traditional norms that govern human relationships. Empathy isn't always logical.

The afternoon progressed with partying at Airstream Park and then an event at Zappos. By then, the group had grown to around fifteen people. I went to PublicUs instead but then, as I was walking past Atomic Liquors, I could see off in the distance Tony's black Zappos T-shirt and a large group trailing behind. It reminded me of the very first time I caught sight of his posse in a flying "V" formation: the night that Jenn Lim invited me into the circle to dance behind the Ogden. A lot has changed in the past three years, but that dynamic remains the same.

I followed the group to the Zappos campus, where there was a large crowd and music blaring as skateboarders flew off the jump that had been constructed in the center of the courtyard. At the gate, one of the workers secured silver VIP wristbands for everyone who was trailing behind Tony. The group paused at the ramp leading up to the campus, and everyone started taking videos and Snapchats of the skateboarders. The crowd went wild every time a skateboarder landed; most of the time the boarders crashed on the pavement. Tony was transfixed by the scene; he held his phone in the air and followed each boarder's every move, posting the images on Snapchat.

Tyler Williams walked over and invited us to the area near the jump. I stood next to a Zappos employee who worked on the new campus. In conversation, he mentioned something about his boss, and I interrupted him. "Boss? Don't you mean 'lead link'?"

He cracked a smile and said, "Well, sure, but for the outside world to understand, I just say boss. Inside Zappos, it's lead link."

Next to us stood Tyler and Zappos's new general counsel, Brandon Hollis. The two have an interesting relationship, as Tyler's core initiative is to push the boundaries as far as possible, while Brandon's is to accommodate that as much as possible without putting the company at risk. Tyler welcomed Brandon to his new job by bringing in a team to outfit his office while he was away into a Tiki room–a sort of initiation and reminder of the company's core values.

Brandon explained some of the tension. "Look at this event, for example. He's asking me if it's okay to invite skateboarders to jump off a high jump in our courtyard. There are a lot of liability issues to consider." Some of the most interesting proposals are those never given the okay by Millie or Brandon. Left to their own devices, Tony and Tyler would turn the campus into a 24/7 festival.

Holacracy is intended to bring more of those crazy ideas to light. Unless there is governance around a particular action, anything is fair game. "It's more the idea of asking for forgiveness than permission," Tony explained. "However, there are rules around resources: you can't just sign a million-dollar contract with a brand."

Though as lead link of the Brand Aura circle, Tyler probably can. Tony now trusts that Tyler's vision and decision-making process are similar to his own. When Tyler was first given the go-ahead to take over Brand Aura, he decided to spend the remainder of the 2015 budget on a nationwide pet-adoption holiday campaign. People warned him that he would surely get kicked out of his role. But he did it anyway–and it was a wild success.

Only a year ago, employees were asking for Tyler's firing. In that instance, the Holacratic system protected him. He had arranged for a toy-drive charity event and then completely forgot about it while in Disneyland attending a conference about event production. His coworkers covered–one even went to Target and bought all the gifts himself–but some were furious. An email made its way to Tony, asking for some explanation around the series of snafus, and Tony responded by saying that he couldn't find anywhere in GlassFrog where Tyler had accountabilities around charity initiatives for the company.

As a result, the system corrected and upgraded itself. Now there is a ticketing system for events, where every proposal gets routed to legal and all of the parties to ensure that there isn't any double booking and that everyone is prepared for what's ahead.

"In most companies, or at least some traditional companies, I would have been fired," Tyler said. "But in this case, my mistake made the system better."

In a way, clarity is a luxury. It allows for the peace of mind around not having to handle something that you're not responsible for.

It's something people can take advantage of, and there are real distractions. Tony shared with me an email thread about approval of a miniature pig on campus. Tyler, who played a key role in getting dogs permitted on campus, attempted to manage the request, but it ultimately got elevated to Tony, who has the most knowledge of the Holacratic system. A security guard signed off, and ultimately the employee was given the okay to bring a mini-pig that she had rescued to sit next to her at work. "There was nothing in governance that prevented mini-pigs from entering our campus, so the default is always that it's okay unless someone raises a tension," Tony explained.

And that's the danger of Holacracy: that it can be deployed for initiatives that are tangential to the company's core function. With the mini-pig, you could argue that saying yes will make that one employee happier, which will ultimately lead to a ripple effect of other happier employees and customers too. But it's still a slippery slope, and there is a lot to be negotiated.

As we looked up at the skateboarders, I turned to the Zappos employee who worked on the campus.

"So why does Zappos invest so much into events like this?" I asked.

He pointed to the ground in front of us, where a bunch of kids were standing wearing Vans skateboarding shoes.

"To sell shoes, of course."

Tyler once said that for Tony, "selling shoes is just a means to an end," and compared his vision for Zappos's marketing to Red Bull, which in 2012 memorably sponsored a space jump from a helium balloon twenty-four miles up in the stratosphere by an Austrian thrill seeker named Felix Baumgartner. "Tony really wants to change the world," Tyler told me enthusiastically.

His role, essentially as chief marketing officer, is valued highly. The company recently put out a directive to raise brand awareness: "It is the lowest since 2006 from Google trends. Need to spread word about our brand." It is under Tyler's purview that Zappos is looking for new ways to capture the eyes of the American consumer again–and not just through the lens of a leader who runs crazy management experiments but as a company that is a cult brand.

The media portrays Tony as an innovator on the cutting edge, and he is, but he loses focus quickly. When Tony was interested and excited about Downtown Project, its employees and entrepreneurs were too. When it appeared that he lost interest and stopped believing in the vision, it began to crumble.

Maybe part of it is that Tony doesn't have a sparring partner. At least that's how Alfred described their relationship. "The way I think of Tony is, 'I'm going to throw a hundred ideas against the wall, and ninety will be bad ideas,' and he knows it, but he doesn't want you to say no to it, he just wants them to be thought through and entertained," Alfred explained. "Nine of them are really good ideas, and we should probably just implement them.

And one of them is genius, but it's very hard to recognize whether it's genius or stupidity."

Yet Tony has not invited an equivalent counterweight into his realm ever since, which explains the current state of things. "Whoever steps up and helps Tony basically has to be the CEO of Zappos," Alfred added. "They have to run Zappos." With Fred now gone, Arun is ostensibly the shadow CEO. He holds several roles, as Alfred once did. But his key initiatives need to prove out more success over the long term.

Internally, the evolution is reflected with the number of employees who are stuck at "the Beach," a place where employees get pushed to when their lead links take away enough of their roles. They have about two weeks to find new roles in the company. Then the HR circle quietly phases them out of the company. Instead of firing the employee outright, being let go is a slower and sometimes more painful process of being figuratively cast off onto an island. In a company that is still wrought with politics and power struggles, even very skilled employees can find themselves at the Beach.

When I asked Tony about how Zappos was doing in spring 2016, he responded differently than he usually does. "It's an SEC violation to talk about finances," he shot back. In the past when I asked him the same question, he always affirmed that Zappos was hitting its numbers. A few days after that discussion, an employee shared with me the company's most recent financial results, and I understood Tony's response: in fact, Zappos was not hitting its numbers.

A then-Zappos employee shared with me the company's financials, which were posted on the company's internal Wikipedia after the company's most recent All Hands. Its 2016 Q1 gross sales were $668 million, 8 percent below target. That puts Zappos in the range of being a $3 to $3.5 billion company, assuming that Q4 (holiday season) gross sales are about twice as much as the other three quarters. Before I shared that number with Alfred, his estimation was that Zappos was in the $3 billion to $4 billion range. I shared with him another piece of information that had been posted to the Zappos internal Wikipedia page: that the company's active customer counts fell from 11.6 million to 9.6 million in the two years since Zappos had stopped discounting and now marked everything at full price. The company expected its active customer count to decline, but the number of customers lost surpassed expectations–down 13.5 percent, on average. The typical Zappos customer–a Midwestern soccer mom–does not want to pay full price for shoes when there are now so many e-commerce options, not to mention Amazon (with the perk of Amazon Prime). After I told Tony's chief of staff Jamie Naughton that I had seen Zappos's official company financials, she followed up with an email: "We do not comment on our confidential financial information. But we can say directionally that the Zappos business is not stagnant and continues to grow in profitability."

After taking in the information, Alfred was quick to point out that a $3 billion company is still significant. "Zulily, when they sold to Liberty, I think they were about a billion in sales," he said, going through a mental checklist. "EBay and Amazon are the largest. There's also Honest Co."

That was a good point. "Maybe Zappos just needs to get through Supercloud and move forward," I offered.

Even so, Alfred had a sense of resignation about where the company is and where it *could* be. That is the general feeling among its current and former employees. There is a large gap between reality and potential–or a tension, in Holacracy terms. The excitement around moving downtown has worn off. It turns out that Zappos employees don't really care much about Downtown Project at all, despite Fred and Tony's relentless push for them to get involved, attend events downtown, and the company adding "Community" into its mission. Maybe that will change in coming years as the residential development gets built up, but today many still commute from their homes closer to the old campus in suburban Henderson. The Zappos parking ramp across from its headquarters fills up every day. Most of its employees see their work as a job. Not everyone wants Zappos to be his or her 24/7 lifestyle.

Zappos was supposed to be done with its migration into Amazon's systems by now. The original goal was 2015, then Q1 2016, and now the date was put into later 2016. Supercloud has led Zappos to lose a lot of its tech talent, and it has delayed innovation. The company hasn't updated its website significantly in nearly a decade.

OLD FRIENDS

Tony still travels mostly in packs, which makes it hard for anyone to spend one-to-one time with him. Even Alfred has to negotiate for time on Tony's calendar. During a recent visit to Vegas, Tony suggested that Alfred meet him at a poker tournament he was playing in. The event went until two in the morning. Alfred said he wouldn't do that, so Tony offered to wake up early for breakfast. During the breakfast, Alfred asked Tony if he wanted help with anything high level for Zappos or Downtown Project, but Tony always says no.

Alfred also noticed that his college friend had gained a lot of weight, an indication that Tony was likely not sleeping and

My friend Lauren Brown, the one who gave me her blessing to go on this adventure instead of her, came to her own conclusion while I was in Vegas. "Happiness is just persistence and sheer will," she wrote in a story for *Quartz*. Lauren said that as an anxious person, she never really believed in happiness. She valued peace more. I could identify with that. "But then I stumbled upon happiness anyway," she wrote of her epiphany in the Joshua Tree desert, where she came to her conclusions around happiness.

INTO THE FURTHER FUTURE

Burning Man has become so popular that now there is a more exclusive, invite-only micro–Burning Man event for the elite called Further Future. The event, now in its second year, is put on by Robot Heart, a community of Burners best known for their iconic Burning Man camp for the 1 percent. The event takes place forty-five minutes outside of Las Vegas in the desert and is held the last weekend in April. The dress code for its four thousand attendees is classic Burning Man rave attire, which has now become common among the Silicon Valley set: entrepreneur Loic Le Meur sported an extravagant fox hat, and Google chairman Eric Schmidt wore a top hat and a vest made of mirrors. Tickets are around the same price as at Burning Man ($350), but most opt to upgrade and live more luxuriously in the desert. When a wellness coach at the event was asked by an attendee about privilege, the instructor responded that "we are the ones meant to be the air, not the earth," reported Nellie Bowles for the *Guardian*.

The festival is on Tony's circuit and a culmination of many of the things he enjoys most. This year, he brought to the event Tyler Williams, Jenn Lim, Heidy and Chad Stamper, Janice Lopez, and a few others. (I did not attend or ask to join the group.) Lauren Randall and Christian Velazquez were at Disneyland that weekend, and besides, they also had just spent several days with Tony at Coachella. For those who travel with Tony regularly, missing one event isn't of much consequence, because there's always another festival around the corner.

Most attendees returned to their comfortable lives in places such as San Francisco, Eden, and around the world. Tony is in a very narrow part of the contingent that returns from a Burning Man–style festival to a Burning Man–style living arrangement: From one Airstream to another Airstream. Not that a large portion of his life isn't an escape from that, but he dedicates a good amount of time there where it's enough to make the average person uncomfortable.

"Further Future is a lot like Burning Man, but it's just four thousand people instead of sixty thousand, so you keep colliding into the same people," he told me over Skype just after returning to Airstream Park. He sounded genuinely excited and even looked more relaxed wearing a plain white T-shirt instead of his regular black Zappos shirt, which went against the dress code at the festival, just like it is at Burning Man. Jenn was in the background, still wearing her sunglasses and arranging her bags after the two nights in the desert. I think she had recently returned to the United States from Dubai.

I asked them both, half joking, if there was a gifting culture at Further Future like there is at Burning Man. It wouldn't have been entirely out of character for the event: among the topics discussed were life in a postcapitalist, postdemocracy society with universal basic income. But the event involved commerce: aside from the $350-plus tickets, food was more expensive than what you'd find in San Francisco's Mission District ($7 mangos, for example), and there was a generally accepted theme that "your every desire can be met"–whether it be acrobatic yoga classes or Michelin-star dinners. Bowles's report from the event for the *Guardian* felt intentionally hollow. Further Future was more of a showcase and aggrandizement of the superficiality of the Silicon Valley start-up world than anything else.

"There's still commerce in the future," Tony quipped.

No doubt that Tony's lifestyle is intoxicating for those who partake. But it's hard to know if, without all the perks, his deputies would truly rally around a community development project or evangelize delivering happiness to the world. Since he launched his Downtown Project five years ago, many of the OGs have disappeared. When the party is over, so to speak, who is really going to stay until the end? Will Tony even stay? I finally understood why he chose five years as the completion date for Downtown Project. Most people don't have the wherewithal to continue dreaming that hard for so long. Changing the world, it turns out, is a lot of work.

FRONT GROUPS

After that Skype Call, I wanted to talk to Tony one more time, so that I could finally ask some of the elephant-in-the-room questions that had been looming. He agreed. In advance of our call, he sent me his Myers-Briggs personality type, INTP (an acronym that stands for "introverted, intuitive, thinking, perceiving"), and asked me to take the test as well. One thing that caught my eye from the INTP description is that the personality type really doesn't like failure. The Myers-Briggs Type Indicator classifies people into one of sixteen psychological types. The first indictor, "introverted" or "extroverted," is one of the most culturally defining elements (especially in the United States, where we tend to place high value on extroversion. Author Susan Cain wrote about this in her 2012 bestselling book *QUIET: The Power of Introverts In A World That Can't Stop Talking*).

I took the test and told him that although it came up ENFP, it could also be INFP, depending upon my mood. I am always split between I/E (introversion/extroversion); it depends on the moment that I take the test. I don't really believe in fixed personality types anyway; I believe that identity is fluid and can alter as we change our circumstances, or new circumstances change us.

Tony told me that he created his own personal "Why?" during an exercise with Simon Sinek, by recalling a childhood memory. He shared something about catching fireflies and wanting to create canvases so that people could find the light. The story seemed too perfect, too contrived, so I didn't really believe it. Why would someone as calculated and confident as Tony feel any need to create a personal "Why?" after all this time? After our call, I even checked his public Evernote to contrast the date on the Evernote he shared with the date of his meeting with Simon Sinek. Even though they aligned, I still wasn't totally convinced of the story.

We also went through the cult-indicator checklist that my friend from Brooklyn had sent me after I told him about Tony's world and what he was doing with Holacracy. There were a lot of parallels. I forwarded the email to Tony, and we started going through the list together, but he conceded only the first point:

Constantly Changing Requirements

Members are kept off balance by continuous changes in the way day-to-day business is conducted. Done under the guise of improving efficiency or maintaining flexibility, it generally results in intensely painful crisis management.

"Black-and-White" Thinking

Complex situations and concepts are often reduced to "catch phrase" simplicity in order to limit free thought.

Multiple Levels of Membership

Most groups have an inner, devoted core with secretive doctrines and/or practices, and an outer congregation that provides a good image to present to the rest of the world.

Deceptive Recruiting or "Staged" Commitment

When joining a group, new converts are not told the "whole story" concerning what will be expected of them as a member.

Excessive Workload/Activities

Members are kept as busy as possible, or at least prevented from spending much time alone.

Control/Oversight

Most groups expend lots of energy in making sure they know where members are and what they're up to. Often includes requiring constant communication or sending "more experienced" members to "check on" others.

Exclusive Doctrine or Special Insight

The group has special knowledge of the scriptures, or a direct line to God (via the leader). As such, they are "special" and often act accordingly.

Front Groups

Cults will often start businesses or community service organizations that perform one or more of the following functions: (1) generate income, (2) recruit new followers, (3) improve the group's image in the community, (4) provide employment for members so they can be more closely controlled.

Double Standards

The leadership is free to do things that are verboten for "regular" members. They receive special privileges and benefits for no reason other than the fact that they are "in charge."

We didn't go through everything in detail because it would have taken too long. He pointed out that companies like Apple could probably also make the list. That's true; Apple is a cult brand and would probably fit some of the requirements. But Tony's ecosystem seemed to be a unique fit. I never considered it a real cult, but it trended more toward yes than no. Even those who had a front-row seat to his world in Airstream Park do not believe that it's a true cult. On a scale of 1 to 10, I'd rank Zappos/DTP/Delivering Happiness and all the rest around a 7. Without a doubt, though, it *is* a cult of personality.

With its unclear intentions and high lack of ambiguity, "Front Groups" seemed to fit Downtown Project perfectly. No one understood what its real purpose was. Group members are encouraged not to spend time alone; the ideal is to have everyone working and playing together 24/7. Airstream Park is a manifestation of this. Beyond that, there are rituals (fernet, tattoos), doctrine (Holacracy is the letter of the law; teal is the spirit of the law). And finally, the idea that "no one is in charge but everyone's in charge." There also appeared to be different levels of membership.

I didn't think that Tony intentionally sought to create a cult, at least not in the beginning. I certainly don't think it was anything that Nick or Alfred would ever support. Alfred left the company when it was starting to turn that corner, by which time Nick had been long gone. The cult of personality emerged with Tony's book tour. During a 2011 appearance on *The Colbert Report* to promote *Delivering Happiness*, comedian Stephen Colbert asked Tony if he was a cult leader. "How much control do you have over these people?" he pressed, and then proceeded to ask Tony if there was a way to "deliver suffering." In her footnotes to her report on Downtown Project, urbanist Leah Meisterlin notes that, "At the time of writing, a Google search for the terms 'Tony Hsieh' and 'cult' yielded a little more than 80,000 results. Under the present circumstances, I am far more troubled knowing that the combination of 'Tony Hsieh' and 'kool-aid' is just as frequent." (As this book went to press, a Google search for "Tony Hsieh" and "cult" provided 300,000 results, though "Tony Hsieh" and "kool-aid" yielded only about 30,000. However, it's also notable that if you do a search for other visionary tech leaders and the word "cult," a high number of results also appear.)

If you ask people why Tony employs people who have no experience, many will say that he wants to give them a chance. But the closer you go into his inner circle, the answer to that question changes. These people talk about how he hires neophytes he can influence. Most of them use the word *control*. I think it's some combination of both.

Even Michael, who has been up close, doesn't understand how things work. "Do you really know that Tony is making the decision?" he reflected. "Or that Fred is making the decision? No, you really don't know because no one will disclose who's making any decision, so the only logical conclusion you can come to is that they are all collectively making the decisions, and one person gives the answer. I've been around Tony so much that I hear interactions that take place, and I've only been surprised by the amount of detail he knows about things. And you'd think, no way he knows that. But he totally does."

Tony has always said that if you become your true self, your tribe will find you. Using that reasoning and the conventional wisdom that we are generally the composite of the five people we spent the most time with, you can figure out Tony by looking at those around him. Within him are Fred Mossler and all of the yes-men and yes-women–those with a fierce desire to please and who avoid conflict at all costs. Andrew Donner reflects his ego, the unforgivingly rational and purely profit-seeking side to him. Scotte Cohen, though more of an acquaintance, uniquely reflects Tony: a counterpart in the dot-com boom, he was also lucky twice, and his Life Cube represents Tony's vision in its purest form. In Tony too are Heidy and Chad Stamper, who represent the raver part of him that is both escapist and idealist; an element of the purity of his vision also lies within them. Then there is Michael, who has leveraged and been scarred by the Vegas underbelly and yet made a decision to devote himself to his wife and daughter; even though that may be more aspirational, that part exists in Tony. Janice Lopez represents his past and his heart. I don't think it's a coincidence that she showed up when she did. And finally, surely there is a part of him that identifies with all of the broken toys and lost souls–the most significant common thread among everyone.

And maybe Tony doesn't want to see himself as a traditional leader, but he is one. Although he won't even claim the title, those who work most closely with him see it that way.

"Tony is the CEO," affirmed Michael Downs, who is executive vice president of operations for Downtown Project and holds a good amount of decision-making power. I asked Michael what was going to happen at the end of the five-year mark, which was January 2017. He told me that the plans to reach sustainability had been pushed back a year to January 2018. The core Downtown Project team is now down to about thirty people, which means that after the Dirty Thirty shake-up in 2014, thirty more employees have since departed–some voluntarily, some not. "We've been really aggressive about not refilling positions," he explained.

Most of Tony's money through Downtown Project has gone to real estate. The biggest winners will be its biggest investors: Tony, Fred, and Andrew.

The costs have been high all around. Many who entered his world have left more broken than when they entered. A former DTP employee shared, years after being let go: "I was traumatized. Lives were lost. People sold their houses to come out here. This upended people's lives." There is a general consensus that too many who engaged closely with the ecosystem endured some degree of psychological and emotional trauma. That former employee likened the experience to now having "war buddies." It's why so many people left the moment they could instead of staying around and finding another job or company to work for in Vegas. Yet most of these same people say that they wouldn't trade what was for them a once-in-a-lifetime experience. If there is an overarching theme that everyone can agree on, that is it: the zeitgeist in downtown Las Vegas during those years will never be replicated again.

A few universal truths have emerged: those who felt most entitled to the money appeared to spend it the fastest. Those who operated more from a place of gratitude, such as Natalie Young of Eat, spent more prudently. She repaid her loans in full faster than anyone else, whereas most of Tony's friends walked away without paying a dime.

Many of the operations that focused on ROC were always viewed primarily as marketing expenses (Life Is Beautiful, Coterie, CatalystCreativ), and I imagine that they were offset by gains from real estate. So what appear to be losses are not always so.

Some ideas were before their time. Take all of the businesses that opened in the newly renovated John E. Carson Building: Grass Roots, O Face Doughnuts, a Bikram hot yoga studio. They were charging customers the equivalent of what someone would pay in San Francisco's Mission District when the neighborhood had not caught up yet to that kind of gentrification.

Downtown Project released a 2016 report stating that it has created $118.9 million in annual economic output. Without seeing a breakdown of the number, it's hard to know what that is all accounting for, but it's fair to say that DTP has had a significant economic impact because of the sheer number of businesses that opened in the past five years.

Michael, one of the biggest beneficiaries of Tony's experiment, lost in some ways too. He lost the Beat, once a central meeting hub and ground zero for Downtown Project, which was announced in summer 2016. His landlord at the El Cortez found someone willing to pay a higher rent. "I would always say, 'Look, if we all get our wish, we are all going to be out of here when it all comes to fruition because rents will go sky high. We will all be displaced.' So, did we help create our own demise? Absolutely. But that's progress."

He shared that deaths of friends and locals such as Kent Johns from Atomic Liquors have clarified what is important. "People work tirelessly and endlessly for the almighty dollar, but what is it all for?" Michael posited.

Fred doesn't have to work another day in his life, but he will. For one, he's focusing on franchising Nacho Daddy, with a new location on the Las Vegas Strip. He will also choose to spend more time with his wife and his kids. So will Michael.

Over time, more details around the reasons behind the many failures may emerge. A number of them will likely trace back to Tony. Many of those who were burned most badly chose to accept a check in exchange for silence. In my opinion, nondisclosure agreements are one of the most unethical business practices in America. NDAs consistently keep the power scales weighed down on the side of employers, and not having to sign an NDA is a unique privilege afforded to those who can afford it. But with the reality of NDAs, many of the details around the failures downtown will remain black-box conversations.

For Alfred's part, he says that Tony's ideas are all a few years too early. Tony wanted to tell the world that Zappos delivered happiness in the mid-2000s, but Alfred told him it wasn't time yet. "People aren't going to believe that we deliver happiness *yet*."

There were certainly magical moments as Downtown Project was being realized–like watching Imagine Dragons, a hometown Vegas rock band that opened the Life Is Beautiful festival that first year, with Sarah Nisperos, her son, and a motley crew. No matter that we were near the back of a crowd of thousands, straining to see the performers, we could see the pyrotechnics and the fireworks. As the band played one of its most popular songs, "Demons," we sang along while lead singer Dan Reynolds held the microphone over the crowd:

> *When your dreams all fail*
> *And the ones we hail*
> *Are the worst of all*

Up near the stage, in the VIP section close to the magic, stood Tony and Rehan Choudhry–at the time, they were still partners and collaborators. Someone who stood near Tony in the VIP section that weekend told me that with the look in his eye, you'd think that he would have been content if everything had stopped then and there.

Only those who were there will ever know how it really felt. Just like the raves of Tony's youth, it's hard to bottle up that sort of thing. Living life according to PLUR–peace, love, unity, respect–is much harder to do outside the context of a rave. Emanuel Sferios, the founder of DanceSafe and producer of the MDMA documentary, told me that the ideal number of times to use MDMA is four times a year. After that, its effects wear off. I told him that I tried the drug as part of my research for this book and was surprised to discover that it did in fact affect my perspective. MDMA is considered an empathogen, and I found that I was able to access a greater empathy and connectedness through that experience. But there were certainly other experiences that impacted my life more profoundly in the past few years.

I feel happier than I did in 2013, when I started on the adventure in earnest. I attribute that to being a by-product of commitment, hard work, and sheer persistence, and developing a set of core values that I abide by no matter what. On the *Delivering Happiness* bus in summer 2013, Tony said that the book would be a good opportunity for personal growth. I guess he was right about that.

My most profound experiences initially presented themselves as prisoner dilemmas and uncomfortable liabilities that required a high degree of humility. It was through those experiences that I discovered who my tribe was. A young woman from Summit Series once confessed to me in a moment of epiphany that deviated from the general ethos of the group, "Following your dreams is dangerous. They don't tell you that." She was right.

My friend Lauren Brown did not discover happiness through a series of highs. At thirty-one, she was diagnosed with stage 3 breast cancer. Through enduring one of the most terrifying experiences of her life, staring down death is when she stumbled upon happiness in the desert. Facebook COO Sheryl Sandberg shared a similar sentiment in the year after her husband Dave Goldberg's sudden death in 2015: "It is the greatest irony of my life that losing my husband helped me find deeper gratitude," she told UC Berkeley students at their graduation.

DTPer Lisa Shufro wrote about this sort of gratitude in her *Medium* post "Delivering Resilience," which she published after the Dirty Thirty layoffs:

> On the day that Malala Yousafzai won the Nobel Peace Prize, Rehan asked me what Shiza Shahid, Malala's mentor and women's rights advocate, would speak about. Resilience, of course. Rehan paused, and said, "What if, in a weird way, what happened to Malala is the best thing that's ever happened to her?"
>
> "That could never be the case," I said. "The best thing that's ever happened to Malala is what she did next with that experience. She chooses to live through it, to journey through the reservoir each day to experience joy."

There's something strange about how coming from a place of loss and failure clarifies things.

In his 2011 interview with Barbara Walters, Tony said that it would be an interesting challenge to build everything back up again from zero. It's one of the most notable things he's said–everyone talks about it when he's not around. I think I now understand more of what he meant: there is nothing like starting with a blank canvas from a place of failure or loss. It's the ultimate opportunity.

AFTERWORD

A few weeks after my final Skype interview with Tony, I went outside the bounds of our Holacracy governance agreement. He never told me what happens when you go outside of its perimeters, but after I did I experienced firsthand what many who had been pushed out of the community recounted over the years. It was painful. The only upside was that I now understood my sources better.

In early July 2016, with my manuscript nearly complete, I emailed Tony. At this point, I finally had the map of the entire ecosystem–the one that I sought to create in summer 2013, after Tony showed me the MIT Labs connectivity tool. With this bird's-eye view, along with intimate knowledge of the psychology of the community, I drew my conclusions. I felt that the book would benefit from him weighing in more and wanted to give him the opportunity to respond to everything. With more of his insights, I thought, readers would find him more empathetic. I even offered him several times the opportunity to review the book in advance and to respond by writing the Afterword.

This was never supposed to be a typical business book. Living the story was the story. I even saw it as something that a progressive bookseller might place in the psychology or spirituality sections. In fact, that was the angle that Tony had suggested when we walked around downtown Las Vegas on Sunday, November 17, 2013. It was the second time I asked him if he'd fund the book, and the second time he gave me an oblique answer. As we approached the Ogden, he said, "You could do something like *The Hitchhiker's Guide To The Galaxy*-your guide through downtown Las Vegas."

Although he didn't fund the book, he provided his support in other ways. For example, he connected me to his book agent from *Delivering Happiness* (we didn't end up working together, but she took the meeting) and offered Downtown Project crash pads so that I could get the project off the ground. His invitation to me was less about the book than it was about walking *the path*-the Zen path, the entrepreneurial path, the one he opens *Delivering Happiness* with:

"There's a difference between knowing the path and walking the path." -Morpheus, *The Matrix*

I always trusted him intuitively because I believe he has a lot of respect for anyone who accepts his challenge. That was really what Downtown Project was about, though it was sugarcoated for the masses. Maybe it had to be that way; following your dreams is brutal and relentless, and that's not a great sales pitch. Walking the path means facing every demon that you have: sheer self-belief is the only way to the other side. So I believed that, at the very end of this path-which for me, was finishing the book-he would come through. That belief gave me the confidence to challenge him with some hard questions, going deeper yet than in our last few interviews. These emails weren't in line with our Holacracy governance agreement; they required emotional energy to answer. He reminded me that we had established "a very specific set of three agreements that originated from our April 9, 2016 meeting where we mutually agreed, in writing, to the following governance between us," and he added the bullet points. Though we had never talked about what happens when you don't follow governance (or how to even go about changing it) I soon realized that he was entirely serious–deviating from governance meant that the relationship was over, at least for now.

It didn't take long for him to stop responding to all communication. It was frustrating, as I believed that he, too, had broken the unspoken terms of our relationship. We never signed a contract but that's because the agreement was based on radical trust.

When I shared this with Sarah Nisperos, previously Downtown Project's "Sorceress" who is now based in Los Angeles, where she opened another Coterie store, she said, "That's apropos–it had to be that way, right?" Reflecting more on how Downtown Project had unfolded, she concluded, "You know, we all experienced ROC after all, just not in the way that we expected."

As the book went to press, there was still a sense of fragility in the community–the wounds cut deep and they haven't yet healed. Sarah was the one who provided me with the Broken Dolls narrative, and that was prescient–it rings truer than ever today. I concluded that there is a unique kind of courage and strength among the Broken Dolls, to admit that they were searching for something and being willing to give up everything to find it.

In one of Tony's last emails to me, he included the quote from *The Matrix* about walking the path and asked if I was stronger today than when I began the journey. He did not ask me if I was happier.

Yes, of course.

Like most everyone else who accepted Tony's challenge–no matter all the pain, heartbreak and uncertainty that came with it–I still wouldn't change my decision for anything.

ACKNOWLEDGMENTS

This book was a start-up and there are so many people to thank. At risk of leaving out some important names:

Mom and Dad, what do I say? Together you made this book happen in all the ways. I love you both so much. To my siblings Dan, Katie, Annalisa, and Kristin; and to Sha Sha, Alex, Trey, and Mark. You all inspire me. Kristin, thank you for pouring your heart and soul into this as my first editor and creative director. Katie and Annalisa, for listening, too, and for your encouragement early on and always.

To the Norm and Helen Groth and the Jack and Vienna Koivula families, for your genuine enthusiasm and clarifying questions that surfaced the story. Uncle Stephen Groth, you are among those who truly brought this project to life. Azy, you too. Grandma, I admire your entrepreneurial spirit.

To Rick Wolff, my agent Jim Levine, and my editor Matthew Benjamin at Touchstone, for believing in the force of my idea. Matthew, you saw the same vision as I did. Thank you for your guidance, your patience, and advocacy as I pulled together all the pieces–even until the very last moment. Amazingly, the final product is what I had in my mind's eye back in summer 2013, before the story had even unfolded. To Lara Blackman, Elisa Rivlin, Kayley Hoffman, Philip Bashe, and the entire Touchstone/Simon & Schuster team for making it happen.

Kevin Delaney, Matt Quinn, Gideon Lichfield, and the rest of the *Quartz* editorial staff: your enthusiasm and support for the book, and the stories that led to it, means the world. At *Quartz* I learned what happens when a newsroom rallies around core values like generosity and empathy. It makes all the difference–to everyone in the newsroom, and to readers.

Henry Blodget, Nich Carlson, Gus Lubin, and my other colleagues from *Business Insider*: I learned a lot from you guys. *BI* was trial by fire and a crash course in what it takes to build a start-up. Start-ups are hard. Andrew Yang, you make a great case for pursuing them anyway.

Lauren Brown, Nina Tomaro, Natalie Parrague, Erin Huebscher, Leah Eyler, Rachel and Jake, Daphne and Austin, Meg and Matt, Natalie and Dusty, Meg and Ev, Katie and Sam, Besse and Aaron, Alicia Hogan, Jill Adrian, Megan Kruggel, Natalie Barnard, Jessi Larson, Christen Dimke, Dylan Love, Zach McCoy, Dan and Brittney, Caitlin Light–you have all been true friends throughout. Heidy and Chad, you guys too. You both made Vegas fun. Nina, I don't know that I could have done Vegas without you either.

Jonathan, Jubi, Asha, and Lyla, you are family–thank you for all the things. Ben Grace, through you I learned to love the process. Jen Wills Fisher, I learned from you, too, about community building. Elisa Duger, for all the work! Lance Schubert, for a copy of *The War of Art* at precisely the right time. Derrick and Yi, BJ and Ryan, Carol and Carlos, Kim and Thomas, Bill Ehninger, Chris Miles, Brady Dale, Jonathan and Heather, Stef Fontela, Emem Offong, and everyone else at Forefront Brooklyn, I feel like I won the lottery. You guys are real.

To Gretchen and Jeff Ryan in Hong Kong: what a way to begin the Year of the Monkey. Anna Dielschneider, Lisa Atkins, Jonathan Wai, Tina Streefland, Lauren and Paige Backenstose, Peeter and Patti Kivestu, the Murdock and Olsen families, Jack Klobuchar, Kurt Kuno, Adam Wahlberg, Ross Pfund, Bill White, Steve Kaplan, Murray and Shirley Baldwin, for cheering me on always.

To those who supported the book in unique ways: Janice Lopez, Michael Cornthwaite, Dave Gould, Lisa Shufro, Mark Rowland, Krissee Danger, Charles Ressler, Phil Pascal, Porter Haney, Jason Miller, Matt Heller, Erica Dhawan, Staci Perkins, Scotte Cohen, Cory Mervis, Hartej Sawhney, Alexis Gonzales-Black, Rachel Murch, Zach Ware, Will Young, Jenn Lim, Maggie Hsu, Aman Advani, Graham Kahr, Frank and Jen, Tyler Williams, Christa Foley, Owen Carver, John Bunch, Lauren Randall, Christian Velazquez, Milena Kellner, Maren Kate Donovan, Jamie Naughton, Jeanne Markel, Kim Schaefer, Liz Gregersen, Mimi Pham, Sara Nisperos, Alfred Lin, Nick Swinmurn, Richard Hsieh, Fred Mossler, Meghan Boyd, Erna Barton, Dylan Jorgensen, Jacqueline Jensen, Zubin Damania, Cathy Brooks, Branden Collinsworth, Arun Rajan, Andy and Oksana, Megan Hannum, Whitney Johnson, Steve Moroney, Sandy Herrera, Andrew Donner, Robbe Richman, Warren Calcove, Byrd Leavell, Greg Lindsay, Ashley Arenson, Jeff Rosenthal, Courtney Boyd Myers, Sean Carasso, Ranielle Rivera. Nadia Sylianou and Alisha Golden, for the right messages at the right time. Paul Iserno and Michael Stoll, for everything you guys did behind the scenes. Henry Kang, you are among those who truly made the book possible. I learned so much from you. Gian Brown, I still have the piece of paper where you mapped out the path. Amanda Slavin, Alex Abelin, Richard Demato, Becky Straw, and everyone else at that first Catalyst Week: still, *wow*. Amanda, you knew exactly what you were doing. Dan Fredinburg, you were a force. You were the ultimate disruptor, in life and in teaching people how to love. Because you were brave, you changed everything.

Tony, this book process revealed to me that my tribe was larger than I realized. As Fred once said, sometimes it takes burning down the ships to learn these things. What a cool gift. I am sincerely grateful for your trust, your generous spirit, and most of all, for the adventure.

NOTES

Downtown Project has been well covered since it launched in 2012, but there are a few journalists whose work I referenced more than others: Max Chafkin, previously at *Inc.* and *Fast Company* and then *Bloomberg Businessweek*; Nellie Bowles, previously at *ReCode* and then the *Guardian*; and locally, Joe Schoenmann ("Joe Downtown") of the *Las Vegas Review-Journal* and *Las Vegas Sun*; and Ben Spillman of the *Las Vegas Review-Journal*. Paul Carr, whose NSFWCORP was acquired by *PandoDaily*, merged local coverage with national discourse.

Greg Lindsay, *Fast Company* journalist and author of the *Aerotropolis: The Way We'll Live Next*, was another key influence. In November 2014 he invited me to an event hosted by the TTSL Foundation, a private foundation that was collecting data on innovative urban planning initiatives around the world. There was high curiosity around the Downtown Project, but a lot of questions around its mission and whether it qualified as an authentic urban development initiative that was intended to improve the community at large. Afterward, Greg sent me an article by urbanist Leah Meisterlin, who engaged with these questions in her article, "Antipublic Urbanism: Las Vegas and the Downtown Project." This book was never intended to be a critical look at the city's redevelopment through an urban planner's eyes, but it was important to understand the general zeitgeist around the Downtown Project.

One of the biggest themes that emerged over the course of reporting the book was the concept of the entrepreneurial struggle. It struck me that there was a huge disconnect between what entrepreneurs were going through personally and what they felt they could reveal publicly. There were a number of news stories published about entrepreneurial suicides and mental health in recent years, in addition to Nellie Bowles's courageous reporting, "The Downtown Project suicides: Can the pursuit of happiness kill you?" *Business Insider*'s Biz Carson furthered the conversation with her piece, "There's a dark side to startups, and it haunts 30% of the world's most brilliant people." Entrepreneur Christina Wallace responded to Carson's article with a *Medium* post, "Let's get real about startups and mental health." *Inc.*'s Jessica Brumder previously wrote an important and defining piece, "The psychological price of entrepreneurship."

Venture capitalists have joined the conversation, too. Boulder, Colorado–based VC Brad Feld has long been outspoken on the topic, as has one of his investments, Moz founder Rand Fishkin. I spoke to Rand a few times and he is one of the few entrepreneurs who walks the walk when it comes to embracing radical transparency–just check out his personal blog. I'm looking forward to reading his book, which as of this writing had a working title of *The Transparent Entrepreneur*.

In October 2015 I met with Dr. Michael Freeman, a University of California, San Francisco, psychiatrist who is researching the links between entrepreneurship and mental health. He had published a research paper, "Are entrepreneurs touched with fire?" six months earlier, which gained a lot of attention in the media. Through our conversation I learned that there is a lot of debate in his profession around the connections between entrepreneurship and mental health, and the research has only scratched the surface. He believes it is a very important topic to delve deeper into because entrepreneurship is what leads to job creation: If we can better understand and support our entrepreneurs, then we will improve the economic and collective well-being.

That same week I met with Dr. Adam Strassberg, who has an office on the Stanford University campus. He is not collecting research data, but has made empirical observations about Silicon Valley culture and how it affects his clients. A few months earlier he had published a story titled "Happiness vs. Success" in *Psychology Today*. In his article, he wrote, "Over the decades–as both a psychiatrist practicing in Silicon Valley and a civilian living here locally–I have witnessed so much success and yet so little happiness. In our valley of material riches and natural beauty, the two are regrettably too often in opposition." He went on to explain that "much of the art of psychotherapy is the art of balance–or rather rebalancing." Dr. Strassberg takes his clients on a recovery path that involves engaging with eight pillars of happiness, which include connection to others, autonomy, self-esteem, competence, purpose, connection to the body, connection to nature, and spirituality:

> "I sell these eight fundamentals to all my patients, though rarely do they come to me initially looking to buy them. They usually would prefer to purchase more success. I warn them all that 'I am in the happiness business, not the success business,' and that 'the two are more and more in opposition in this valley,'

and finally that 'you will get what you pay for.' I sell the eight fundamentals of happiness to all who knock on my door. They soon leave my office satisfied customers, less depressed, less anxious, on a path towards far less success, but paradoxically far happier than ever imaginable."

This book was designed to mirror the chaos and self-organizing nature of Tony's universe, so I didn't follow a typical storytelling format, but Donald Miller's *Blue Like Jazz* influenced the stream of consciousness style throughout parts of the book.

INDEX

Hsieh, Tony (*cont.*)
  finances and, x–xiii, xv, 2–4, 8, 10,
    13, 16–19, 23, 26, 28, 34–35, 39–40,
    44, 48–50, 54, 56, 59–61, 63–64,
    66–67, 70, 72, 76, 83, 88, 94, 111,
    122, 124, 131–32, 150, 158–60,
    184–85, 198, 222, 227–28, 238–40,
    246–47, 250, 267, 273, 282–83, 290
  and firing of Kang, 85–86
  as game theorist, 145–46, 192, 261
  girlfriends and dating of, 45–46,
    72–74, 112, 134, 179–81
  Gould's Op-Ed and, 155–57
  Groth's entrepreneurial ideas and,
    60, 62
  Groth's unwritten agreement with,
    289–91
  Groth's Zappos job application
    and, 113–14
  happiness movement and, 143, 145,
    148, 209, 212, 258
  Hawaiian trips of, 42, 57–61
  and health care in Las Vegas, 60–61
  heritage of, ix, 1, 222, 233, 255
  Holacracy and, 69–71, 76, 101–2,
    108, 135, 137, 142, 146, 149–50,
    161, 171, 173–74, 176, 184, 193–
    94, 206, 213, 252, 255, 258–63,
    265, 267–68, 278, 289–90
  as inspirational happiness guru,
    12, 17
  on integrity, 119–20
  Kang's relationship with, 137–38
  leadership and, 25, 123, 136, 146,
    150, 153–55, 158, 160–62, 164–66,
    207–9, 226, 246, 282
  libertarian ethos of, xii–xiii
  Life Cube Burn and, 105–6, 127
  Lim's relationship with, 39, 41, 43,
    183
  Lin's relationship with, 1–4, 145–46,
    162, 239, 269–70, 272–74
  llamas and, 44, 179, 209
  Lopez's relationship with, 164,
    166, 264–65, 282
  management books of, 77
  on MDMA, 40–41
  media and, xv, 2, 12–13, 21–24,
    27–28, 33, 54, 57–58, 63, 88, 110,

116, 122, 138, 150–51, 161, 169,
  171, 183–84, 213, 218, 229–30,
  269, 273, 287
Mossler's relationship with, x–xi,
  37, 98, 257–58, 282
and narrative around
  entrepreneurship, 245–46
national book tour of, 12–14, 27, 33,
  43, 85, 155, 168, 233, 281
Nisperos's relationship with, 29–30
Ogden apartment of, 16–17, 22–23,
  31–32, 42–45, 56, 88–89, 112–13,
  143, 167, 170
Ogden leases of, 15, 166–67
as Oz in Emerald City, 116
parents and family of, 1, 112, 114,
  166–67, 169, 213–14, 254–57
parties and partying of, 41–46,
  49–50, 53, 61, 75–79, 82, 88–89,
  98, 109–12, 128, 133, 169
people collected by, 28, 42–43
personal Why? of, 278
Pham's relationship with, 16, 86
physical appearance of, x, 8–9,
  36–38, 40, 43, 53, 76, 79, 83,
  97–98, 148, 166, 177, 181, 209,
  231, 266, 273, 276
PLUR code of conduct of, x, 1
poker playing of, 4, 70, 145–46,
  148, 272
popularity and fame of, xiii, 12–14,
  27–28, 68, 76, 90, 100, 114, 155,
  179, 182, 233, 240, 266
PR and, 33, 152, 175, 227–28
punctuality of, 112
Rajan's relationship with, 205
real estate prices and, 63–64
recruiting of, 23, 27, 36–37, 42,
  46–47, 52, 56, 60–62, 64, 66–69,
  79, 83, 85, 102, 105, 121, 149, 163
Romotive and, 19–20, 53, 61, 93
sadness in reaction to, 229–30
Santa Monica trip of, 72–75, 246
self-organization interests of,
  69–70, 137, 146, 161, 171, 174,
  183–84
serendipity and, 54, 68, 98, 116,
  135, 137
Shift and, 54, 90, 185, 243

ABOUT THE AUTHOR

AIMEE GROTH is an independent business journalist who writes primarily for *Quartz*, a division of Atlantic Media. She previously served as a senior editor at *Business Insider*. Her work has been highlighted by several publications, including the *Wall Street Journal*, NPR, and the *Harvard Business Review*. In December 2013 she broke the news about Zappos's adoption of Holacracy, which led to coverage by dozens of news organizations around the world, including CNN and the *New York Times*.